Teen Finance Series

PERSONAL AND AUTOMOBILE LOAN INFORMATION FOR TEENS FIRST EDITION

Teen Finance Series

PERSONAL AND AUTOMOBILE LOAN INFORMATION FOR TEENS FIRST EDITION

Basic Financial Information for Teens Seeking Personal and Automobile Loans

Including Facts about Loan Options, Credit Score, Debt Management, and Identity Theft, along with Information about Buying or Renting a Car, Vehicle Repossession, Auto Warranties, Maintenance, Insurance, and Legal Rights of Consumers

OMNIGRAPHICS
615 Griswold St., Ste. 520
Detroit, MI 48226

* * *

OMNIGRAPHICS
Angela L. Williams, *Managing Editor*

* * *

ISBN 978-0-7808-1788-3
E-ISBN 978-0-7808-1789-0

Library of Congress Cataloging-in-Publication Data

Names: Williams, Angela, 1963- editor.

Title: Personal and automobile loan information for teens / edited by Angela L. Williams.

Description: First Edition. | Detroit: Omnigraphics, Inc., 2020. | Series: Teen finance series | Includes index. | Audience: Ages 13 | Audience: Grades 7-9 | Summary: ""Provides basic financial information for teens about loans and credits including procedures and risks involved in availing personal and automobile loans, building credit score, managing debts, along with facts about financial scams and consumer rights. Includes index and other resources for teens seeking financial assistance.""-- Provided by publisher.

Identifiers: LCCN 2019055831 (print) | LCCN 2019055832 (ebook) | ISBN 9780780817883 (library binding) | ISBN 9780780817890 (ebook)

Subjects: LCSH: Teenagers--Finance, Personal--Juvenile literature. | Bank loans--Juvenile literature. | Automobile industry and trade--Finance--Juvenile literature. | Finance charges--Juvenile literature.

Classification: LCC HG179 .P36847 2020 (print) | LCC HG179 (ebook) | DDC 332.7/43--dc23

LC record available at https://lccn.loc.gov/2019055831

LC ebook record available at https://lccn.loc.gov/2019055832

Printed in the United States

TABLE OF CONTENTS

Part 3 | Add-On Expenses: Car Maintenance and Insurance

Part 4 | Your Legal Rights as a Consumer

Part 5 | If You Need More Help or Information

PREFACE

About This Book

Today's teens face economic challenges unlike previous generations as they transition to managing their own money. This book provides teens with the information they need to gain the basic financial literacy necessary to efficiently manage their earnings, savings, and loans. Loans can be of great help when one runs out of the money needed to meet your needs or make large purchases. There are many types of loans, such as automobile loans, home loans, personal loans, student loans, and so on. A clear understanding of how loans and credit work can help teens avoid financial pitfalls and build economic stability.

Personal and Automobile Loan Information for Teens, First Edition provides teens with the financial literacy they need to navigate loans and credit. It provides basic information about various loan options available for teens and talks extensively about the procedures and risks involved in taking out personal and automobile loans. It highlights the importance of credit scoring and gives insight into how teens can build their credit while avoiding common financial pitfalls. It discusses various considerations to be taken into account before buying, renting, or leasing a car and provides information about car repair, warranties, and insurance. The legal rights of consumers are explained in detail along with tips for avoiding loan scams and identity theft. It also includes additional resources for teens seeking personal and automobile loans.

How to Use This Book

This book is divided into parts and chapters. Parts focus on broad areas of interest; chapters are devoted to single topics within a part.

Part 1: Understanding Personal Loans and Credit provides information about various loan options available for teens. It highlights the importance of credit scoring and explains how teens can build their credit while avoiding common financial pitfalls. It also offers tips for avoiding credit repair scams and identity theft.

Part 2: What a Teen Needs to Know before Buying Their First Car gives insight into the ways teens can plan their finance when buying a car. It discusses various things to be taken into account before buying, renting, or leasing a car. It also explains how to avail an auto loan and describes various loan choices.

Part 3: Add-On Expenses: Car Maintenance And Insurance tells how to plan for the additional expenses of a car, such as gasoline and repairs, warranties and service contracts, insurance, and so on. It also explains how to get a good deal when buying a used car.

Part 4: Your Legal Rights As a Consumer gives information about various consumer rights and explains how consumers can protect themselves from various issues that may arise while pursuing a loan. Facts about negative automobile equity and prepayment penalty are provided, along with a brief description about bankruptcy.

Part 5: If You Need More Information provides key financial terms with their definitions, along with directories of resources that can help people seeking loans and credits.

Bibliographic Note

This volume contains documents and excerpts from publications issued by the following U.S. government agencies: Consumer Financial Protection Bureau (CFPB); Federal Bureau of Investigation (FBI); Federal Deposit Insurance Corporation (FDIC); Federal Trade Commission (FTC); National Credit Union Administration (NCUA); National Motor Vehicle Title Information System (NMVTIS); U.S. Courts; and USA.gov.

It may also contain original material produced by Omnigraphics and reviewed by professional consultants.

The photograph on the front cover is © Shutterstock.

PART 1 | UNDERSTANDING PERSONAL LOANS AND CREDIT

CHAPTER 1
TYPES OF LOANS

About This Chapter: This chapter includes text excerpted from "Personal Loans: Secured versus Unsecured," MyCreditUnion.gov, National Credit Union Administration (NCUA), June 23, 2018.

Loans provide you with money you might not currently have for making large purchases and lets you pay back the money over a stated period of time. Many loan types, such as home loans, car loans, and student loans, are available. Loans are either secured or unsecured.

Secured Loans

With secured loans, your property is used as collateral. If you cannot repay the loan, the lender may take your collateral to get its money back. Common secured loans are mortgages, home equity loans, and installment loans.

Mortgages

A mortgage loan is used to buy real estate such as a home. Fixed-rate and adjustable-rate mortgages are the two main types of mortgages, but there is a wide variety of mortgage products available. Typical sources for mortgage loans include credit unions, commercial banks, thrift institutions, mortgage brokers, and online lenders. When shopping for a home mortgage, you should consider contacting several lenders to compare offers.

If you do not make your mortgage payments when due, foreclosure proceedings may occur. This action provides the legal means for your lender to take possession of your home. Foreclosures have a negative impact on your credit history. Beware of predatory mortgage lending, where creditors impose unfair or abusive terms on you. Deceptive mortgage-lending practices can strip you of home equity and threaten foreclosure.

Home Equity Loans

A home equity loan is a form of mortgage loan where your home is used as collateral to borrow money. It is typically used to pay for major expenses (education, medical bills, or home repairs). These loans may be a one-time lump-sum amount, or a more flexible

Personal Line of Credit

A Personal Line of Credit is a loan that you access from time to time. You write special checks or request a transfer to your checking account by phone or online.

Like a credit card account, you have a credit limit, receive a monthly bill, make at least a minimum payment, pay interest based on your outstanding balance, and possibly pay a fee each time you use the account.

Personal Lines of Credit are unsecured and are offered by banks and credit unions and usually require that you also have a checking account with the same institution.

(Source: "What Is a Personal Line of Credit?" Consumer Financial Protection Bureau (CFPB))

revolving line of credit that allows you to withdraw funds at any time. In either case, if you cannot pay back the loan, the lender could foreclose on your home.

Installment Loans

With an installment loan, you repay the loan over time with a set number of scheduled payments. Car loans are the most common installment loans. Before you sign an agreement for a loan to buy a car or other large purchase, make sure you fully understand all of the lender's terms and conditions.

In particular, know the dollar amount you are borrowing, payment amounts and when they are due, the total finance charge (including all interest and fees you must pay to get the loan), and the rate of interest you will pay over the full term of the loan. Be aware of penalties for late payments or for paying the loan back early. Know what the lender will do if you cannot repay the loan.

Lenders are required by federal law to provide this information before you agree to make a purchase, so you can compare different offers.

Unsecured Loans

Unsecured loans do not use property as collateral. Lenders consider these to be riskier than secured loans, so they charge a higher rate of interest for them. Two common unsecured loans are credit cards and student loans.

Credit Cards

Credit cards allow you to purchase products and services now, but you need to repay the balance before the end of your billing cycle to avoid paying interest on your purchase. The credit card issuer sets a credit limit on how much you can charge on your card. When applying for credit cards, it is important to shop around. Fees, interest rates, finance charges, and benefits can vary greatly.

Student Loans

Student loans are available from a variety of sources, including the federal government, individual states, colleges and universities, and other public and private agencies and organizations. To help pay for higher-education expenses, students and parents can

Free Money from the Government

The federal government does not offer grants or "free money" to individuals to start a business or cover personal expenses, contrary to what you might see online or in the media. Websites or other publications claiming to offer "free money from the government" are often scams. Report them to the Federal Trade Commission (FTC).

(Source: "Government Grants and Loans," USA.gov)

borrow funds that must be repaid-with interest. As a general rule, federal loans have more favorable terms and lower interest rates than traditional consumer loans.

CHAPTER 2
LOAN OPTIONS FOR PEOPLE UNDER 18

When you are younger than 18, it can be difficult to get a loan approved, but it is not impossible. When a loan provider performs a credit check on you, they will be assessing their risk and, in particular, checking to determine how likely it is that you will be able to repay the loan. However, because of your age, the lender may find it hard to judge how reliable you might be.

There are many reasons why a young person may opt for a loan. They might, for example, want to get a loan to buy their first car or to fund their studies. Other reasons include buying a house, going on a vacation, paying for a wedding, or paying off debts.

Types of Loans for Young People

There is a prime age set for borrowing based on the risk factors that age carries. To put it simply, the older you are, the less time you will have to repay your debt and the younger you are, the less income and experience you will have to indicate the likelihood that you will repay your debt. Despite these obstacles, a person younger than 18 can be eligible for certain types of loans. Some of these are listed below.

Personal Loans

If you are under 18 with little credit history, then you may be eligible for a personal loan. However, the amount that you are offered might be less, or at a higher rate of interest than advertised. This is because the lender may consider a person below the age of 18 to be a potentially risky prospect.

It is also important to note that your credit score drops each time you apply for a loan, so applying for many is unwise and a lower credit score will make it difficult to get a loan or credit product in the future.

Search tools, such as insurance.com, allow you to see whether you are eligible for a loan. Since rejection of a loan adversely affects your credit score, it is always better to take advantage of online tools such as these.

Student Loans

There are three types of student loans:

- Federal loans
- Private loans
- Refinance loans (once you leave school)

Federal loans are funded by the government, while private and refinanced loans are provided by banks, credit unions, and states. Federal loans are more flexible than private loans. However, the loan that is best suited to you will be determined by several factors, including your financial need, grade point average (GPA), and credit history.

A "Free Application for Federal Student Aid" (FAFSA) application must be filled out in order to get a federal loan. A borrower usually must apply with the bank or financial institution directly for private or refinanced loans.

Cosigner Loans

Since few people under the age of 18 will be approved for a loan, they may wish to consider asking their parents, relatives, or even an older friend to be a guarantor for them. This person takes on the responsibility of repaying the loan if the borrower is unable to pay it.

Alternatives to Loans

There are other options that a person can consider before taking out a loan. Some of the options are listed below:

Check with Peers

Even though peers may not always have money they can lend, they may be able to direct you to someone who can help. Hence, checking with peers is always worth the effort.

Check with Family

If a family member or close friend is able to lend money to you, then you may wish to consider asking them. However, it is also important to remember that even if the money is being borrowed from a person of trust, it is recommended that you draw up a contract that lists details about the repayment amount, loan period, and whether or not interest will be paid on the loan.

Government Support

People who receive federal benefits may be eligible for an interest-free loan that can be used for everyday essentials such as rent; therefore, check your eligibility for such benefits.

Credit Cards

Interest-free credit cards can be used as an alternative to a loan. However, it is important to note when the interest-free period ends, or you could end up paying interest

> **Debt-to-Income Ratio**
> The debt-to-income ratio is a simple calculation:
> Total of your monthly debt payments ÷ Monthly gross income (income before taxes).
> The result is a percentage that tells you how much of your income is going toward covering your debt. For example, if you have a debt to income ratio of 36 percent, you have 64 cents out of every dollar you earn to pay for everything else, including all of your living expenses and taxes.
> *(Source: "Your Money, Your Goals," Consumer Financial Protection Bureau (CFPB))*

that is higher than the typical interest rate on payments made after the interest-free period ends.

Savings

If the loan is desire in order to purchase a car or move out, then start saving for the expense as early as possible. This could result in not having to take out a loan at all.

Tips for Getting a Loan at 18

Here are some suggestions to consider if you are 18 and trying to get a loan:

- Show evidence that you can save.
- Offer collateral.
- Get a letter of recommendation and/or proof of employment from your employer if employed.
- Apply for a lower amount.
- Opt for a secured loan.

Taking out a loan at a young age can give you access to quick funds and help you build a credit history, but it may come with certain negative consequences such as a high-interest rate and an increased risk of defaulting on your payment. Hence, it is always important to think of alternative ways to raise the funds before you choose to pursue a loan. Finally, if you are considering a loan, make sure you can afford to repay it.

References

1. "Loans for Young People," GoCompare, January 17, 2016.
2. "Compare Loans for 18-Year-Olds," Finder, January 5, 2020.
3. "Types of Student Loans: Which Is Best for You?" NerdWallet, June 13, 2019.

CHAPTER 3
BASIC FACTS ABOUT BANKS AND BANKING

About This Chapter: "Basic Facts about Banks and Banking," © 2016 Omnigraphics.

The monetary system of the modern world is built around banks. They account for trillions of dollars in assets, making them a crucial driver of the global economy. And, closer to home, they provide a number of services that can help you manage your money wisely. But, not everyone understands what banks are, what they do, and how they operate. Increasing your knowledge about banks can guide you to make better financial decisions and save you money in the long run.

The Origin of Banks

Although money-lending and the exchange of money for goods dates back to ancient times, the first institution most of us would recognize as a bank arose in fourteenth-century Italy. In the cities of Florence, Genoa, and Venice, prominent families established banks to loan money to merchants, finance military operations, and facilitate trade between city-states and regions.

Banks gradually sprang up throughout Europe from the fifteen to the seventeenth centuries. Most of them dealt in bullion (gold and silver bars or ingots) or coins made from gold, silver, copper, or other metals. But, late in the seventeenth century, in Sweden, banks started issuing paper money, notes of credit that promised the holder could exchange the paper for a specified amount of precious metal. Banking continued to expand worldwide, and during the Industrial Revolution in the nineteenth-century banks became the key component in international trade that they remain today.

Types of Banks

You are probably familiar with one kind of bank, the one near you with the drive-through automated teller machine (ATM) and where you may have a savings account. But, there are actually a number of different types of banks, including:

- **Retail banks.** These are the ones you know. Also called "consumer banks," they are usually local branches of larger banking systems that provide a variety of services to individual customers, including savings and checking accounts, loans, and credit and debit cards.

- **Savings and loans.** Less common than they once were, these institutions function similarly to a retail bank, but usually offer more limited services. Their main purpose is to take in savings deposits and make loans, primarily home mortgages.
- **Commercial banks.** These banks cater to business customers with basic services like savings and checking accounts. But they can also accept payments for customers, extend lines of credit to help businesses manage cash flow, and facilitate cash transfers from overseas customers.
- **Investment banks.** Investment banks are set up to facilitate large transactions. Their services can include handling investors' funds, guaranteeing payments, helping institutional clients with mergers or corporate reorganizations, and acting as a broker or financial adviser.
- **Online banks.** These are retail banks that have no physical location, operating instead completely via the Internet. They provide most of the same services as a traditional bank but frequently offer better savings interest rates and more favorable terms on loans.
- **Central banks.** Central banks are national banks that provide services for their country's government. They also implement the government's monetary policy and issue the country's currency. In the United States, this function is served by the Federal Reserve Bank, which was founded in 1913.

Retail Bank Services

Since it is unlikely that you will need the services of other types of banks at the moment, it might be useful to concentrate on your interaction with retail banks, which can include online banks. Some of the services these banks provide include:

- **Savings accounts.** There pay a relatively small amount of interest on your deposits but allow you to withdraw your money at any time. Then there are other types of accounts that earn a higher rate of interest in exchange for leaving your money in the bank for longer periods, such as certificates of deposit (CDs).
- **Checking accounts.** When you open a checking account you deposit funds and receive a book of checks, slips of paper that are a promise to pay a specified amount of money from your account. Checking accounts also let you make deposits and withdrawals from an ATM using a debit card, pay bills online, and transfer money between accounts.
- **Loans.** One of the primary ways banks make money is by taking funds it receives from depositors and lending it to people who need it. The bank makes money by charging a higher fee for these loans than it pays out in interest.

Deposit Advance Loans

Deposit advance loans are short-term loans made by banks. The loan is secured by the borrower's deposit account to which the bank has access. The loan is limited to a percentage of the recurring direct deposit: the lesser of $500 or 50 percent of the scheduled direct deposit based on the amount from the previous deposit into the account.

Repayment is due the next time the direct deposit is made into the account. The bank withdraws the amount of the loan plus the fees from the account before any transactions can be made from the account. In some instances, this puts borrowers into overdraft status (in which they are charged more fees for any subsequent withdrawals on the account).

Many banks are discontinuing this product, but clients may still find them at some banks.

(Source: "Your Money, Your Goals," Consumer Financial Protection Bureau (CFPB))

- **Credit cards.** These are actually a kind of loan. The bank advances funds to a merchant or other payee with the understanding that the customer will pay the money back to the bank at the end of the month, usually with no fee, or over time with a finance charge added.
- **Online and mobile banking.** Even physical banks now provide customers with access to their secure web sites. This allows you to check your balances, transfer funds between accounts, and pay bills from any computer with an Internet connection. Most banks now also have mobile apps that allow you to perform these same functions from a phone or tablet.

Banking Regulation

Through the many centuries of banking, there have been numerous abuses that have sometimes led to personal bankruptcies, bank failures, and even the collapse of the monetary systems of entire countries. As a result, governments place restrictions on banks that regulate the way they handle money and interact with customers. In the United States, banking is regulated by the federal government, as well as by individual states. Many regulations were enacted after the bank failures of the Great Depression that began in 1929, and more were passed following the financial crisis that started in 2007. A few of the federal agencies responsible for overseeing the huge number of bank regulations include:

- **Federal Deposit Insurance Corporation.** Created in 1933, the Federal Deposit Insurance Corporation (FDIC) insures the money in your savings and checking accounts. This agency guarantees that your funds will be there when you need them.
- **Federal Reserve Board.** Often called "The Fed," this is the governing body of the Federal Reserve System (FRS), which provides central control of the country's monetary system. This includes regulating banks, ensuring a stable economy, and providing services to individual banks.

- **Office of the Comptroller of the Currency.** Established in 1863, the purpose of the office of the comptroller of the currency (OCC) is to charter, supervise, and regulate banks to help ensure the stability and proper functioning of the entire banking system.
- **Office of Thrift Supervision.** This agency was created in 1989 by the Financial Institutions Reform, Recovery and Enforcement Act (FIRREA) of that year. It primarily regulates savings and loans in the same way the OCC regulates other banks.

Credit Unions

These financial institutions perform many of the functions of banks, providing customers with services like savings and checking accounts and loans. There are some differences, however, including:

- **Structure.** Most banks are corporations owned by shareholders who elect their governing boards. Credit unions are owned by their customers, called "members." All members, regardless of the size of their deposits, get a vote when electing board members, and while banks pay their board members, credit unions are run by volunteers.
- **Profits.** Banks are in business to make money for their shareholders. Credit unions, on the other hand, are nonprofit organizations. When they make a profit from loans or other investments, they use it to increase interest rates on savings accounts or reduce the finance charges on loans to members.
- **Size.** Through the years, changes in regulations have resulted in the elimination of some restrictions on the way credit unions do business, bringing them more in line with banks. However, the fact remains that today even the biggest credit unions are tiny compared to most banks.
- **Regulations.** As we have seen, the many regulations on banks are overseen by a number of federal and state agencies. But, national regulation of credit unions is handled by the National Credit Union Administration (NCUA), as well as individual state authorities. One of the responsibilities of the NCUA is to manage the National Credit Union Share Insurance Fund (NCUSIF), which is similar to the FDIC in that it insures depositor funds.

Which is better, a bank or a credit union? Like a lot of questions, the answer depends on your individual circumstances. Credit unions have the reputation of providing better, more personal, customer service, which is an important factor for many people. They also generally pay higher interest rates on savings and charge lower fees for loans. But, unlike banks, credit unions may offer limited access to ATMs. And you cannot open an account at just any credit union; most of them have been created to serve specific organizations, employee groups, or geographic regions. But, if you qualify for membership, a credit union may meet your needs. As with any financial decision, do your homework carefully before choosing an option.

References

1. Maxfield, John. "Credit Union versus Bank: 4 Major Differences," Fool.com, June 7, 2015.
2. Roche, Cullen. "The Basics of Banking," Pragcap.com, n.d.
3. "The Role of Banks," ING.com, n.d.
4. Sylla, Richard. "The U.S. Banking System: Origin, Development, and Regulation," Gilderlehrman.org, n.d.
5. "Types of Banks and Federal Deposit Insurance Corporation (FDIC)," Teensguidetomoney.com, n.d.

CHAPTER 4
WHAT IS CREDIT SCORING?

About This Chapter: This chapter includes text excerpted from "Credit Scores," Federal Trade Commission (FTC), September 2013.

Ever wonder how a lender decides whether to grant you credit? For years, creditors have been using credit scoring systems to determine if you would be a good risk for credit cards, auto loans, and mortgages. These days, other types of businesses—including auto and homeowners insurance companies and phone companies—are using credit scores to decide whether to issue you a policy or provide you with a service and on what terms. A higher credit score is taken to mean you are less of a risk, which, in turn, means you are more likely to get credit or insurance—or pay less for it.

Credit scoring is a system creditor use to help determine whether to give you credit. It also may be used to help decide the terms you are offered or the rate you will pay for the loan.

Information about you and your credit experiences, such as your bill-paying history, the number and type of accounts you have, whether you pay your bills by the date they are due, collection actions, outstanding debt, and the age of your accounts, is collected from your credit report. Using a statistical program, creditors compare this information to the loan repayment history of consumers with similar profiles. For example, a credit scoring system awards points for each factor that helps predict who is most likely to repay a debt. A total number of points—a credit score—helps predict how creditworthy you are: how likely it is that you will repay a loan and make the payments when they are due.

Some insurance companies also use credit report information, along with other factors, to help predict your likelihood of filing an insurance claim and the amount of the claim. They may consider this information when they decide whether to grant you insurance and the amount of the premium they charge. The credit scores insurance companies use sometimes are called "insurance scores" or "credit-based insurance scores."

You Have Different Credit Scores

It is normal to see slightly different numbers. At a given point in time, lenders are probably looking at slightly different scores than the ones you see.

Scores are calculated at different times, in different ways.

- **Credit report data.** A score uses data from a credit reporting company, and each may have slightly different data, such as; Equifax, TransUnion, Experian, or others.
- **Timing.** Your scores are not calculated on a fixed schedule, so they depend on when data is updated at a reporting company and when your score is actually calculated.
- **Scoring models.** Companies have created multiple versions of their scoring models and update them frequently. e.g., FICO, VantageScore, etc.

(Source: "What Is a Credit Score?" Consumer Financial Protection Bureau (CFPB))

Credit Scores and Credit Reports

Your credit report is a key part of many credit scoring systems. That is why it is critical to make sure your credit report is accurate. Federal law gives you the right to get a free copy of your credit reports from each of the three national credit reporting companies once every 12 months.

The Fair Credit Reporting Act (FCRA) also gives you the right to get your credit score from the national credit reporting companies. They are allowed to charge a reasonable fee for the score. When you buy your score, you often get information on how you can improve it.

To order your free annual credit report from one or all of the national credit reporting companies, and to purchase your credit score, visit www.annualcreditreport.com, call toll-free 877-322-8228, or complete the Annual Credit Report Request Form and mail it to:

Annual Credit Report Request Service
P.O. Box 105281
Atlanta, GA 30348-5281

How Is a Credit Scoring System Developed?

To develop a credit scoring system or model, a creditor or insurance company selects a random sample of customers and analyzes it statistically to identify characteristics that relate to risk. Each of the characteristics then is assigned a weight based on how strong a predictor it is of who would be a good risk. Each company may use its own scoring model, different scoring models for different types of credit or insurance, or a generic model developed by a scoring company.

Under the Equal Credit Opportunity Act (ECOA), a creditor's scoring system may not use certain characteristics—for example, race, sex, marital status, national origin, or religion—as factors. The law allows creditors to use age, but any credit scoring system that includes age must give equal treatment to applicants who are elderly.

Fair and Accurate Credit Transactions

The Fair and Accurate Credit Transactions Act (FACTA) provides you with better access to your credit information. Under FACTA, consumers are entitled to one free credit report every 12 months from each of the three credit bureaus (Equifax, TransUnion, and Experian). Reviewing these reports allows you to correct any errors in your credit history and protect your credit identity.

(Source: "Credit Reporting," Office of the Comptroller of the Currency (OCC), U.S. Department of the Treasury)

What Can You Do to Improve Your Score?

Credit scoring systems are complex and vary among creditors or insurance companies and for different types of credit or insurance. Even if a single factor changes, your score may change—but improvement generally depends on how that factor relates to others the system considers. Only the business using the system knows what might improve your score under the particular model they use to evaluate your application.

Nevertheless, scoring models usually consider the following types of information in your credit report to help compute your credit score:

- **Have you paid your bills on time?** You can count on payment history to be a significant factor. If your credit report indicates that you have paid bills late, had an account referred to collections, or declared bankruptcy, it is likely to affect your score negatively.
- **Are you maxed out?** Many scoring systems evaluate the amount of debt you have compared to your credit limits. If the amount you owe is close to your credit limit, it's likely to have a negative effect on your score.
- **How long have you had credit?** Generally, scoring systems consider your credit track record. Insufficient credit history may affect your score negatively, but factors such as timely payments and low balances can offset that.
- **Have you applied for new credit recently?** Many scoring systems consider whether you have applied for credit recently by looking at "inquiries" on your credit report. If you have applied for too many new accounts recently, it could have a negative effect on your score. Every inquiry is not counted: for example, inquiries by creditors who are monitoring your account or looking at credit reports to make "prescreened" credit offers are not considered liabilities.
- **How many credit accounts do you have and what kinds of accounts are they?** Although it is generally considered a plus to have established credit accounts, too many credit card accounts may have a negative effect on your score. In addition, many scoring systems consider the type of credit accounts you have. For example, under some scoring models, loans from finance companies may have a negative effect on your credit score.

Scoring models may be based on more than the information in your credit report. When you are applying for a mortgage loan, for example, the system may consider the amount of your down payment, your total debt, and your income, among other things.

Improving your score significantly is likely to take some time, but it can be done. To improve your credit score under most systems, focus on paying your bills in a timely way, paying down any outstanding balances, and staying away from new debt.

Are Credit Scoring Systems Reliable?

Credit scoring systems enable creditors or insurance companies to evaluate millions of applicants consistently on many different characteristics. To be statistically valid, these systems must be based on a big enough sample. They generally vary among businesses that use them.

Properly designed, credit scoring systems generally enable faster, more accurate, and more impartial decisions than individual people can make. And some creditors design their systems so that some applicants—those with scores not high enough to pass easily or low enough to fail absolutely—are referred to a credit manager who decides whether the company or lender will extend credit. Referrals can result in discussion and negotiation between the credit manager and the would-be borrower.

What If You Are Denied Credit or Insurance, or Do Not Get the Terms You Want?

If you are denied credit, the ECOA requires that the creditor give you a notice with the specific reasons your application was rejected or the news that you have the right to learn the reasons if you ask within 60 days. Ask the creditor to be specific: Indefinite and vague reasons for the denial are illegal. Acceptable reasons might be "your income was low" or "you haven't been employed long enough." Unacceptable reasons include "you didn't meet our minimum standards" or "you didn't receive enough points on our credit scoring system."

Sometimes you can be denied credit or insurance—or offered less favorable terms—because of information in your credit report. In that case, the FCRA requires the creditor or insurance company to give you a notice that includes, among other things, the name, address, and phone number of the credit reporting company that supplied the information. If a credit score was a factor in the decision to deny you credit or to offer you terms less favorable than most other customers receive, the notice also will include that credit score. If you receive one of these notices, you are entitled to a free copy of your credit report. Contact the company to find out what your report said. The credit reporting company can tell you what is in your report, but only the creditor or insurance company can tell you why your application was denied.

If a creditor or insurance company says you were denied credit or insurance because you are too near your credit limits on your credit cards, you may want to reapply after paying down your balances. Because credit scores are based on credit report information, a score often changes when the information in the credit report changes.

If you have been denied credit or insurance or did not get the rate or terms you want, ask questions:

- Ask the creditor or insurance company if a credit scoring system was used. If it was, ask what characteristics or factors were used in the system, and how you can improve your application.
- If you receive a notice explaining that you are being offered less favorable credit terms than those offered to most other consumers, ask the creditor or insurance company why you are not getting its best offer.
- If you are denied credit or not offered the best rate available because of inaccuracies in your credit report, be sure to dispute inaccurate information with the credit reporting company.

CHAPTER 5
A CREDIT REPORT

About This Chapter: Text in this chapter begins with excerpts from "What Is a Credit Report?" Consumer Financial Protection Bureau (CFPB), June 8, 2017; Text under the heading "Tips for Credit Reports" is excerpted from "Consumer Protection Topics—Credit Reports," Federal Deposit Insurance Corporation (FDIC), February 29, 2016.

A credit report is a statement that has information about your credit activity and current credit situation, such as loan paying history and the status of your credit accounts.

Most people have more than one credit report. Credit reporting companies, also known as "credit bureaus" or "consumer reporting agencies," collect and store financial data about you that is submitted to them by creditors, such as lenders, credit card companies, and other financial companies. Creditors are not required to report to every credit reporting company.

Lenders use these reports to help them decide if they will loan you money, what interest rates they will offer you. Lenders also use your credit report to determine whether you continue to meet the terms of an existing credit account. Other businesses might use your credit reports to determine whether to offer you insurance; rent a house or apartment to you; provide you with cable TV, Internet, utility, or cell phone service. If you agree to let an employer look at your credit report, it may also be used to make employment decisions about you.

Components of a Credit Report

Credit reports contain the following information.

Personal Information

- Your name and any name you may have used in the past in connection with a credit account, including nicknames
- Current and former addresses
- Birthdate
- Social Security number (SSN)
- Phone number(s)

How You Can Order Your Free Report

The three nationwide credit-reporting companies have set up a central website, a toll-free telephone number, and a mailing address through which you can order your free annual report.

To order, visit annualcreditreport.com, call 877-322-8228. Or complete the Annual Credit Report RequestForm(www.consumer.ftc.gov/sites/www.consumer.ftc.gov/files/articles/pdf/pdf-0093-annual-report-request-form.pdf) and mail it to Annual Credit Report Request Service, P.O. Box 105281, Atlanta, GA 30348-5281. Do not contact the three nationwide credit reporting companies individually. They are providing free annual credit reports only through annualcreditreport.com, 877-322-8228 or mailing to Annual Credit Report Request Service.

You may order your reports from each of the three nationwide credit reporting companies at the same time, or you can order your report from each of the companies one at a time. The law allows you to order one free copy of your report from each of the nationwide credit reporting companies every 12 months.

(Source: "Free Credit Reports," Federal Trade Commission (FTC))

Credit Accounts

- Current and historical credit accounts, including the type of account (mortgage, installment, revolving, etc.)
- The credit limit or amount
- Account balance
- Account payment history
- The date and the account was opened and closed
- The name of the creditor

Collection Items

Public Records

- Liens
- Foreclosures
- Bankruptcies
- Civil suits and judgments

A credit report may include information on overdue child support provided by a state or local child support agency or verified by any local, state, or federal government agency.

Inquiries

- Companies that have accessed your credit report

Tips for Credit Reports

- Pay your loans and other bills on time. Even if you fell into trouble in the past, you can rebuild your credit history by beginning to make payments as agreed. Paying your debts on time will have a positive effect on your credit score and can improve your access to credit.

Equal Credit Opportunity Act

The Equal Credit Opportunity Act (ECOA) prohibits credit discrimination on the basis of sex, race, marital status, religion, national origin, age, or receipt of public assistance. Creditors may ask for this information (except religion) in certain situations, but they may not use it to discriminate against you when deciding whether to grant you credit.

The ECOA protects consumers who deal with companies that regularly extend credit, including banks, small loans, and finance companies, retail and department stores, credit-card companies, and credit unions. Everyone who participates in the decision to grant credit, including real estate brokers who arrange to finance, must follow this law. Businesses applying for credit also are protected by this law.

(Source: "Credit and Your Consumer Rights," Federal Trade Commission (FTC))

- To help show that you have not borrowed too much, try to minimize how much you owe in relation to your credit limit. Do not automatically close credit-card accounts that have been paid in full and have not been used recently because that may lower your available credit. However, you may want to close a card with a zero balance if you pay a monthly fee for the card.
- If you believe you cannot repay your creditors, contact them immediately and explain your situation. Ask about renegotiating the terms of your loan, including the amount you repay. Reputable credit counseling organizations also can help you develop a personalized plan to solve your money problems, but less-reputable providers offer questionable or expensive services or make unsubstantiated claims.

CHAPTER 6
DISPUTING ERRORS ON CREDIT REPORTS

About This Chapter: This chapter includes text excerpted from "Disputing Errors on Credit Reports," Federal Trade Commission (FTC), February 2017.

Your credit report contains information about where you live, how you pay your bills, and whether you have been sued or arrested, or have filed for bankruptcy. Credit reporting companies sell the information in your report to creditors, insurers, employers, and other businesses that use it to evaluate your applications for credit, insurance, employment, or renting a home. The federal Fair Credit Reporting Act (FCRA) promotes the accuracy and privacy of information in the files of the nation's credit reporting companies.

Some financial advisors and consumer advocates suggest that you review your credit report periodically. Why?

- Because the information it contains affects whether you can get a loan—and how much you will have to pay to borrow money.
- To make sure the information is accurate, complete, and up-to-date before you apply for a loan for a major purchase such as a house or car, buy insurance, or apply for a job.
- To help guard against identity theft. That is when someone uses your personal information—such as your name, your Social Security number (SSN), or your credit card number—to commit fraud. Identity thieves may use your information to open a new credit card account in your name. Then, when they do not pay the bills, the delinquent account is reported on your credit report. Inaccurate information like that could affect your ability to get credit, insurance, or even a job.

How to Order Your Free Report

An amendment to the FCRA requires each of the nationwide credit reporting companies—Equifax, Experian, and TransUnion—to provide you with a free copy of your credit report, at your request, once every 12 months.

Managing Debt—Where Do I Start?

- Make a budget
  - Write down what you make and spend in a month
  - Look at where your money goes
  - Look for ways to save money
- Call the companies where you owe money
  - Explain why you have trouble paying the bill
  - Ask for a plan to let you pay less each month
- Get help from a credit counselor

(Source: "Managing Debt," Federal Trade Commission (FTC))

The three nationwide credit reporting companies have set up one website, toll-free telephone number, and mailing address through which you can order your free annual report. To order, visit www.annualcreditreport.com, call 877-322-8228, or complete the Annual Credit Report Request Form and mail it to:

Annual Credit Report Request Service
P.O. Box 105281
Atlanta, GA 30348-5281

Do not contact the three nationwide credit reporting companies individually.

You may order your reports from each of the three nationwide credit reporting companies at the same time, or you can order from only one or two. The FCRA allows you to order one free copy from each of the nationwide credit reporting companies every 12 months.

You need to provide your name, address, SSN, and date of birth. If you have moved in the last two years, you may have to provide your previous address. To maintain the security of your file, each nationwide credit reporting company may ask you for some information that only you would know, like the amount of your monthly mortgage payment. Each company may ask you for different information because the information each has in your file may come from different sources.

Other Situations Where You Might Be Eligible for a Free Report

You are also entitled to a free report if a company takes adverse action against you, such as denying your application for credit, insurance, or employment, based on information in your report. You must ask for your report within 60 days of receiving notice of the action. The notice will give you the name, address, and phone number of the credit reporting company.

You are also entitled to one free report a year if you are unemployed and plan to look for a job within 60 days; if you are on welfare; or if your report is inaccurate because of fraud, including identity theft.

Otherwise, a credit reporting company may charge you a reasonable amount for another copy of your report within a 12-month period. To buy a copy of your report, contact the three credit report companies:

Experian-888-397-3742 (www.experian.com)
TransUnion-800-916-8800 (www.transunion.com)
Equifax-800-685-1111 (www.equifax.com)

Correcting Errors

Under the FCRA, both the credit reporting company and the information provider (that is, the person, company, or organization that provides information about you to a credit reporting company) are responsible for correcting inaccurate or incomplete information in your report. To take advantage of all your rights under this law, contact the credit reporting company and the information provider.

Tell the credit reporting company, in writing, what information you think is inaccurate. Include copies (NOT originals) of documents that support your position. In addition to providing your complete name and address, your letter should clearly identify each item in your report you dispute, state the facts and explain why you dispute the information and request that it be removed or corrected. You may want to enclose a copy of your report with the items in question circled. Send your letter by certified mail, "return receipt requested," so you can document what the credit reporting company received. Keep copies of your dispute letter and enclosures.

Credit reporting companies must investigate the items in question—usually within 30 days—unless they consider your dispute frivolous. They also must forward all the relevant data you provide about the inaccuracy to the organization that provided the information. After the information provider receives notice of a dispute from the credit reporting company, it must investigate, review the relevant information, and report the results back to the credit reporting company. If the information provider finds the disputed information is inaccurate, it must notify all three nationwide credit reporting companies so they can correct the information in your file.

When the investigation is complete, the credit reporting company must give you the results in writing and a free copy of your report if the dispute results in a change. This free report does not count as your annual free report. If an item is changed or deleted, the credit reporting company cannot put the disputed information back in your file unless the information provider verifies that it is accurate and complete. The credit reporting company also must send you written notice that includes the name, address, and phone number of the information provider.

If you ask, the credit reporting company must send notices of any corrections to anyone who received your report in the past six months. You can have a corrected copy of your report sent to anyone who received a copy during the past two years for employment purposes.

If an investigation does not resolve your dispute with the credit reporting company, you can ask that a statement of the dispute be included in your file and in future reports. You also can ask the credit reporting company to provide your statement to anyone who received a copy of your report in the recent past. You can expect to pay a fee for this service.

Step Two

Tell the information provider (that is, the person, company, or organization that provides information about you to a credit reporting company), in writing, that you dispute an item in your credit report. Include copies (NOT originals) of documents that support your position. If the provider listed an address on your credit report, send your letter to that address. If no address is listed, contact the provider and ask for the correct address to send your letter. If the information provider does not give you an address, you can send your letter to any business address for that provider.

If the provider continues to report the item you disputed to a credit reporting company, it must let the credit reporting company know about your dispute. And if you are correct—that is, if the information you dispute is found to be inaccurate or incomplete—the information provider must tell the credit reporting company to update or delete the item.

About Your File

Your credit file may not reflect all your credit accounts. Although most national department store and all-purpose bank credit card accounts will be included in your file, not all creditors supply information to credit reporting companies: some local retailers, credit unions, travel, entertainment, and gasoline card companies are among the creditors that do not.

When negative information in your report is accurate, only the passage of time can assure its removal. A credit reporting company can report most accurate negative information for seven years and bankruptcy information for 10 years. Information about an unpaid judgment against you can be reported for seven years or until the statute of limitations runs out, whichever is longer. There is no time limit on reporting: information about criminal convictions; information reported in response to your application for a job that pays more than $75,000 a year; and information reported because you have applied for more than $150,000 worth of credit or life insurance. There is a standard method for calculating the seven-year reporting period. Generally, the period runs from the date that the event took place.

CHAPTER 7

CREDIT ISSUES AND WHAT YOU CAN DO TO FIX THEM

About This Chapter: This chapter includes text excerpted from "Three Common Credit Issues and What You Can Do to Fix Them," Consumer Financial Protection Bureau (CFPB), April 13, 2018.

Your credit history can determine if you can get a loan, and even where you live or work. Credit scores are built from your credit history and can determine how much you pay to borrow money for a car or house. Yet, many people do not know where to start when it comes to building, improving, or protecting their credit history. Three common credit problems are:

- Lack of enough credit history
- Denied credit application
- Fraud and identity theft

Lack of Enough Credit History

Many people may not know that having no credit history, or a limited credit history, can create issues similar to having negative information in your credit history. If you do not currently have a credit history, you are not alone. One in ten adults experiences "credit invisibility," meaning they do not have any credit history with one of the three nationwide credit-reporting companies. Many more do not have enough credit history, sometimes referred to as having "thin" credit, to generate a credit score. People with thin or no credit history may find it difficult to apply for a loan or rent an apartment.

What You Can Do

Take action to help build your credit history responsibly. There are a number of products considered helpful in establishing or rebuilding credit histories, and they provide you with the opportunity to practice making on-time payments that are reported to the credit-reporting companies. These may include secured credit cards, credit-builder loans, or retail store credit cards.

Denied Credit Application

If you have been denied an application for a loan or line of credit, there are steps you can take to improve your credit score or dispute inaccurate information on your credit report.

What You Can Do

- Find out why your application was denied. If a lender rejects your application, they are required under the Equal Credit Opportunity Act (ECOA) to tell you why your application was rejected or tell you that you have the right to learn the reasons if you ask within 60 days.
    - If you were denied due to an "insufficient credit file," you can use this checklist to learn how to build and keep good credit (files.consumerfinance.gov/f/documents/201612_cfpb_credit_invisible_checklist.PDF).
    - If a lender rejected your application based on your credit report, they must provide specific information about why your application was rejected or tell you that you have the right to learn more about why you were denied if you ask within 60 days.
- Review your credit reports. Make sure the information in your credit reports is accurate. If you find errors, take steps to correct them.
- Improve your credit history with a few best practices, such as paying your bills on time and limiting your credit use to no more than a third of your credit limit.

Fraud or Identity Theft

Identity theft occurs when someone uses your name, Social Security number (SSN), date of birth, or other identifying information, without authority, to commit fraud.

What You Can Do

If you think you have been a victim of fraud or identity theft, there are several steps you can take to protect your personal information from being misused. These steps include:

- Reviewing your credit reports each year to make sure they contain only information about you
- Immediately reporting any inaccurate or suspicious information on your credit reports
- Placing a fraud alert or security freeze on your credit reports
- Consider signing up for identity monitoring or credit monitoring services. Some of these services are free, and others cost money. If you are considering these services, be aware that there are other free and low-cost services to protect consumers, including a security freeze or fraud alert. If you are considering signing up for identity or credit monitoring services, make sure you fully understand the terms and conditions related to trial

periods, fees, cancellation requirements, and other conditions so that you do not face unexpected fees, charges, or other limitations.

Next Steps

Building or rebuilding your credit will take time and planning. The steps above can guide you on your journey.

If you want more help, consider talking to a credit counselor. Most reputable credit counseling organizations do provide free educational materials and workshops, though some do not. Building or improving on your credit will not happen overnight. Anyone who claims to be able to do this for you may be scamming you.

CHAPTER 8
UNDERSTANDING DEBT

About This Chapter: This chapter includes text excerpted from "Managing Debt," Federal Trade Commission (FTC), September 28, 2012.

What Is Debt?

When you owe money to someone, you are in debt. Owing money is not always bad. You might have a loan. You might use a credit card. If you do, you might be in debt. But, if you pay your bills when they are due, it might help your credit history.

When Is Debt Bad?

Debt is bad when you owe money you cannot pay back. Debt collectors might call you. You might have legal problems if you cannot pay back the money.

Does Debt Hurt My Credit History?

Sometimes, debt can hurt your credit history. For example:

- Owing a lot of money on credit cards
- Paying bills late
- Not paying the minimum amount due
- Skipping payments

These things can hurt your credit history.

Who Can Help Me with Debt?

You can do some things yourself. A credit counselor can help you. Credit counselors can help you make a budget. Credit counselors also can help you make a plan to repay your debts.

Debt-relief services companies might offer to help. These companies are different from credit counselors. They might charge you high prices. And they might not really help.

> **How to Reduce Your Debt**
> Getting out of debt is possible when you know what you owe and what you can do to repay it. If you are ready to begin paying down your debt, start with these three steps:
> - Step one: Understand debt-reduction strategies
> - Step two: Create your debt-reduction plan
> - Step three: Organize your monthly bills
>
> *(Source: "How to Reduce Your Debt," Consumer Financial Protection Bureau (CFPB))*

Who Are Debt Collectors?

Debt collectors try to collect the money you owe to someone else. Debt collectors must follow rules when they call you. If they do not follow the rules, you can complain about them to the Federal Trade Commission (FTC).

Can I Stop Debt Collectors from Bothering Me?

You can ask a debt collector to stop calling you. Legally, they must stop. If they do not, you can report them to the FTC.

What to Know

What Can I Do to Get Out of Debt?

Start by making a budget. Write down how much money you make every month. Write down how much you spend every month. Include:

- Rent
- Car payment
- Insurance
- Utilities
- Food
- Gas
- Credit card bills
- Other bills

Look for ways to spend less money. You might not find ways to save. But, it helps to write down what you spend. Then you can make a budget.

How Else Can I Try to Get Out of Debt?

Call the companies you owe money to. Explain why you have trouble paying your bill. Ask for a "payment plan." Some companies might let you pay less every month until you have repaid all the money.

Call the company before it sends your debt to a debt collector. Many debt collectors will not accept a payment plan.

How Can I Get Help?

Credit counselors can help you make a budget. Credit counselors also can help you plan to repay your debt.

A good credit counselor will spend time with you. The counselor will ask you all about your finances. A good counselor will:

- Talk with you
- Help make a plan that works for you

A good counselor will not:

- Promise to fix all your problems
- Charge you a lot of money before doing anything

How Do I Find a Credit Counselor?

Look for a credit counselor you can meet in person. Look here first:

- Credit unions
- Universities
- Military bases
- The U.S. Cooperative Extension Service (CES)

These groups sometimes have credit counselors who charge low fees to help you.

How Do I Choose a Credit Counselor?

When you find a credit counselor, ask questions. Choose a counselor who can help you make a budget. Choose a counselor who also can help you plan to stay out of debt.

Some counselors might suggest a "debt-management plan" as your only choice. Others might talk about a "debt-settlement plan." If they do either of these things, go somewhere else.

What Is a Debt-Management Plan?

A debt-management plan is one way to repay the money you owe. Here is how it works:

- A credit counselor works with you and the companies you owe money to.
- You all agree to a plan for how you will repay the money you owe.
- Sometimes the companies agree to a lower interest rate. Sometimes they do not.
- Every month, you deposit money into an account with the credit counselor.
- The credit counselor pays your credit card, medical, or student loan bills.
- This continues until your debt is repaid.

Debt-management plans might help some people. These plans do not help everyone. A good credit counselor can help you decide what might help you.

What Is a Debt-Settlement Plan?

Some people say a debt-settlement plan is a way to repay money you owe. But, many companies that offer these plans make promises they cannot keep.

Some companies say:

- They can help you pay less than you owe and get out of debt
- They can get bad information taken off your credit report
- You should stop paying your bills and send the money to their company

Many people who use debt-settlement plans find they owe more money, not less. These companies charge you a lot of money, and then they do not help you.

What Does a Debt Collector Do?

A debt collector is someone who tries to collect money owed to someone else.

The company you owe money to hires a debt collector. The debt collector only makes money if he gets money from you. The debt collector starts calling you to get that money. If the debt collector does not get the money, he might take you to court.

What Rules Must Debt Collectors Follow?

U.S. law stipulates that a debt collector:

- Can call only from 8 a.m. to 9 p.m.
- Cannot tell anyone else about your debt
- Can talk to someone else only to find out your address, home phone number, or where you work
- Cannot harass you—for example, they cannot curse at you or threaten to hurt you
- Cannot lie to you

The law also says debt collectors must send you a written notice about your debt. This is called a "validation notice." The notice must say:

- How much you owe
- Who you owe the money to
- What to do if you do not owe the money

Are There Problems with Debt Collectors?

The government gets complaints from thousands of people about debt collectors. Some of the complaints say, debt collectors:

- Break the rules
- Threaten people
- Call the wrong person
- Lie while they try to collect a debt that is not yours

What Can I Do If a Debt Collector Calls?

To prepare for a possible debt-collector call:

- Keep a notebook by your phone or with you.
- Ask the debt collector his name, his company's name, address, phone number, and why he is calling.
- Write the answers in your notebook.
- Write the date and time you talked.

Then you have a record if you need to complain, or if you need to go to court to defend yourself.

How Can I Stop Calls from a Debt Collector?

Do you want the debt collector to stop calling you? You must send a letter telling the debt collector to stop calling. The law says he must stop calling you then.

If a debt collector breaks the law, file a complaint. The FTC tries to catch debt collectors who break the law.

You can help. Report bad debt collectors to the FTC at 877-382-4357.

What Happens If I Get Sued

Stopping calls does not mean the debt goes away. The debt collector might still sue you to collect money. If you are being sued, you should get a notice in the mail. Sometimes, this is called a "summons."

In a lawsuit, the debt collector usually asks the court to:

- Say how much you owe
- Make you repay that amount

The court might even tell your employer to take money out of your paycheck until you repay what you owe. This is called "garnishing" your wages.

Do not ignore notices about a lawsuit. If you do not go to court, you automatically lose.

CHAPTER 9
SEEKING CREDIT COUNSELING

About This Chapter: This chapter includes text excerpted from "What Is Credit Counseling?" Consumer Financial Protection Bureau (CFPB), February 2, 2018.

Credit-counseling organizations can advise you on your money and debts, help you with a budget, and offer money management workshops.

Credit counseling organizations are usually nonprofit organizations. Typically, their counselors are certified and trained in the areas of consumer credit, money and debt management, and budgeting. Counselors discuss your financial situation with you and help you develop a personalized plan to solve your money problems. Here are some examples of what credit counselors might do:

- Advise you on managing your money and debts
- Help you develop a budget
- Help you get a copy of your credit report and scores
- May offer free educational materials and workshops
- Organize a "debt management plan (DMP)" to pay down your debts

Tip: If you are having trouble making payments on your debts, a credit counselor may be able to help you with advice or by organizing a "debt management plan" (DMP) for all of your debts. Typically, under a DMP, you make a single payment to the credit counseling organization each month or pay period and the credit counseling organization makes monthly payments to each of your creditors. Under DMPs, credit counselors usually do not negotiate any reduction in the amounts you owe—instead, they can lower your overall monthly payment. They do so by negotiating extensions of the periods over which you can repay a loan and by asking creditors to lower the interest rates and waive certain fees.

How Do You Find a Credit Counselor?

Most credit counselors offer services through in-person meetings at local offices, the Internet, or on the telephone. To get started, you can try the Financial Counseling

Regarding Nonprofit Status

Be aware that "nonprofit" status does not guarantee that services are free, affordable, or even legitimate. In fact, some credit-counseling organizations charge high fees, which they may hide; others might urge their clients to make "voluntary" contributions that can cause more debt.

(Source: "Choosing a Credit Counselor," Federal Trade Commission (FTC))

Association of America (FCAA), on their website or by phone at 800-450-1794, or the National Foundation for Credit Counseling (NFCC), on their website or by phone at 800-388-2227.

Once you have developed a list of potential credit counseling organizations, check them out with your state Attorney General and state consumer protection agency (CPA). Ask the counselors for free information about their services.

How Do You Choose Which Credit Counselor Is Right for You?

A reputable credit counseling organization should be willing to send you free information about itself and the services it provides without requiring you to provide any details about your situation. If a service does not do that, consider this a red flag and go elsewhere for help.

Here are some questions to ask to help you find the best credit counseling service for you.

What Services Do You Offer?

Look for an organization that offers a range of services, including budget counseling and classes for managing spending and debt. Avoid organizations that push a debt management plan as your only option before they have spent a significant amount of time analyzing your financial situation.

How Is Credit Counseling Offered?

Services may be offered in-person, by phone, or online. An initial counseling session typically lasts an hour, with an offer of follow-up sessions.

Do You Offer Free Educational Materials?

Avoid organizations that charge for the information.

What Are Your Fees?

Is there set-up or monthly fees? Get a specific price quote in writing. Although most credit counseling organizations are nonprofits, credit counselors may charge fees for some of their services that they take out of the payments you make to them.

What If I Cannot Afford to Pay Your Fees or Make Contributions?

If an organization would not help you because you cannot afford to pay, look elsewhere.

Will I Have a Formal Written Agreement or Contract?

Do not sign anything without reading it first. Make sure all verbal promises are also in writing. As with any contract, do not sign anything that you do not understand.

What Are the Counselor's Qualifications?

Is the organization or counselor accredited or certified? What are the qualifications of its credit counselors? Find out about what training or professional certifications the counselor has received.

How Are Your Employees Paid?

Are the employees paid more if I sign up for certain services, if I pay a fee, or if I make a contribution to your organization? If the answer is yes, consider this a red flag and go elsewhere.

CHAPTER 10
CREDIT REPAIR

About This Chapter: This chapter includes text excerpted from "Credit Repair: How to Help Yourself," Federal Trade Commission (FTC), November 2012.

You see the ads in newspapers, on TV, and online. You hear them on the radio. You get fliers in the mail, email messages, and maybe even calls offering credit repair services.

They all make the same claims:

"Credit problems? No problem!"

"We can remove bankruptcies, judgments, liens, and bad loans from your credit file forever!"

"We can erase your bad credit—100 percent guaranteed."

"Create a new credit identity—legally."

Do yourself a favor and save some money, too. Do not believe these claims: they are very likely signs of a scam. Indeed, attorneys at the Federal Trade Commission (FTC), the nation's consumer protection agency (CPA), say they have never seen a legitimate credit repair operation making those claims. The fact is there is no quick fix for creditworthiness. You can improve your credit report legitimately, but it takes time, a conscious effort, and sticking to a personal debt repayment plan.

Your Rights

No one can legally remove accurate and timely negative information from a credit report. You can ask for an investigation—at no charge to you—of information in your file that you dispute as inaccurate or incomplete. Some people hire a company to investigate for them, but anything a credit repair company can do legally, you can do for yourself at little or no cost. By law:

- You are entitled to a free credit report if a company takes "adverse action" against you, such as denying your application for credit, insurance, or employment. You have to ask for your report within 60 days of receiving notice of the action. The notice includes the name, address, and phone number of the consumer reporting company. You are also entitled to one free report a year if you are unemployed and plan to look for a job within 60 days; if you are on welfare; or if your report is inaccurate because of fraud, including identity theft.

- Each of the nationwide credit-reporting companies—Equifax, Experian, and TransUnion—is required to provide you with a free copy of your credit report once every 12 months, if you ask for it. To order, visit www.annualcreditreport.com, or call 877-322-8228. You may order reports from each of the three credit-reporting companies at the same time, or you can stagger your requests throughout the year.
- It does not cost anything to dispute mistakes or outdated items on your credit report. Both the credit-reporting company and the information provider (the person, company, or organization that provides information about you to a credit-reporting company) are responsible for correcting inaccurate or incomplete information in your report. To take advantage of all your rights, contact both the credit reporting company and the information provider.

Do It Yourself

Step 1: Tell the credit-reporting company, in writing, what information you think is inaccurate. Include copies (not originals) of any documents that support your position. In addition to including your complete name and address, your letter should identify each item in your report that you dispute; state the facts and the reasons you dispute the information, and ask that it be removed or corrected. You may want to enclose a copy of your report, and circle the items in question. Send your letter by certified mail, "return receipt requested," so you can document that the credit reporting company got it. Keep copies of your dispute letter and enclosures.

Credit-reporting companies must investigate the items you question within 30 days—unless they consider your dispute frivolous. They also must forward all the relevant data you provide about the inaccuracy to the organization that provided the information. After the information provider gets notice of a dispute from the credit-reporting company, it must investigate, review the relevant information, and report the results back to the credit-reporting company. If the investigation reveals that the disputed information is inaccurate, the information provider has to notify the nationwide credit-reporting companies so they can correct it in your file.

When the investigation is complete, the credit-reporting company must give you the results in writing, too, and a free copy of your report if the dispute results in a change. If an item is changed or deleted, the credit-reporting company cannot put the disputed information back in your file unless the information provider verifies that it is accurate and complete. The credit-reporting company also must send you written notice that includes the name, address, and phone number of the information provider. If you ask, the credit-reporting company must send notices of any correction to anyone who got your report in the past six months. You also can ask that a corrected copy of your report be sent to anyone who got a copy during the past two years for employment purposes.

If an investigation does not resolve your dispute with the credit-reporting company, you can ask that a statement of the dispute be included in your file and in future reports. You also can ask the credit-reporting company to give your statement to anyone who got a copy of your report in the recent past. You will probably have to pay for this service.

Step 2: Tell the creditor or other information provider, in writing, that you dispute an item. Include copies (not originals) of documents that support your position. Many providers specify an address for disputes. If the provider reports the item to a consumer reporting company, it must include a notice of your dispute. And if the information is found to be inaccurate, the provider may not report it again.

Reporting Accurate Negative Information

When negative information in your report is accurate, only time can make it go away. A credit-reporting company can report most accurate negative information for seven years and bankruptcy information for 10 years. Information about an unpaid judgment against you can be reported for seven years or until the statute of limitations runs out, whichever is longer. The seven-year reporting period starts from the date the event took place. There is no time limit on reporting information about criminal convictions; information reported in response to your application for a job that pays more than $75,000 a year; and information reported because you have applied for more than $150,000 worth of credit or life insurance.

The Credit Repair Organizations Act

The Credit Repair Organizations Act (CROA) makes it illegal for credit-repair companies to lie about what they can do for you, and to charge you before they have performed their services. The CROA is enforced by the FTC and requires credit-repair companies to explain:

- Your legal rights in a written contract that also details the services they will perform
- Your three-day right to cancel without any charge
- How long it will take to get results
- The total cost you will pay
- Any guarantees

What if a credit repair-company you hired does not live up to its promises? You have some options. You can:

- Sue them in federal court for your actual losses or for what you paid them, whichever is more

- Seek punitive damages—money to punish the company for violating the law
- Join other people in a class action lawsuit against the company, and if you win, the company has to pay your attorney's fees

Report Credit-Repair Fraud

State Attorneys General

Many states also have laws regulating credit-repair companies. If you have a problem with a credit-repair company, report it to your local consumer affairs office or to your state Attorney General (AG).

Federal Trade Commission

You also can file a complaint with the FTC. Although the FTC cannot resolve individual credit disputes, it can take action against a company if there is a pattern of possible law violations. File your complaint online at www.ftc.gov/complaint, or call 877-FTC-HELP (877-382-4357).

Where to Get Legitimate Help

Just because you have a poor credit history does not mean you cannot get credit. Creditors set their own standards, and not all look at your credit history the same way. Some may look only at recent years to evaluate you for credit, and they may give you credit if your bill-paying history has improved. It may be worthwhile to contact creditors informally to discuss their credit standards.

If you are not disciplined enough to create a budget and stick to it, to work out a repayment plan with your creditors, or to keep track of your mounting bills, you might consider contacting a credit-counseling organization. Many are nonprofits and work with you to solve your financial problems. But, remember that "nonprofit" status does not guarantee free, affordable, or even legitimate services. In fact, some credit-counseling organizations—even some that claim nonprofit status—may charge high fees or hide their fees by pressuring people to make "voluntary" contributions that only cause more debt.

Most credit counselors offer services through local offices, online, or on the phone. If possible, find an organization that offers in-person counseling. Many universities, military bases, credit unions, housing authorities, and branches of the U.S. Cooperative Extension Service operate nonprofit credit-counseling programs. Your financial institution, local consumer protection agency, and friends and family also may be good sources of information and referrals.

If you are thinking about filing for bankruptcy, be aware that bankruptcy laws require that you get credit counseling from a government-approved organization within six months before you file for bankruptcy relief. You can find a state-by-state list of government-approved organizations at www.usdoj.gov/ust, the website of the U.S. Trustee Program. That is the organization within the U.S. Department of Justice (DOJ) that supervises bankruptcy cases and trustees. Be wary of credit-counseling organizations that say they are government-approved, but do not appear on the list of approved organizations.

Reputable credit-counseling organizations can advise you on managing your money and debts, help you develop a budget, and offer free educational materials and workshops. Their counselors are certified and trained in the areas of consumer credit, money and debt management, and budgeting. Counselors discuss your entire financial situation with you, and can help you develop a personalized plan to solve your money problems. An initial counseling session typically lasts an hour, with an offer of follow-up sessions.

CHAPTER 11
A CREDIT-REPAIR SCAM

About This Chapter: Text in this chapter begins with excerpts from "How Can I Tell a Credit Repair Scam from a Reputable Credit Counselor?" Consumer Financial Protection Bureau (CFPB), June 8, 2017; Text beginning with the heading "How to Avoid Credit-Repair Service Scams" is excerpted from "How to Avoid Credit Repair Service Scams," Consumer Financial Protection Bureau (CFPB), September 23, 2016.

There are counselors who can help you with your credit report, and others who take your money but do not help you.

Recognizing a Credit-Repair Scam

Warning signs for credit-repair scams include companies that ask you to pay before providing services. The company may tell you it can guarantee a specific increase in your credit score or get rid of negative credit information in your credit report, even though the information is accurate and current.

If you see advertisements or receive offers to repair or fix your credit, it could be a warning sign if the company:

- **Pressures you to pay upfront fees.** The company wants you to pay before it provides any services. A simple rule to follow is "Do not pay upfront." If the company uses telemarketing such that the federal Telemarketing Sales Rule (TSR) applies, the credit-repair company may not request or receive fees until it gives you a credit-report generated more than six months after the promised results that shows the results. Under the federal Credit Repair Organizations Act (CROA), credit-repair companies cannot request or receive payment until they have completed the services they have promised. Some companies will structure monthly payment plans to try to avoid this requirement. You should know that all forms of upfront payment before services are completed are illegal.
- **Promises to remove negative information from your credit report.** The company tells you it can get rid of the negative credit information, even if that information is accurate and current. No one can do this.

You have probably seen ads from companies promising a "new credit identity"—that is, a fresh start for your credit history. It may seem like just the thing you need to get your credit back on track, but it is actually a scam. These companies often sell Social Security numbers (SSN) illegally. If you use a number other than your own to apply for credit, not only will you not get credit, but you also could face fines or prison.

If your credit is less than golden, there are steps you can take to repair it on your own, at no cost. Only time and a personal debt repayment plan will improve your credit.

(Source: "Credit Repair Scams," Federal Trade Commission (FTC))

- **Requests you dispute accurate information in your credit report.** The company advises you to dispute all the information in your credit report, regardless of its accuracy or timeliness.
- **Refuses or avoids explaining your rights to you.** The company does not tell you your rights and what you can do for yourself for free. Disputing errors in your credit reports is a free legal right available to you under the Fair Credit Reporting Act (FCRA); you do not need to pay a credit-repair organization to do it for you. Also, if you have just signed up for a credit-repair service, you have the right to cancel your contract with any credit-repair organization for any reason within three business days at no charge to you.
- **Tells you to not contact credit-reporting companies.** The company recommends that you do not contact any of the nationwide credit-reporting companies directly.

Credit-repair companies are subject to numerous federal laws, including the CROA and often the TSR, both of which forbid credit-repair organizations from using deceptive practices and from accepting upfront fees. These laws prohibit many deceptive practices by credit-repair organizations. You may have a right to sue a credit-repair organization using these laws.

How Do You Find a Reputable Credit Counselor?

Most credit counselors offer services through local offices, online, or on the telephone. You can find a list of approved credit counselors online.

Once you have developed a list of potential counseling agencies, check them out with your State Attorney General's office and local consumer protection agency (CPA).

Finally, ask the credit-counseling agency for free information about their services and what they provide. A reputable credit-counseling agency should be willing to send you free information about itself and the services it provides without requiring you to provide any details about your situation. If a service does not do that, consider it a red flag and go elsewhere for help.

How to Avoid Credit-Repair Service Scams

Repairing your credit history after a setback can feel overwhelming. Unfortunately, that is why some credit-repair companies use confusing and misleading messaging to target anxious consumers who are just trying to get their financial lives back on track.

Over the course of several months, more than half of people who submitted complaints with the Consumer Financial Protection Bureau (CFPB) about credit repair chose the issue "fraud or scam" to describe their complaints.

Many people do not know the full set of protections they have or understand the laws that govern credit-repair companies. These companies must follow numerous federal laws, including the CROA and often the TSR, both of which forbid credit-repair organizations from using deceptive practices and from accepting upfront fees.

If you see advertisements or receive offers to fix your credit, look out for these red flags:

They demand payment upfront: The company wants you to pay before it provides any services. Under the CROA, credit-repair companies cannot request or receive payment until they have completed the services they have promised. Some companies will structure monthly payment plans to avoid this requirement, and you should know that no form of upfront payment is legal. A simple rule to follow is "Don't pay upfront." If the company uses telemarketing such that the TSR applies, the company may not request or receive fees until it has provided you with a credit report generated more than six months after the promised results that shows the results.

It sounds too good to be true: The company tells you it can get rid of the negative credit information in your credit report in a short period, even if that information is accurate and current. Also, if they promise a specific increase in your credit score or guarantee a certain result. No one can guarantee this. It simply takes time to repair your credit file.

They cannot answer questions: The company representative cannot explain the specifics of the services they are offering you or the total cost for those services. Asking a few simple questions can help you determine if you are dealing with a reputable organization.

They hold back or provide misinformation: The company does not inform you of your rights, including your right to obtain a written contract outlining the details of your arrangement, as well as having the ability to cancel your contract with the company within three business days. The company does not disclose the full cost of its services, and/or the company suggests that you should not (or cannot) contact any of the nationwide credit-reporting companies directly (you can).

They ask you to misrepresent information: The company suggests that you try to invent a "new" credit identity—resulting in a new credit report—by applying for an Employer Identification Number (EIN) instead of your Social Security number (SSN).

Know Your Rights

Do not pay a company upfront. According to the TSR, it is illegal for a telemarketing or sales company to charge you for credit-repair services unless it has been six months since the company achieved the promised results and the company has proven to you that it achieved those results.

Under the Fair Credit Reporting Act (FCRA), you have a legal right to dispute credit-history errors yourself for free. You do not have to pay a credit-repair company to do it for you. The first step is to get your free annual credit report from one or more of the three nationwide credit-reporting companies to identify any errors. Check out our information on how to correct inaccuracies on your credit reports, including sample dispute letters and contact information for each of the three nationwide credit-reporting companies. You can also go online to any of the credit reporting companies' websites and dispute errors.

CHAPTER 12
HOW TO REBUILD YOUR CREDIT

About This Chapter: This chapter includes text excerpted from "How to Rebuild Your Credit," Consumer Financial Protection Bureau (CFPB), July 2017.

When you experience a financial challenge, your credit record could suffer. Rebuilding it takes time. There are no shortcuts or secrets.

The steps below can help.

Pay Your Bills on Time, Every Time

"On time" means the payment gets to the company by the day the bill is due. Mail your bills a few days before they are due. Think about signing up for text alerts to make sure you do not pay late or miss a payment. Or, consider automatic payments from your bank to help make sure your bills get paid on time. Keep track of automatic payments so you know you have enough money in your account to cover them.

Do Not Get Too Close to Your Credit Limit

Credit scores consider how close you are to being "maxed out" on credit cards. If you use too much of your available credit, you can hurt your credit score. Experts advise using no more than 30 percent of your available credit—some even say you should use less than 10 percent.

Do Not Apply for Too Much Credit in a Short Time

Your credit score may go down if you apply for or open a lot of new accounts in a short period of time. This includes getting a new card so you can transfer balances or opening a new store account so you can get a discount.

If You Cannot Qualify for a Regular Credit Card, Try a Secured Card

Many banks and credit unions offer secured credit cards. With most of these cards, your credit line starts out small. You put an amount equal to your credit limit in an account as a deposit. As you show you can pay on time, your credit limit may grow and

These four things do not help rebuild your credit:

1. **Using a debit card or paying cash.** These transactions do not help you prove you can repay debts.
2. **Using a prepaid card.** A prepaid card is your own money, loaded on to the card in advance.
3. **Taking out a payday loan.** Even making on-time repayments might not help your credit.
4. **Taking out an auto loan from a "buy here, pay here" car lot,** unless they promise in writing to report your on-time payments.

you may have your deposit refunded. Fees and interest rates can be high for secured cards, but using one can help you to establish a credit record.

If You Pay with a Credit Card, Pay Your Balance off Every Month

You will build credit by using your credit card and paying on time, every time. Pay off your balances in full each month to avoid paying finance charges. Paying off your balance each month can also build better credit than carrying a balance.

Keep It Up

Credit scores are partly based on experience over time. The longer you have credit and pay on time, the more information there is to show you are a good credit risk.

Check Your Credit Reports and Fix Errors Right Away

You can get a free copy of each of your credit reports from the three nationwide credit reporting companies every year at annualcreditreport.com. You may find incorrect information that is bringing your score down. If you do, file a dispute with the credit-reporting company and with the company that was the source of the information.

CHAPTER 13
DEBT-RELIEF OPTIONS

About This Chapter: This chapter includes text excerpted from "Choosing a Credit Counselor," Federal Trade Commission (FTC), November 2012.

Working with a credit-counseling organization is just one option for dealing with your debt. You also could:

- Negotiate directly with your credit-card company
- Work with a debt-settlement company
- Consider bankruptcy

Talk with your credit-card company, even if you have been turned down before. Rather than pay a company to talk to your creditor on your behalf, remember that you can do it yourself for free. You can find the telephone number on your card or your statement. Be persistent and polite. Keep good records of your debts, so that when you reach the credit-card company, you can explain your situation. Your goal is to work out a modified payment plan that reduces your payments to a level you can manage.

If you do not pay on your debt for 180 days, your creditor will write your debt off as a loss; your credit score will take a big hit, and you will still owe the debt. Creditors are often willing to negotiate with you even after they write your debt off as a loss.

Bankruptcy

Declaring bankruptcy has serious consequences, including lowering your credit score, but credit counselors and other experts say that, in some cases, it may make the most sense. Filing for bankruptcy allows people with a steady income to keep the property, such as a mortgaged house or a car that they might otherwise lose through the bankruptcy process. The court approves a repayment plan that allows you to pay off your debts over a three- to five-year period, without surrendering any property. After you have made all the payments under the plan, your debts are discharged. As part of the process, you will have to pay a lawyer, and you must get credit counseling from a

The Telemarketing Sales Rule

The Telemarketing Sales Rule (TSR), enforced by the Federal Trade Commission (FTC), requires companies that sell debt-relief services to explain their fees and tell you about any conditions on their services before you sign up; it also prohibits companies that sell debt-relief services by phone from charging a fee before they settle or reduce your debt. For credit counseling that promises to get you into a debt-management plan (DMP), that means the company cannot collect a fee until you have entered the DMP and made at least one payment to your creditors using the DMP.

government-approved organization within six months before you file for any bankruptcy relief.

You can find a state-by-state list of government-approved organizations at the U.S. Trustee Program (USTP), the organization within the U.S. Department of Justice (DOJ) that supervises bankruptcy cases and trustees. Also, before you file a bankruptcy case, you must satisfy a "means test." This test requires you to confirm that your income does not exceed a certain amount. The amount varies by state and is publicized by the USTP.

Filing fees are several hundred dollars. Attorney fees are extra and vary.

Debt Settlement

Debt-settlement programs typically are offered by for-profit companies and involve them negotiating with your creditors to allow you to pay a "settlement" to resolve your debt—a lump sum that is less than the full amount that you owe. To make that lump-sum payment, the program asks that you set aside a specific amount of money every month in savings. Debt-settlement companies usually ask that you transfer this amount every month into an escrow-like account to accumulate enough savings to pay off any settlement that is eventually reached. Further, these programs often encourage or instruct their clients to stop making any monthly payments to their creditors.

Although a debt-settlement company may be able to settle one or more of your debts, these programs can be very risky and have serious negative financial consequences for consumers. Additionally, some debt-settlement companies deceive consumers by making promises they do not keep and engaging in other illegal conduct (such as charging fees before obtaining any settlements, in violation of the Telemarketing Sales Rule (TSR)).

CHAPTER 14

HOW TO PREPARE A LOAN PROPOSAL

About This Chapter: This chapter includes text excerpted from "Create a Loan Application Packet," Consumer Financial Protection Bureau (CFPB), September 17, 2015.

In the course of exploring your loan options, you will talk with several lenders to get acquainted. You will need to give these lenders some information about your finances. It is best to gather this information in advance, so you will have it ready at your fingertips.

What to Do Now

Gather your personal and financial information

- Pay stub for the last 30 days
- W-2 forms, last 2 years
- Signed federal tax return, last 2 years
- Documentation of any other sources of income
- Bank statements, 2 most recent
- Documentation of the source of your down payment: investment or savings account statements showing at least 2 months' history of ownership. If some of the funds were a gift, get a signed statement from the giver stating that the funds were a gift.
- Documentation of name change, if recent
- Proof of your identity (typically a drivers' license or nondriver ID)
- Social security number
- Certificate of housing counseling or home-buyer education, if you have it

What to Know

The More Organized You Are, the Faster the Loan-Approval Process Is Likely to Be

Make sure your documents are accurate and complete.

Your lenders use the information you provide to decide how much they are willing to lend to you and at what interest rate. If your information is inaccurate, you could

> **Keep Your Documents Up-to-Date**
> Update your application packet to make sure you have everything
> - Gather the most recent copies of any time-sensitive paperwork, such as paystubs, bank statements, etc.
> - Now is a good time to ask the lenders you have been talking with what additional documents you might need based on your specific situation.
>
> When in doubt, gather it anyway. Even if one of the lenders you are considering does not need a particular piece of paperwork right now, they may want to see it once you get further into the application process. Having everything in the same place makes the rest of the process easier.
> *(Source: "Exploring Loan Choices," Consumer Financial Protection Bureau (CFPB))*

encounter costly surprises down the road. If your documents are incomplete, lenders may reject them.

- Make sure to include every page of multi-page documents, even ones marked "intentionally left blank."
- Make sure when printing online documents that the full URL is included on the bottom of each page.

Chances Are, You Will Need to Update Your Loan Application Packet at Least Once during This Process

Lenders like to see your most-recent bank statements, pay stubs, and so on. If you access any of these items online, write a reminder to yourself on how to find the information again so you can update your packet easily.

If You Are Self-Employed or Have Irregular or Nonwage Income, You May Need Additional Documentation

Requirements vary from lender to lender and depending on your specific situation. Share your situation when you meet with loan officers or a housing counselor and ask what kind of documentation you need.

CHAPTER 15

WHY YOU MIGHT NEED A COSIGNER IN ORDER TO GET VEHICLE FINANCING

About This Chapter: Text under the heading "What Is a Cosigner?" is excerpted from "What Is a Co-Signer?" Consumer Financial Protection Bureau (CFPB), August 4, 2016; Text under the heading "Why You Might Need a Cosigner" is excerpted from "Why Might I Need a Co-Signer in Order to Get Vehicle Financing?" Consumer Financial Protection Bureau (CFPB), August 5, 2016.

What Is a Cosigner?

A cosigner is another person who also takes full responsibility to pay back your loan.

Often a cosigner will be a family member. The cosigner is obligated to pay any missed payments and even the full amount of the loan if the borrower does not pay. The cosigner's credit also can be harmed if the borrower is late making payments.

Having a cosigner on your loan gives your lender additional assurance that the loan will be repaid.

Why You Might Need a Cosigner

A cosigner is a person—such as a parent, close family member, or friend—who pledges to pay back the loan if you do not. This can be a benefit both to you and your lender.

A lender cannot require you to have a cosigner if you qualify on your own. If you are told that you need a cosigner for a loan, it means that the lender will not offer you the loan based solely on your own income and credit record. The lender wants another person to also promise to pay the loan. This is what a cosigner does. A cosigner is a person who is obligated to pay back the loan just as you, the borrower, are obligated to pay. A cosigner could be your spouse, a parent, or a friend. The lender cannot require your spouse to be a cosigner unless you are both applying for the loan.

Having a cosigner on your loan can be a benefit to both you and your lender. Cosigning gives your lender additional assurance that the loan will be repaid. You may get a better interest rate with a cosigner.

Obstacles to Releasing Cosigners from the Loan

Borrowers face bureaucratic barriers when seeking to release their cosigner, even though this benefit was advertised before the loan was taken out and could help avoid auto default. Consumers continue to complain that the rigid and opaque standards for cosigner release make for a mysterious process. For example, consumers note that required forms are often not available on websites or in an electronic form. In addition, servicers do not seem to be proactively notifying consumers about the specific requirements to process a release.

(Source: "CFPB Finds Private Student Loan Borrowers Face "Auto-Default" When Co-Signer Dies or Goes Bankrupt," Consumer Financial Protection Bureau (CFPB))

There are risks for the cosigner. The cosigner is also obligated on the loan. If you do not repay your loan, your cosigner will be liable for repayment even if the cosigner never drove your vehicle. In addition, if you pay late or default on the loan, both your credit and your cosigner's could be negatively affected.

CHAPTER 16
IF YOU ARE A COSIGNER

About This Chapter: Text in this chapter begins with excerpts from "Co-Signing a Loan," Federal Trade Commission (FTC), October 2012; Text under the heading "Three Things You Should Consider before Cosigning for an Auto Loan" is excerpted from "3 Things You Should Consider before Co-Signing for an Auto Loan," Federal Trade Commission (FTC), June 14, 2016.

What do you do if a friend or relative asks you to cosign a loan? Before you say yes, think about the obligations involved and how they may affect your own finances and creditworthiness. When you agree to cosign a loan, you are taking a risk a lender will not take.

The Cosigner's Notice

When you cosign a loan, the lender (known as the "creditor") must spell out your obligations in a cosigner's notice, which says:

- You are being asked to guarantee this debt. Think carefully before you do. If the borrower does not pay the debt, you will have to. Be sure you can afford to pay if you have to and that you want to accept this responsibility.
- You may have to pay up to the full amount of the debt if the borrower does not pay. You may also have to pay late fees or collection costs, which increase this amount.
- The creditor can collect this debt from you without first trying to collect from the borrower.* The creditor can use the same collection methods against you that can be used against the borrower, including suing you or garnishing your wages. If this debt is ever in default, that fact may become a part of your credit record.
- This notice is not the contract that makes you liable for the debt.

**Depending on the laws in your state, this may not apply. If state law forbids a creditor from collecting from a cosigner without first trying to collect from the primary debtor, this sentence may be crossed out or omitted.*

Before You Cosign

Despite the risks, there may be times when you want to cosign. Your child may need a first loan, or a close friend may need help. Before you cosign, consider how it might affect your financial well-being.

- Can you afford to pay the loan? If you are asked to pay and cannot, you could be sued, or your credit rating could be damaged.
- Even if you are not asked to repay the debt, your liability for the loan may keep you from getting other credit. Creditors will consider the cosigned loan as one of your obligations.
- Before you pledge the property to secure the loan, such as your car, furniture or jewelry, make sure you understand the consequences. If the borrower defaults, you could lose these items.
- Ask the creditor to calculate the amount you might owe. The creditor does not have to do this, but might if you ask. You also may be able to negotiate specific terms of your obligation. For example, you may want to limit your liability to the principal on the loan, and not include late charges, court costs, or attorneys' fees. In this case, ask the creditor to include a statement in the contract—such as "The cosigner will be responsible only for the principal balance on this loan at the time of default."—before you cosign.
- Ask the creditor to agree, in writing, to notify you if the borrower misses a payment or the terms on the loan change. That will give you time to deal with the problem or make back payments without having to repay the entire amount immediately.
- If you are cosigning for purchase, make sure you get copies of all important papers, such as the loan contract, the Truth-in-Lending Disclosure Statement, and warranties. These documents may come in handy if there is a dispute between the borrower and the seller. The creditor does not have to give you these papers; you may have to get copies from the borrower.
- Check your state law for additional cosigner rights.

Three Things You Should Consider before Cosigning for an Auto Loan

Cosigning an auto loan obligates you to repay the loan.

Young adults with limited or spotty credit histories often ask older family members, such as a parent or grandparent, to cosign for a loan to help them buy a vehicle. However, cosigning for an auto loan includes real risks and responsibilities.

If you have been asked to cosign a loan, you can use or share Take Control of Your Auto Loan resources (www.consumerfinance.gov/consumer-tools/getting-an-auto-loan). This chapter gives you a road map to help you and the other borrower navigate and understand the total cost of your loan and other terms, and help you both repay the loan on schedule.

Here are three things to consider before you cosign a loan to help someone else buy a vehicle.

Cosigners Are Responsible for Repaying the Loan

As a cosigner, you are not merely vouching for someone's ability to repay a loan. Rather, as a cosigner, you are taking full responsibility to pay back the loan. If the other borrower stops paying the loan, you are responsible for making the monthly payments. If you are thinking about cosigning an auto loan, ask yourself whether you could make those monthly payments now and in the future.

If the other borrower defaults on the auto loan, the lender might repossess and sell the vehicle. Depending on your state law, the lender could then sue both of you for any outstanding loan balance. If the lender successfully sues you, the lender could try to garnish your bank account or wages or place a lien on your home.

Cosigning an Auto Loan Could Affect Your Credit

Your ability to borrow more money in the future may be affected by cosigning a loan. Lenders usually weigh the total amount of debt you are carrying (including loans you cosigned) and your income before providing you with a new credit card, mortgage, or another auto loan.

Lenders usually consider your payment history too. Any missed payments on the auto loan that you cosign also can make it harder to get new credit at a later time.

Before agreeing to cosign, consider your current personal balance sheet and whether cosigning may affect your ability to get new credit in the future.

Cosigners Can Ask to Receive Monthly Statements

Lenders sometimes send monthly statements only to the primary borrower. If you cosigned for an auto loan and do not receive statements, ask the lender to start sending you monthly statements. If the lender agrees to send them, monthly statements will alert you about any missed payments.

If the loan is in default, the lender may try to repossess the vehicle. Many states provide consumer protections regarding how a lender repossesses and resells a vehicle after a loan default.

Financing a vehicle, especially as a cosigner for someone else, can often be a challenging process for consumers. Remember, you are on the hook like the other borrower. There are a few things you should consider before you become a cosigner. But, before shopping for an auto loan, you can also play an active role by helping the primary borrower navigate and understand the auto loan process.

If you choose to cosign a loan to help a family member buy a vehicle, you are encouraged to share auto loan resources (www.consumerfinance.gov/consumer-tools/getting-an-auto-loan) with your other borrower.

CHAPTER 17
BEWARE OF IDENTITY THEFT

About This Chapter: Text under heading "What Is Identity Theft?" is excerpted from "Recovering from Identity Theft," Federal Trade Commission (FTC), September 2, 2016; Text beginning with the heading "What Do Thieves Do with Your Information?" is excerpted from "Warning Signs of Identity Theft," IdentityTheft.gov, Federal Trade Commission (FTC), February 7, 2012; Text under the heading "Know Your Rights" is excerpted from "Know Your Rights," IdentityTheft.gov, Federal Trade Commission (FTC), February 8, 2016.

What Is Identity Theft?

Identity theft is a serious crime. Identity theft happens when someone uses information about you without your permission.

They could use your:

- Name and address
- Credit card or bank account numbers
- Social Security number (SSN)
- Phone or utility account numbers

What Do Thieves Do with Your Information?

Once identity thieves have your personal information, they can drain your bank account, run up charges on your credit cards, open new utility accounts, or get medical treatment on your health insurance. An identity thief can file a tax refund in your name and get your refund. In some extreme cases, a thief might even give your name to the police during an arrest.

Clues That Someone Has Stolen Your Information

- You see withdrawals from your bank account that you cannot explain.
- You do not get your bills or other mail.
- Merchants refuse your checks.
- Debt collectors call you about debts that are not yours.
- You find unfamiliar accounts or charges on your credit report.

Prevent Identity Theft

Keep these tips in mind to protect yourself from identity theft:

- **Secure your Social Security number (SSN).** Do not carry your Social Security card in your wallet. Only give out your SSN when necessary.
- **Do not share personal information** (birthdate, SSN, or bank account number) because someone asks for it.
- **Collect mail every day.** Place a hold on your mail when you are away from home for several days.
- **Pay attention to your billing cycle.** If bills or financial statements are late, contact the sender.
- **Use the security features available on your mobile phone.**
- **Update sharing and firewall settings** when you are on a public wi-fi network. Use a virtual private network (VPN) if you use public wi-fi.
- **Review your credit card and bank account statements.** Compare receipts with account statements. Watch for unauthorized transactions.
- **Shred receipts, credit offers, account statements, and expired credit cards.** This can prevent "dumpster divers" from getting your personal information.
- **Store personal information in a safe place.**
- **Install firewalls and virus-detection software** on your home computer.
- **Create complex passwords that identity thieves cannot guess.** Change your passwords if a company that you do business with has a breach of its databases
- **Review your credit reports once a year.** Be certain that they do not include accounts that you have not opened. You can order it for free from Annualcreditreport.com.
- **Freeze your credit files** with Equifax, Experian, Innovis, TransUnion, and the National Consumer Telecommunications and Utilities Exchange for free. Credit freezes prevent someone from applying for and getting approval for a credit account or utility services in your name.

(Source: "Identity Theft," USA.gov)

- Medical providers bill you for services you did not use.
- Your health plan rejects your legitimate medical claim because the records show you have reached your benefits limit.
- A health plan will not cover you because your medical records show a condition you do not have.
- The Internal Revenue Service (IRS) notifies you that more than one tax return was filed in your name, or that you have income from an employer you do not work for.
- You get a notice that your information was compromised by a data breach at a company where you do business or have an account.

If your wallet, Social Security number (SSN), or other personal information is lost or stolen, there are steps you can take to help protect yourself from identity theft.

Know Your Rights

Here is an overview of your rights when recovering from identity theft. If someone is using your information to open new accounts or make purchases, report it and get help.

If someone steals your identity, you have the right to:

- Create an FTC Identity Theft Report
- Place a one-year fraud alert on your credit report
- Place a seven-year extended fraud alert on your credit report
- Get free copies of your credit report
- Get fraudulent information removed (or "blocked") from your credit report
- Dispute fraudulent or inaccurate information on your credit report
- Stop creditors and debt collectors from reporting fraudulent accounts
- Get copies of documents related to identity theft
- Stop a debt collector from contacting you

Documenting the Theft

You have the right to create an FTC Identity Theft Report. This report helps prove to businesses that someone stole your identity, and makes it easier to correct problems caused by identity theft.

You can create an FTC Identity Theft Report by filing a report with the FTC.

Working with Credit Bureaus

You have the right to:

- **Place a one-year fraud alert on your credit report.** The fraud alert tells creditors that they must take reasonable steps to verify who is applying for credit in your name. To place this alert, contact one of the three national credit bureaus. The one you contact must notify the others. When you place a one-year fraud alert, you are also entitled to a free copy of your credit reports. You will get a confirmation letter from each credit bureau with instructions on how to get your free reports.
- **Place a seven-year extended fraud alert on your credit report.** To do this, send a copy of your FTC Identity Theft Report to each credit bureau. The extended fraud alert means potential creditors must contact you before they issue a credit in your name. In your letter, be sure to give the best way for a creditor to reach you. Each credit bureau will send you a letter confirming that they placed an extended fraud alert on your file. That letter also will include instructions about how to get free copies of your credit report.
- **Get credit bureaus to remove fraudulent information from your credit report.** This is called "blocking." You must send them a copy of your FTC Identity Theft Report, proof of your identity, and a letter stating which information is fraudulent. Then the credit bureau must tell the relevant creditor that someone stole your identity. Creditors cannot turn fraudulent debts over to debt collectors.
- **Dispute fraudulent or inaccurate information on your credit report.** Do this by writing to the credit bureau. They must investigate your dispute and amend your report if you are right.

Table 17.1. Loss of Debit Card

If You Report Your Debit Card Lost	Your Maximum Loss Is
Before any unauthorized charges are made.	$0
Within 2 business days after you learn about the loss or theft.	$50
More than 2 business days after you learn about the loss or theft, but less than 60 calendar days after your statement is sent to you.	$500
More than 60 calendar days after your statement is sent to you.	Possibly unlimited

- **You have the right to place a free credit freeze on your credit report.** A credit freeze, also called a "security freeze," makes it less likely that an identity thief could open a new account in your name.

Communicating with Creditors and Debt Collectors

You have the right to:

- **Stop creditors and debt collectors from reporting fraudulent accounts.** After you give them a copy of a valid FTC Identity Theft Report, they may not report fraudulent accounts to the credit-reporting companies.
- **Get copies of documents related to the theft of your identity,** such as transaction records or applications for new accounts. Write to the company that has the documents, and include a copy of your FTC Identity Theft Report. You also can tell the company to give the documents to a specific law-enforcement agency (LEA).
- **Stop a debt collector from contacting you.** In most cases, debt collectors must stop contacting you after you send them a letter telling them to stop.
- **Get written information from a debt collector about debt,** including the name of the creditor and the amount you supposedly owe. If a debt collector contacts you about a debt, request this information in writing.

Limits on Financial Losses

You have limited liability for fraudulent debts caused by identity theft.

- Under most state laws, you are not responsible for any debt incurred on fraudulent new accounts opened in your name without your permission.
- Under federal law, the amount you have to pay for unauthorized use of your credit card is limited to $50. If you report the loss to the credit-card company before your credit card is used by a thief, you are not responsible for any unauthorized charges.
- If your ATM or debit card is lost or stolen, you can limit your liability by reporting the loss immediately to your bank or credit union.

- If someone makes unauthorized debits to your bank or credit-union account using your debit-card number (not your card), you are not responsible if you report the problem within 60 days after they send your account statement showing the unauthorized debits.
- Most state laws limit your liability for fraudulent checks issued on your bank or credit-union account if you notify the bank or credit union promptly.

CHAPTER 18

FEDERAL LAW ON IDENTITY THEFT FOR MINORS UNDER 16

About This Chapter: Text in this chapter begins with excerpts from "New Protections Available for Minors under 16," Federal Trade Commission (FTC), March 11, 2019; Text under the heading "Other Federal Rights" is excerpted from "Know Your Rights," IdentityTheft.gov, Federal Trade Commission (FTC), February 8, 2016.

Young people now have more protection from identity theft and fraud, thanks to a new federal law that went into effect on September 21st, 2018. The new law lets parents and child-welfare representatives of people under 16, as well as legal guardians, request a security freeze, also called a "credit freeze," on their behalf. Taking this step can help protect a young person from identity theft and fraud—and it is free.

Identity theft happens when someone misuses your personal information, such as a Social Security number (SSN), to open accounts, file taxes, or make purchases. Hackers, thieves, and even people you know might steal your identity. Minors typically do not have credit reports, which means that a young person may not find out about issues with their credit reports until they first try to get credit—perhaps even years later.

While a security freeze will not affect anything already on your credit report, it restricts access to your report. That makes it harder for identity thieves to open new accounts using your personal information. With the new law, it is free to freeze and unfreeze your credit file at the three nationwide consumer reporting agencies—Equifax, Experian, and TransUnion. To find contact information for placing a free credit freeze, visit IdentityTheft.gov.

The new law also lets people, such as parents, guardians, and representatives acting on behalf of a young person in foster care, proactively protect a young person's credit file by freezing it.

If the nationwide credit-reporting agencies do not have a file on the child, they will create one so they can freeze it. This record cannot be used for credit purposes. It is

Free Credit Freezes

Security freezes, also known as "credit freezes," restrict access to your credit file, making it harder for identity thieves to open new accounts in your name. Starting September 21, 2018, you can freeze and unfreeze your credit file for free. You also can get a free freeze for children who are under 16. And if you are someone's guardian, conservator, or have a valid power of attorney, you can get a free freeze for that person, too.

How will these freezes work? Contact all three of the nationwide credit reporting agencies—Equifax, Experian, and TransUnion. If you request a freeze online or by phone, the agency must place the freeze within one business day. If you request a lift of the freeze, the agency must lift it within one hour. If you make your request by mail, the agency must place or lift the freeze within three business days after it receives your request. You also can lift the freeze temporarily without a fee.

Do not confuse freezes with locks. They work in a similar way, but locks may have monthly fees. If you want a free freeze guaranteed by federal law, then opt for a freeze, not a lock.

(Source: "Free Credit Freezes Are Here," Federal Trade Commission (FTC))

there just to make sure the child's record is frozen and protected against identity theft and fraud.

Depending on the adult's relationship with the child, there are different procedures to put a freeze in place. Parents need to show proof of their authority, such as a birth certificate, to freeze or unfreeze the credit file for their child under 16. The new law says that child-welfare or probation-agency representatives acting on behalf of a young person in foster care can request a security freeze for that child. They have to show documentation certifying that the child is in the agency's care, such as written communication or an official letter from the child-welfare or probation agency or its designee. Child-welfare agencies who already work with consumer reporting agencies to pull and review credit reports for youth in their care can use the same company contacts and liaisons to facilitate the security-freeze process.

Other Federal Rights

Under the Justice for All Act, you have additional rights when the identity thief is criminally prosecuted in federal court. You have the right to:

- Reasonable protection from the accused
- Reasonable, accurate, and timely notice about any public court proceeding, parole proceeding involving the crime, or release or escape of the accused
- Not be excluded from any public court proceeding unless the judge decides that your testimony would change significantly if you heard other testimony
- Be reasonably heard at any public proceeding in the district court that involves release, plea, sentencing, or parole
- Confer with the attorney for the government in the case

- Full and timely restitution as provided in the law proceedings free from unreasonable delay
- Be treated with fairness and respect for your dignity and privacy

PART 2 | WHAT A TEEN NEEDS TO KNOW BEFORE BUYING THEIR FIRST CAR

CHAPTER 19
CONSIDER RENTING A CAR

About This Chapter: This chapter includes text excerpted from "Renting a Car," Federal Trade Commission (FTC), September 2012.

Need to rent a car for your vacation or business travels? Comparing prices online can save you a bundle. But, make sure you compare the total cost—not just the advertised rate—because fees and options can increase the base price dramatically.

What to Know

Keep these things in mind as you start your search for a rental car.

Size Matters

The size of the rental car can impact the price you pay. Terms such as "compact," "mid-size," and "luxury" can vary across rental-car companies. To illustrate car sizes, companies usually provide car models or suggest how many passengers the car seats safely.

Shop and Compare

Search across several websites for the type of car you are interested in renting. To get an idea of the best price you can get, search for rates at individual rental-car company websites and price-comparison websites.

Money-Saving Deals or Specials

If your travel plans are flexible, you may be able to rent a car when price breaks are available. Try searching for specials geared to the length of time you need the vehicle. You may find better deals if you book in advance, or book in combination with a flight or hotel. Read any fine print about restrictions on special offers, including blackout dates when an advertised price may not be available. Some companies also offer special rates for seniors or members of particular organizations, such as motor clubs.

Figure 19.1. Compare Products ***(Source: "Shopping Online Infographic," Federal Trade Commission (FTC))***

Question Fees

Comparing advertised rates for rental cars may not give you an accurate picture of the price you will pay. Try to make an "apples to apples" comparison of car rental prices that includes all mandatory fees and charges, as well as charges for options.

Some fees may be quoted when you reserve a car online, though you may not find out about all of the charges until you go to the rental office to pick up your car. Read your contract carefully, and look for fees triggered by specific events—such as accidents.

Your Driving Record Is Important

Many companies check driving records when customers arrive at the counter and reject those whose records do not meet company standards. Even if you have a confirmed reservation, you may be disqualified from renting a car for recent violations, including:

- Reckless driving
- Seat belt law violations
- Accidents, regardless of fault
- Leaving the scene of an accident
- Convictions for driving while intoxicated (DWI) or driving under the influence (DUI)
- Driving with an invalid, suspended, or revoked license

Ask the rental-car company in advance whether they check customers' driving records.

Coverage Options

Rental companies usually offer drivers additional coverage options—for a price. If you buy their coverage, they say you can minimize your liability while driving their rental car. However, you may be covered already through your own auto or homeowner's policies. Read your insurance policies for specifics, and call your insurers if you are

Car Sharing

Car-sharing services allow you to rent a car on an hourly basis. They offer flexibility in where and when you can pick up a vehicle.

- **Fees.** What fees does the company charge (annual fees, application fee)? Are they refundable, even if you cancel or are denied membership?
- **Availability of cars.** Are there cars available at times when you need one? How far in advance do you need to reserve a vehicle?
- **Attendants.** Are staff on-site when you check out a car and return it? On-site staff can verify that you returned the car in the same condition as when you borrowed it.
- **Fuel.** Do you have to pay for gas out of your own pocket or does the company pay for it?
- **Extension of time.** How easy is it to extend the length of your rental? Is it done through an app or is there a dedicated customer-service hotline?
- **Cancellation.** How far in advance must you give the notice to cancel a reservation or your membership? Can the company cancel your membership without notification?
- **Damages.** Are you responsible for damages, even if they were not your fault or they happened after you returned the car?
- **Insurance.** Is insurance included in the membership fee?

(Source: "Buying a Car," USA.gov)

uncertain about the coverage. If you are traveling on business, you may be covered under your employer's insurance. Some credit-card companies and motor clubs provide members with free rental protection when you use their cards to pay for rentals.

Salespeople also may try to sell you a collision damage waiver (CDW), or a Loss Damage Waiver. These waivers guarantee that the rental company will pay for damages to your rental car. It is not technically collision insurance—the company would not pay for any injuries to you or damages to your personal property. Coverage under your medical insurance plan might offer protection that CDW coverage lacks.

If you do not buy CDW coverage or are not covered by your personal auto-insurance policy, you accept responsibility for any damages—and could be liable for the full value of the car. Some rental companies hold you liable only for a portion of the value.

If you purchase CDW, your coverage still could be revoked if you damage the rental car while:

- Driving in a negligent manner
- Driving on unpaved roads
- Driving out of state
- Driving while intoxicated
- An unauthorized driver operates the car

Rental-car companies may offer other coverage options for additional charges. Prices and policies for coverage vary among companies. If you decide to pay for extra coverage, ask for details.

Ask about Fees

Ask about fees before you rent a car to avoid surprises when you pay your bill. Here are some common fees and charges you may encounter.

Taxes

The rental company will add on the required state, city, or county taxes—and their own sales tax rates—to the price of your rental car. You may see other fees, too, such as a "vehicle licensing fee" or an "energy recovery fee."

Early or Late Return Fees

Being early is not always a good thing. Some rental companies may charge a fee if you return the car more than 24 hours before your reservation was supposed to end. If you must return the car early, call the company to talk to an agent.

Running a little late? Many rental car companies have short grace periods that allow you to return the car without a fee if you are late by less than 30 minutes. However, you still may have to pay a full day's charge for optional items, such as navigation systems, and liability coverage options. If you are running more than a half-hour late, call the company to see if it is cheaper to pay late charges or extend your rental.

Airport Surcharges

If you are renting a car at the airport, fees can increase the rental rate considerably. These surcharges can apply even when rental car companies shuttle you to their off-site lot.

Fuel Charges

Most companies require you to return your rental car with a full tank of gas. If you do not, you will be charged the rental company's price for gas, which is virtually always more expensive than if you refill the tank yourself at a local station. Companies might give you the option of prepurchasing a full tank of gas when you first take the car, so you can return the car without paying an additional fee to fuel up. There is usually no refund for unused fuel.

Mileage Fees

Most rental car companies now offer unlimited miles. But, daily mileage caps may apply based on the type of vehicle you rent (for example, some Sport utility vehicles (SUV) or high-performance vehicles). It helps to know about how far you plan to drive so you can select the company that offers the most favorable mileage terms.

Roadside Assistance Fees

Ask whether roadside assistance is included in the price of your rental car, or if the company will charge you a fee for it. If the company charges for a roadside service plan, find out exactly what it will cover if you need help—for example, if you have a flat tire or lock your keys in the car. If you are a member of a motor club, you may have free or low-cost roadside assistance through your membership.

Out-of-State Charges

Before you head out on a road trip, check whether your rental company allows you to drive out of the state or geographical area in which you rented the car. Ask about the charges to drive out of state.

Drop-Off Fees

Need to drop your car off at a location other than where you picked it up? You may have to pay a steep fee for that.

Equipment-Rental Fees

If you would prefer to include extra items in your rental car—such as a navigation system or a car seat—you will have to pay a fee. Reserve these items in advance; availability varies based on the location of the rental.

Additional-Driver Fees

Want to switch off driving duties? Some companies charge a fee to add another driver—even your spouse—to your contract.

Underage-Driver Fees

You do not have to be 25 to rent a car. Drivers between the ages of 21 and 24 are allowed to rent cars—for an additional fee.

Debit and Credit-Card Blocking

Most rental companies place a hold—or a block—on your debit or credit card to protect themselves from possible charges beyond the authorized amount. They do not process the blocked amount unless you fail to return the car as specified in your contract. Your spending limit on your card may be reduced by the blocked amount until shortly after you return the car.

CHAPTER 20
IS IT BETTER TO LEASE OR BUY A CAR?

About This Chapter: This chapter includes text excerpted from "Financing or Leasing a Car," Federal Trade Commission (FTC), August 2017.

When you lease a car, you have the right to use it for an agreed number of months and miles.

How Is Leasing Different from Buying?

The monthly payments on a lease usually are lower than monthly finance payments if you bought the same car. You are paying to drive the car, not buy it. That means you are paying for the car's expected depreciation during the lease period, plus a rent charge, taxes, and fees. But, at the end of a lease, you must return the car unless the lease agreement lets you buy it.

To figure out if leasing fits your situation:

- Consider the beginning, middle, and end of lease costs
- Consider how long you may want to keep the car
- Compare different lease offers and terms, including mileage limits

Think about How Much You Drive

The mileage limit in most standard leases is typically 15,000 or fewer per year. You can negotiate a higher mileage limit, but that normally increases the monthly payment, because the car depreciates more during the life of the lease. If you go beyond the mileage limit in the lease agreement, you probably will have to pay an additional charge when you return the car.

Consider All of the Lease Terms

When you lease, you are responsible for excess wear and damage and any missing equipment. You also must service the car according to the manufacturer's recommendations and maintain insurance that meets the leasing company's standards. If you

The Time Value of Money

If the lease requires an initial payment of $1,200 and the finance agreement requires an initial payment of $2,000, the $800 difference could be invested to generate earnings or used to pay off other bills and thereby save interest payments. These earnings or savings will generate investment earnings or interest savings that should be applied to the cost of the lease. Generally, it is better to do this calculation after deducting any income tax due on the earnings.

If the $800 difference is deposited in an account that earns 5 percent and the earnings are taxable at your tax rate of 30 percent, the effective monthly after-tax interest rate is 5% ÷ 12 × (1–30%) = 0.2917%. The benefit for each month in the lease term is $800 × 0.2917% = $2.33 per month. If the $800 difference is instead used to pay a nondeductible credit card debt on which the APR is 16 percent, the benefit received each month in the lease term is $800 × 16% ÷ 12 = $10.67 per month.

Just as the value of a difference in the up-front costs of a lease and purchase should be included in the buy-versus-lease comparison, so, too, should the value of any difference in monthly payments. The methodology is similar to that used for a difference in upfront costs; the amount of the savings will be different each month and should include amounts gained from the reinvestment of any interest earnings on investments and interest savings resulting from debt repayments. Thus, a table would have to be developed that shows how the monthly payment savings, and the earnings from those savings, accumulate.

(Source: "Example: The Time Value of Money," Board of Governors of the Federal Reserve System)

end the lease early, you often have to pay an early termination charge that could be substantial.

Might You Move during the Lease Period?

Some leases may not let you move the car out of state or out of the country. Find out the rules for the deal you are considering.

Are You a Service Member Who Leased a Car?

Federal law lets you terminate the lease with no early termination charges if:

- You leased before you went into military service and then went on active duty for at least 180 days
- You leased a car during military service and then got a permanent change of duty station outside the continental United States, or got deployment orders for at least 180 days

Other fees may still apply, including those for excess wear, use, and mileage.

Factors in Buying and Leasing

Below are some of the factors in buying and leasing to help you compare your choices.

Leasing a vehicle:

- Monthly payments may be lower than buying but the payments are going towards the depreciation of the vehicle during the lease term plus rent charges (similar to interest on a loan) and other fees.
- You may be responsible for early termination charges if you end the lease early. These fees can be very expensive. You will not be able to simply return the vehicle and stop making payments.
- At the end of your lease term, you can either turn the vehicle in and pay any end-of-lease fees or purchase the vehicle if your lease includes a purchase option.
- For most leases, the company or person leasing the vehicle to you assumes the risk of depreciation.
- Most leases include mileage restrictions of 10,000 to 15,000 miles per year. At the end of the lease, most leases also include fees for excessive mileage and wear and tear. The amount of excessive wear and tear is usually determined by the lessor.
- A typical lease is two to four years.

Buying a vehicle:

- Monthly payments may be higher than leasing but part of each payment is going towards the purchase price of the vehicle.
- You might sell or trade-in the vehicle when you want to purchase a new one.
- You assume the risk of depreciation to your vehicle in regards to what it will be worth when you decide to sell or trade it in.
- You can drive as many miles as you want. High mileage and excessive wear and tear will affect the vehicle's resale value.
- A typical auto loan term is four to six years.
- You own the vehicle and get to keep it at the end of the financing term.

If you decide to lease, you can and should negotiate the lease terms.

(Source: "What Should I Know about the Differences between Leasing and Buying a Vehicle?" Consumer Financial Protection Bureau (CFPB))

CHAPTER 21
RESEARCHING YOUR NEW CAR

About This Chapter: This chapter includes text excerpted from documents published by two public domain sources. Text under the headings marked 1 are excerpted from "Buying a Car," MyCreditUnion.gov, National Credit Union Administration (NCUA), October 9, 2019; Text under the heading marked 2 is excerpted from "Looking to Buy a Car? Four Things to Keep in Mind," Federal Trade Commission (FTC), December 1, 2017.

A new car is second only to a home as the most expensive purchase many consumers make. That is why it is important to know how to make a smart deal.

Things to Consider When Buying a New Car[1]

Think about what car model and options you want and how much you are willing to spend. Do some research. You will be less likely to feel pressured into making a hasty or expensive decision at the showroom and more likely to get a better deal.

Consider these suggestions:

- Check publications online or at a library or bookstore that discuss new car features and prices. These may provide information on the dealer's costs for specific models and options.
- Shop around to get the best possible price by comparing models and prices in advertisements and at dealer showrooms. You also may want to contact your credit union or a car-buying service to make comparisons.
- Plan to negotiate on price. Dealers may be willing to bargain on their profit margin, often between 10 and 20 percent. Usually, this is the difference between the manufacturer's suggested retail price (MSRP) and the invoice price.
- Because the price is a factor in the dealer's calculations regardless of whether you pay cash or finance your car—and also affects your monthly payments—negotiating the price can save you money.
- Consider ordering your new car if you do not see what you want on the dealer's lot. This may involve a delay, but cars on the lot may have options you do not want—and that can raise the price. However, dealers often want

to sell their current inventory quickly, so you may be able to negotiate a good deal if an in-stock car meets your needs.

Looking to Buy a Car? Four Things to Keep in Mind[2]

Buying a car can be overwhelming. There are many things to consider, including your budget, your needs and preferences, and the inventory available at the time. And you see car ads when searching online when watching TV while reading the newspaper or listening to the radio. So how do you know those offers are the real deal?

Here are four things to keep in mind when you are considering an offer in a car ad:

1. **The fine print is important.** Read the entire ad. The small print should not contradict the big print.
2. **Compare offers from multiple dealers.** If you do not understand what an ad is offering, you can look for an offer from another dealer.
3. **Speak Spanish?** All of the ads should be in the same language. A company should give you all the important information in the same language, so you can understand the entire offer. Be skeptical if the ad you see is in Spanish, but parts of it are in English. The Federal Trade Commission (FTC) recently announced a case against a dealership that advertised attractive terms in Spanish but had other important information in English.
4. **Asking questions is important.** When you visit the dealer, you should ask many questions. If you decide to buy, be clear on the terms you are agreeing to before signing anything.

When you see a car ad, keep a critical eye. If the ad offers, for example, low monthly payments or zero-percent rates, and if the fine print at the bottom of the ad contradicts the offers in large print on the same ad, the ad may not be telling the whole story.

What to Know before You Buy[1]

Shopping for a car can be stressful. Before making the big purchase learn about common car-buying terms, financing options, trading in your old car, service contracts, and more.

Learning the Terms

Negotiations often have a vocabulary of their own. Here are some terms you may hear when you are talking price.

- **Invoice price** is the manufacturer's initial charge to the dealer. This usually is higher than the dealer's final cost because dealers receive rebates, allowances, discounts and incentive awards. Generally, the invoice price should include freight (also known as "destination" and "delivery"). If you are buying a car based on the invoice price (for example, "at invoice," "$100 below invoice," "two percent above invoice") and if freight is already included, make sure freight is not added again to the sales contract.

- **Base price** is the cost of the car without options but includes standard equipment and a factory warranty. This price is printed on the Monroney sticker.
- **Monroney sticker price** shows the base price, the manufacturer's installed options with the manufacturer's suggested retail price, the manufacturer's transportation charge, and the fuel economy (mileage). Affixed to the car window, this label is required by federal law and may be removed only by the purchaser.
- **Dealer sticker price**, usually on a supplemental sticker, is the Monroney sticker price plus the suggested retail price of dealer-installed options, such as additional dealer markup (ADM) or additional dealer profit (ADP), dealer preparation, and undercoating.

Financing Your Car

If you decide to finance your car, be aware that the financing obtained by the dealer, even if the dealer contacts lenders on your behalf, may not be the best deal you can get. Contact lenders directly. A credit union can also discuss car loan options with you. Compare the financing they offer you with the financing the dealer offers you. Because offers vary, shop around for the best deal, comparing the annual percentage rate (APR) and the length of the loan. When negotiating to finance a car, be wary of focusing only on the monthly payment. The total amount you will pay depends on the price of the car you negotiate, the APR, and the length of the loan.

Sometimes, dealers offer very low financing rates for specific cars or models, but may not be willing to negotiate on the price of these cars. To qualify for the special rates, you may be required to make a large down payment. With these conditions, you may find that it is sometimes more affordable to pay higher financing charges on a car that is lower in price or to buy a car that requires a smaller down payment.

Before you sign a contract to purchase or finance the car, consider the terms of the financing and evaluate whether it is affordable. Before you drive off the lot, be sure to have a copy of the contract that both you and the dealer have signed and be sure that all blanks are filled in.

Some dealers and lenders may ask you to buy credit insurance to pay off your loan if you should die or become disabled. Before you buy credit insurance, consider the cost and whether it is worthwhile. Check your existing policies to avoid duplicating benefits.

Credit insurance is not required by federal law. If your dealer requires you to buy credit insurance for car financing, it must be included in the cost of credit. That is, it must be reflected in the APR. Your state Attorney General also may have requirements about credit insurance. Check with your state Insurance Commissioner or state consumer protection agency (CPA).

Tips to Get the Best Deal and Avoid Problems

If you are buying or leasing a new car, consider these tips to get the best deal and avoid problems:

- Compare car makes and models. Visit dealerships in person and manufacturers' websites to research car models.
- Research the dealer's price (or wholesale price) for the car and options. This price can help you negotiate the final price.
- Learn if the manufacturer offers rebates that will lower the cost.
- Read car advertisements closely. Ads may overpromise on the deals, or offer deals that apply to a small group of buyers.
- Ask how long the manufacturer's warranty lasts and the repairs it covers.
- Get price quotes from several dealers. Ask if the prices quoted are before or after rebates are deducted.
- Research financing options. You are not required to finance your car through the dealer.
- Avoid low-value extras such as credit insurance, auto-club memberships, or extended warranties.
- Get estimates for how much your auto insurance would cost for each model you are considering.

(Source: "Buying a Car," USA.gov)

Tip: You can get the invoice price by looking at the dealer's invoice or reviewing car publications.

CHAPTER 22

DECIDING HOW MUCH YOU CAN AFFORD TO BORROW FOR AN AUTO LOAN

About This Chapter: This chapter includes text excerpted from "How Should I Decide How Much I Can Afford to Borrow for an Auto Loan?" Consumer Financial Protection Bureau (CFPB), June 9, 2016.

Figuring out how much you can afford to borrow before you sign on the dotted line is a great way to stay in control of your finances. It can be very helpful to break the process down into several steps.

Assess Your Financial Situation by Creating a Monthly Budget

- First, add up all of your fixed expenses (these include rent/mortgage, utilities, phone, and other recurring monthly bills, amounts you set aside each month for savings, child-support payments, insurance premiums, and payments on any existing loans, including outstanding credit-card debt).
- Second, add up your estimated additional expenses—for food, gas, entertainment, emergencies, unexpected expenses, and whatever else is not a set monthly expense.
- Third, if you did not have a vehicle before, do not forget you will also have to pay for insurance, maintenance, and registration. Shop around for auto insurance before you shop for a vehicle to get a sense of how that will affect your budget. If you are going from a used vehicle to a new vehicle, your insurance rates may be higher.
- Fourth, if you will be trading in a vehicle but still owe money on it, be sure to find out how much you owe on that loan. If what you owe is more than the trade-in or private sale amount, you will need to account for how you will pay that amount. Your loan amount, monthly payment, and total interest cost will be higher if this old debt is rolled into the loan for your new vehicle.

Tip: Most accurate negative information on your credit report must be removed after seven years and bankruptcy information after ten years. If you find a negative item on your report that should have been removed, you should dispute the error on your credit report.

- Now, subtract all expenses from your take-home pay and any other income you receive on a regular monthly basis.
- Your auto loan payment should be less than the amount you have left.

Review Your Credit

One of the first things you should do before applying for an auto loan is to review your credit report at all of the largest consumer reporting agencies—Equifax, TransUnion, and Experian. You are entitled to a free copy of your credit report from each of these agencies every 12 months, and you can request the free report at www.annualcreditreport.com or by calling 877-322-8228.

Review your credit report and dispute any errors that you find. A negative error on your credit report could affect the interest rate you get for an auto loan and cost you hundreds or thousands of dollars.

Any negative information on your credit report (such as late payments, delinquencies, court judgments and settlements, or bankruptcy filings) will influence your ability to obtain a loan or to obtain one at a low interest rate.

Save for a Down Payment

It is important to know how much of a down payment you can afford before you call around for loan quotes or go to a dealer. This will help you decide the size of the loan you can afford. Remember the more you put on a down payment, the less you will need to borrow.

Research Loan Options and Consider Getting Prequalified or Preapproved for a Loan

It is a good idea to shop around for a loan before heading to a dealer. You may want to consider getting prequalified or preapproved for an auto loan from a bank, credit union, or other lenders before visiting an auto dealer.

Shopping for the best deal on an auto loan will generally have little to no impact on your credit score(s). The benefit of shopping will far outweigh any impact on your credit. In some cases, applying for multiple loans over a long period of time can lower your credit score(s). Depending on the credit scoring model used, generally, any requests or inquiries by these lenders for your credit score(s) that took place within a time span ranging from 14 to 45 days will only count as a single inquiry.

Tip: Do not forget to read the fine print of any loan contract before you sign. Check to see if your loan has a "prepayment penalty," which means that you will have to pay a penalty if you pay off your loan before the end of the loan term. Even if you are not planning to pay off your loan before the end of the term, you may want to avoid loans that have a prepayment penalty in case your situation changes. Check the amount you are borrowing to be sure it is the amount you expected. Check that you are getting the amount of credit you agreed on for your trade-in.

This means shopping around for an auto loan during that time span will count the same as applying for just one loan. You can minimize any negative impact on your credit score by doing all your rate shopping in a short amount of time.

When you are offered different loans, compare all of the loan terms. You will look at:

- The amount you will borrow
- The interest rate and the annual percentage rate (APR)
- The length or term of the loan (number of months)
- The monthly payment (and whether you will be able to make that payment given your budget)

A higher interest rate or a longer loan term will result in additional interest costs for your loan.

CHAPTER 23

PLAN TO SHOP FOR YOUR AUTO LOAN

About This Chapter: This chapter includes text excerpted from "Plan to Shop for Your Auto Loan," Consumer Financial Protection Bureau (CFPB), June 9, 2016.

Planning ahead to shop for your loan can save money, time, and stress. Making decisions early gives you time to think about your alternatives and helps you make the right choices.

Decisions to Make at This Step

- How much can I afford?
- How much can I pay as a down payment?
- Do I want or need a co-signer?
- How much is my trade-in worth?

Actions to Take

Budget Wisely

If you have a budget, you have a better chance of ending up with a loan you can afford and are able to pay on time. A budget also helps you think about ongoing costs, such as vehicle maintenance and insurance. You want to be sure that there is room in your budget for both the loan and the other costs of ownership, such as:

- Additional costs at the time of purchase (taxes, title fees, and dealer fees)
- Ongoing costs throughout the time you own the vehicle (insurance, gas, annual registration fees, maintenance, and repairs)

If you are having trouble coming up with a budget that works for you, think about ways that you can reduce the cost of your auto loan, such as:

- Saving for a larger down payment
- Buying a less expensive vehicle
- Getting fewer add-ons, features, or options

Check Your Credit Reports before You Apply

The information in your credit report determines your credit scores. Your credit score(s) plays a large part in determining what kind of auto loan you can get, and how much interest you will pay for the loan. You can get a free copy of your credit report annually from each of the three nationwide credit-reporting agencies at www.annualcreditreport.com. Check your credit report for errors and dispute any errors you find.

> When you apply for a loan and the lender checks your credit, a credit score(s) is created for the lender. Depending on the credit scoring model used, any inquiries that took place within a short period of time—usually within a time span ranging from 14 to 45 days—generally, will only count as one inquiry. So it is a good idea to do your loan comparison shopping within that short time span to minimize any impact on your credit score(s).

Decide If You Want or Need a Cosigner

A cosigner is a person—such as a parent, family member, or friend—who is contractually obligated to pay back the loan just as you are. If your credit history is limited or needs improvement and you have a low (or no) credit score, a cosigner with good or excellent credit could significantly lower your interest rate. That is because the lender will rely on the cosigner's credit history and score in deciding to make the loan.

If you are considering having a cosigner, you and the potential cosigner should think carefully about this decision. If you do not repay your loan, you and your cosigner will be responsible for repayment. The cosigner is responsible for the loan even though she or he has no right to possession of the vehicle. In addition, any late payments made on the loan would affect both your credit record and score(s) and your cosigner's credit record and score(s). Federal law generally prohibits a lender from requiring you to have a cosigner if you apply for a loan individually and you qualify under the lender's standards for creditworthiness for the loan.

Think about Optional Add-Ons Ahead of Time

It is a good idea to think about add-ons ahead of time so that you are prepared and know what you want on the day you finance your vehicle. These products and services are optional and negotiable. If you buy them it can increase the total cost of your loan. Shopping around for any add-ons that you decide you want can save you money.

Some common add-ons are:

- **Service contracts or extended warranties.** These optional agreements provide protection for repair costs on certain mechanical and electrical components of the vehicle.
- **Guaranteed auto protection (GAP) insurance.** In case of loss or destruction of the vehicle, optional GAP insurance can pay the difference between the value of the vehicle and the amount you owe on your loan.

- **Credit insurance.** This is optional insurance that makes your auto loan payments in certain situations, such as death or injury, or loss of employment or property.

> **If you finance add-ons as part of your loan, the amount you borrow and pay will increase.**

- **Optional physical features for the vehicle.** These are features such as alarm systems, window tinting, tire and wheel protection, and other products.

Your own auto-insurance company may offer GAP insurance, credit insurance, or similar products. If you want one or more of these products, check and see if you can get a better price. Lowering the amount you need to borrow results in you paying less in interest over the life of your loan.

If Trading in a Vehicle, Research Its Approximate Value

You can look up the value of your vehicle using online commercial websites such as Consumer Reports, Edmunds, Kelley Blue Book, and the National Automobile Dealers Association's (NADA) Guides. These resources may also be available at your local library. Finding examples of similar vehicles that have sold recently in your area will help you figure out a fair price.

Once you know how much your current vehicle is worth, you can decide whether to trade it in or sell it yourself. If you trade it in at a dealership, you and the dealer will decide on the value that will be credited toward the purchase price of your next vehicle. If you sell it yourself, you can use the money you get as a down payment.

If you owe more on your current vehicle than it is worth—referred to as being "upside-down"—then you have negative equity. If you roll the balance of your existing auto loan into your new auto loan, this could make the new auto loan much more expensive. Your total loan cost may be much higher because you will be borrowing more than just the price of your new vehicle. Being upside-down can also reduce your options if you later decide you want to refinance your auto loan.

Make sure during any negotiations that you consider whether you are getting fair value for your trade-in and whether you are able to fully pay off the old auto loan.

Now that you have done your homework, you are ready to take the next step: shopping for your auto loan.

CHAPTER 24
GUIDELINES FOR GETTING AN AUTO LOAN

About This Chapter: Text beginning with the heading "What Happens If You Still Owe Money on the Vehicle You Want to Trade-In?" is excerpted from "Auto Loans How-To Guides," Consumer Financial Protection Bureau (CFPB), June 9, 2016; Text under the heading "What Are Manufacturer Incentives?" is excerpted from "What Are Manufacturer Incentives?" Consumer Financial Protection Bureau (CFPB), August 5, 2016;

What Happens If You Still Owe Money on the Vehicle You Want to Trade-In

If you still have a loan for the vehicle you plan to trade in, there are steps you should take to carefully consider whether to take on new debt for another vehicle before you have paid off your old vehicle.

These are the steps you should take:

- Find out how much you still owe on your current vehicle. Get the "payoff amount" from your current lender. This is the amount it will take to pay off your existing loan, and it may be different from any outstanding balance listed on your statement or coupon book. This difference may be because of a prepayment penalty or the way interest is calculated.
- Research your trade-in's value, so you will know if the amount you still owe on your trade-in is less than it is worth and make sure during any negotiations that you consider whether you are getting fair value for your trade-in and are able to fully pay off the old auto loan.
- Decide if you are going to pay off your existing loan now, wait until you pay off your old auto loan before you borrow for another vehicle, or include the amount that you still owe on your current vehicle in your new auto loan.
- If you owe more on your current vehicle than it is worth and you roll the balance of your existing auto loan into your new auto loan, this could make the new auto loan much more expensive. Your total loan cost will be higher because you will be borrowing more than just the price of your new vehicle.

Tip: Research your trade-in's value so you know whether the amount you still owe on your trade-in is more or less than it is worth. Then, during any negotiations, you can decide whether you are getting fair value for your trade-in and whether you are able to fully pay off the old auto loan. If your auto loan payoff amount is more than the dealer is willing to give you for your trade-in then you will still have to pay off what you owe on your old vehicle even if you trade it in. You should consider whether it makes sense to go through with the new purchase because in this circumstance your new loan will include the amount you still owe from your old vehicle and the amount you are borrowing for your next vehicle. Be very careful to make sure you understand the total cost of the new loan, the monthly payments, and the loan term (in months), before you agree to anything.

If you decide to roll the balance of your existing auto loan into your new loan:

- Find out which department of your current lender to contact in order to confirm that, once you have your new loan, your old loan has been paid off.
- After about a week, use the contact information to find out if your old loan has been paid off.
- If your loan has not been paid off, contact the lender. If, after reasonable efforts, your loan has still not been paid off, you may want to consider submitting a complaint to the Federal Trade Commission (FTC), or with the Consumer Financial Protection Bureau (CFPB) online or by calling toll-free at 855-411-CFPB (855-411-2372). You can also tell the CFPB about your experience without submitting a formal complaint. You can also contact your state Attorney General.

What Should You Do If You Have Problems Making Your Auto Loan Payments?

If you are having problems making payments, contact your lender or loan servicer and ask what options are available to you.

You can try to work out a payment plan. If you do, confirm any payment plan in writing. Also, be sure to ask about any negative impact that the plan might have on your credit report. If you are told there will not be any negative impact if you select one of the options you are offered, ask for confirmation in writing. If you have trouble making your auto loan payment, the sooner you contact the lender the better chance you have of working out an arrangement that gives you time to get back on track.

How Do You Qualify for Advertised Zero-Percent Auto Financing?

In general, only consumers with the highest credit scores qualify for zero-percent financing offers. Before you shop, check your credit report at one of the three nationwide consumer reporting agencies—TransUnion, Equifax, and Experian—and check for errors. Incorrect, negative information in your file could prevent you from qualifying for some offers. If there are errors, you can ask that the credit errors be corrected.

You should also know that zero-percent financing deals often require you to pay back the loan in a relatively short period of time, such as 36 months. In general, a shorter loan duration can be good for you because it means you will pay less interest over the course of the loan, but it means a higher monthly payment.

Sometimes you get a choice between the promotional financing (which provides a lower interest rate) and a manufacturer's rebate (which pays you cash). You should shop around for other loans from banks or credit unions to find out whether you will save more money by taking the manufacturer's rebate and arranging your own financing.

Do You Have to Negotiate Your Vehicle Purchase at the Same Time as You Negotiate How Much You Get for Your Trade-In or the Terms of a Loan from the Dealer?

You are not required to get a loan from a dealer or trade in a vehicle in order to purchase a vehicle from a dealer. You should negotiate each part of the deal separately and comparison shop to get the best overall deal.

Here are some steps you can take:

- **Step 1:** You can shop around and research vehicle prices as if you are buying for cash. Even if you think you might trade-in your vehicle, you do not have to decide that when you are shopping around.
- **Step 2:** You can get an approximate value for your trade-in. You should look up the value of your current vehicle by comparing what you could sell the vehicle for at other dealers or to other persons directly (the "private sale" value). You can estimate its value by checking newspaper or online classifieds as well as resources, such as Consumer Reports, Edmunds, Kelley Blue Book, and the National Automobile Dealers Association's (NADA) Guides (online or at your local library).
- **Step 3:** If you still have an outstanding balance on the vehicle you are trading in, find out the payoff amount from your lender so you know how much you will have to pay before your old loan is fully paid.
- **Step 4:** Negotiate the interest rate for your loan separately, comparing interest rates obtained from your bank, credit union, or other lenders. Before you go to the dealer, you can find out what interest rates you may qualify for based on your credit history, how much you want to pay for the vehicle, what your trade-in is worth, and what you can make for a down payment.

Negotiating the price, the trade-in value, and financing rates separately and deciding whether to finance the new purchase with someone other than the dealer if you get your best offer there may improve your overall deal. Breaking the transaction into different pieces may take some of the pressure off you while you shop around. This can save you money in the long run.

Be sure to talk to your dealer and your lender about any outstanding loans or financing on your trade-in. Make sure that your dealer or lender arranges to pay off your current loan if you trade in a vehicle with a balance due on your current loan.

You Owe More on Your Current Loan than Your Current Vehicle Is Worth. What Do You Need to Know If You Buy a New Vehicle?

If you are considering rolling the balance of the old auto loan into your new auto loan, make sure you understand how this will affect the total cost of your new loan.

Carefully look at the total cost of the new loan (including the amount borrowed), the annual percentage rate (APR), the interest rate, the loan term (in months), and the monthly payment—before you agree to anything. If you do not roll the amount you still owe on your old vehicle into the new loan and keep your current vehicle while buying a new one, then you will have two loans and two monthly payments to make. Either way, you may want to consider whether it makes sense to go through with the transaction and purchase the next vehicle if you still owe money on your trade-in.

If you owe more than your current vehicle is worth—sometimes referred to as "negative equity"—you should consider whether you can afford a new vehicle.

To find out if you have negative equity, you should look up the approximate value of your current vehicle using websites such as the Consumer Reports, Edmunds, Kelley Blue Book, NADA Guides, and online classifieds. You may also find these and other resources at your local library. Look up the "private sale" value, because that is what you can get if you sell your vehicle to an individual. Look up "Trade-In to Dealer" if you want to see a range of prices for similar vehicles. Then call your lender to find out how much you still owe on your loan.

A dealer may offer to "roll in" the balance of your old loan into a loan for a new vehicle. This is called a "negative trade-in," because the trade-in adds to the cost of the new loan, rather than reducing it. This might make the new loan unaffordable. Be very careful to make sure you understand the total cost of the new loan and the monthly payments—and the loan term (in months)—before you agree to anything.

How Can You Find Out What Your Trade-In Vehicle Is Worth?

You can look up the approximate value using online commercial websites such as the Consumer Reports, Edmunds, Kelley Blue Book, NADA Guides, and online classifieds. These resources may be available at your local library. Finding examples of similar vehicles that have sold recently in your area will help you know a fair price.

Once you know how much your current vehicle is worth, you can decide whether to trade it in or sell it yourself. If you trade it in at a dealership, you and the dealer will decide on the value that will be credited toward the purchase price of your next vehicle. If you sell it yourself, you can use the money you get as a down payment.

Table 24.1. Comparison Table of Short Loan Term

Loan Term	Monthly Payment	Total Interest Paid
36 months (3 years)	$597	$1,498
48 months (4 years)	$458	$1,999
60 months (5 years)	$375	$2,508
72 months (6 years)	$320	$3,024

If you still owe money on a vehicle that you want to trade-in, there is more to consider.

How Do You Compare Auto Loan Offers? What Should You Look at besides the Monthly Payment?

When comparing auto loan offers to determine the best deal, focus on the annual percentage rate (APR), the interest rate, and the length of the loan—and not just on the monthly payment. If you do not get the best deal available to you on the interest rate, you could end up paying significant additional interest amounts over the life of the loan.

The length of the loan term is also important in considering the overall cost of the loan. A longer loan term may mean smaller monthly payments, but you will pay more in interest over the life of the loan. You should consider carefully whether you want to lengthen the loan term just to get your monthly payments down. Making your loan term longer may not be worth the extra costs and you could be left with a vehicle that's worth less than what you owe. So do not focus on the monthly payment alone. The big picture is the total cost of the loan. The total cost of your auto loan depends on the cost of borrowing (interest rate and APR), which is reflected in your monthly payment and in how many months you will have to make that monthly payment (the loan term). In other words, how much you will pay overall depends partly on how long you will have to pay.

Understanding the parts of a loan—the amount the loan, the interest rate and the length of the loan—is necessary in order to negotiate the best auto loan for you. Negotiating the interest rate and the loan term are key factors in getting the best auto loan. You might want to use a loan calculator to help you with the math. There are a number of auto loan calculators available online. For example, Consumer Reports and the NADA Guides provide online auto loan calculators that may be helpful in evaluating and comparing the costs and terms of various auto loans.

The comparison samples in Table 24.1 illustrate how you will pay less in the long run if you have a shorter loan term. The table assumes a $20,000 loan and an interest rate of 4.75 percent.

While the longer loan term gives you a lower monthly payment, consider the total cost over the term of the loan. If you paid off a $20,000 loan in 3 years, you will pay

$1,498 in interest. For a 6-year loan, you will pay $3,024 in interest—more than twice as much. Some financial advisers recommend keeping the length of your auto loan to 5 years or less, reasoning that the longer the loan, the more likely you will owe more than the vehicle is worth.

When you think about your auto loan, it is also important to think about the total cost of ownership for your new vehicle. Consider the costs (such as taxes and insurance) that are higher for a new vehicle than for an older one, as well as other costs resulting from the purchase (such as annual registration fees). Maintenance and repairs may also factor into your calculations.

What Are Manufacturer Incentives?

Manufacturer incentives are special deals, such as zero-percent financing or cash rebates, that you may have seen advertised for new vehicles. Often, they are offered only for certain models.

Manufacturers offer these deals many times when they are having campaigns to sell certain models, or because they have a large inventory that they want to sell more quickly.

If you are interested in these types of offers, read the fine print to see if you qualify. Sometimes promotional interest rates are limited to people with high credit scores or to loans of a shorter duration.

CHAPTER 25
EXPLORE LOAN CHOICES

About This Chapter: This chapter includes text excerpted from "Learn to Explore Loan Choices," Consumer Financial Protection Bureau (CFPB), June 9, 2016.

As soon as you know your budget, shop around. Banks, credit unions, and other lenders are common places to get preapproved. Comparing offers will help you get the loan that is right for you.

Decisions to Make at This Step

- Where do I want to look for preapprovals or financing?
- How long do I want to be paying this auto loan?
- Should I make a down payment to reduce the loan's cost?
- Which lender can get me the best deal?

Actions to Take

Learn More about Sources of Auto Financing

While some consumers are able to pay cash for their new vehicle, most buyers use financing. Understanding your choices and the loan process will help you save money.

Banks, Credit Unions, and Nonbank Auto Finance Companies

You can get preapproved for your auto loan before selecting a vehicle. Check out banks, credit unions, and other lenders. You usually do not have to have an account with the bank or other lenders to get a preapproval. Generally, you do need to be or become a member of a credit union in order to apply for an auto loan.

The preapproval will give you a loan quote with an interest rate, loan length, and maximum loan amount based on factors such as your creditworthiness, the terms of the loan, and the type of vehicle you have in mind. The rate you are offered may be negotiable. This quote allows you to compare different lenders' offers against each other, giving you a stronger hand in negotiations.

Tip: Use the auto loan worksheet at www.files.consumerfinance.gov/f/documents/201606_cfpb_auto-loan-worksheet.pdf to compare the financing offered through the dealership with the rate and terms of any preapproval you received from a bank, credit union, or other lenders. Because you have preapproved loan offers in your pocket, you can choose whether to stick with one of them or ask the dealer to match or beat your best preapproval. Choose the option that best fits your budget.

Lenders and dealers are not required to offer the best interest rates available. You may be able to save a lot of money over the life of the loan by negotiating the interest rate.

Dealer-Arranged Financing

With dealer-arranged financing, you obtain financing from a lender through a dealership. The dealer collects information from you and forwards that information to one or more prospective auto lenders. If the lender(s) agrees to finance your loan, they may authorize or quote a rate to the dealer, referred to as the "buy rate." The interest rate that you negotiate with the dealer may be higher than the "buy rate" because it may include an amount that compensates the dealer for handling the financing.

Dealers may have the discretion to charge you more than the buy rate they receive from a lender, so you may be able to negotiate the interest rate the dealer quotes to you. Ask or negotiate for a loan with better terms. After the auto purchase is finalized, a dealer-arranged loan may then be sold to a lender who has already indicated a willingness to extend the credit. That lender may own your loan and collect the monthly payments, or transfer those responsibilities and rights to other companies.

Buy Here Pay Here Dealership Financing

Some types of dealerships finance auto loans "in-house" to borrowers with no credit or poor credit. At Buy Here Pay Here dealerships, you might see signs with messages like "No Credit, No Problem!" The interest rate on these loans can be higher. You may want to consider if the cost of the loan outweighs the benefit of buying the vehicle.

Even if you have poor or no credit, it may be worth seeing if there is a bank, credit union, other lenders, or another dealer that is willing to extend a loan to you.

Check Current and Auto Loan Interest Rates

Start by researching rates and loan terms by contacting several banks, credit unions, or other lenders. You can also look online at many commercial sites that may give you an estimate of interest rates nationwide and by your Zone Improvement Plan (ZIP) code. Some commercial sites will link you to specific lenders and dealers for estimates, so you should be careful about entering your personal information.

Get Preapproved for a Loan

Shopping ahead of time will get you ready for negotiating your auto loan and make the process less stressful. Getting preapproved by multiple lenders can mean that they

> **Tip**: When you apply for a loan and the lender checks your credit, a credit score is created for the lender. Depending on the credit scoring model used, generally, any credit inquiries that took place within a 14 to 45-day time span will only count as one inquiry. So it is a good idea to do your loan-comparison shopping within a short time period to minimize any negative impact on your credit score.

may compete for your business. This puts you in a stronger negotiating position for whichever lender you choose. This can help you lower your total cost.

When you are heading over to a bank, credit union, or dealership, make sure to gather all the information you will need. Lenders will generally ask for this information in a loan application:

- Name
- Social Security Number (SSN) or Individual Taxpayer Identification Number (ITIN)
- Date of birth
- Current and previous address(es) and length of stay
- Current and previous employer(s) and length of employment
- Occupation
- Sources of income
- Total gross monthly income
- Financial information on current credit accounts, including debts

In addition to giving you more options and power in negotiations, a preapproval helps you stay within your budget and save time. Preapprovals allow you to compare interest rates without the time pressure you may feel once you are at the dealership. Then, at the dealership, you can focus more attention on items such as your trade-in or auto choice. Because you have preapproved loan offers in your pocket, you get to choose whether to stick with one of them or negotiate with the dealer for the best financing option.

Once your application is preapproved, the lender will give you documents to take to the dealership. When you are ready to buy, the dealer will contact your lender to make the arrangements.

Understand How Loan Shopping Impacts Your Credit Scores

Shopping for the best deal on an auto loan will generally have little to no impact on your credit score(s). The benefit of shopping will far outweigh any impact on your credit. In some cases, applying for multiple loans over a long period of time can lower your credit score. You can minimize any negative impact on your credit score by doing all your rate shopping in a short amount of time.

Know Your Rights

A lender cannot discourage or deny your application for credit, or offer different prices or other terms and conditions of the loan, based on your race, color, religion, national origin, sex, marital status, age, receipt of public-assistance income, or good faith exercise of any right under the Consumer Credit Protection Act (CCPA).

You can submit a complaint with the Consumer Financial Protection Bureau (CFPB) online or by calling toll-free at 855-411-CFPB (855-411-2372) or with the Federal Trade Commission (FTC). You can also tell CFPB about your experience without submitting a formal complaint.

CHAPTER 26

SIX SURE SIGNS OF AN ADVANCE-FEE LOAN SCAM

About This Chapter: This chapter includes text excerpted from "Advance-Fee Loans," Federal Trade Commission (FTC), August 2012.

Looking for a loan or credit card but do not think you will qualify? Have you been turned down by a bank because of your poor credit history? You may be tempted by advertisements and websites that guarantee loans or credit cards, regardless of your credit history. Rule number one: Legitimate lenders never "guarantee" or say that you are likely to get a loan or a credit card before you apply, especially if you have bad credit, no credit, or bankruptcy.

Some red flags can tip you off to scam artists' tricks. For example:

1. **A lender who is not interested in your credit history.** A lender may offer loans or credit cards for many purposes—for example, so you can start a business or consolidate your bills. But, one who does not care about your credit record should worry you. Advertisements that say "Bad credit? No problem" or "We don't care about your past. You deserve a loan" or "Get money fast" or even "No hassle—guaranteed" often indicate a scam. Banks and other legitimate lenders generally evaluate creditworthiness and confirm the information in an application before they grant firm offers of credit to anyone.
2. **Fees that are not disclosed clearly or prominently.** Scam lenders may say you have been approved for a loan, then call or email demanding a fee before you can get the money. Any upfront fee that the lender wants to collect before granting the loan is a cue to walk away, especially if you are told it is for "insurance," "processing," or just "paperwork."

   Legitimate lenders often charge application, appraisal, or credit report fees. The differences? They disclose their fees clearly and prominently; they take their fees from the amount you borrow, and the fees usually are paid to the lender or broker after the loan is approved.

And if a lender says they will not check your credit history but wants your personal information, such as your Social Security number (SSN) or bank account number? Go somewhere else. They may use your information to debit your bank account to pay a fee they are hiding.

3. **A loan that is offered by phone.** It is illegal for companies doing business by phone in the United States to promise you a loan or credit card and ask you to pay for it before they deliver.
4. **A lender who uses a copy-cat or wanna-be name.** Crooks give their companies names that sound like well-known or respected organizations and create websites that look professional. Some scam artists have pretended to be the Better Business Bureau (BBB), a major bank, or another reputable organization; some even produce forged paperwork or pay people to pretend to be referenced. Always get a company's phone number from the phone book or directory assistance and call to check that they are who they say they are. Get a physical address, too; a company that advertises a P.O. box as its address is one to check out with the appropriate authorities.
5. **A lender who is not registered in your state.** Lenders and loan brokers are required to register in the states where they do business. To check registration, call your state Attorney General's office or your state's Department of Banking or Financial Regulation. Checking registration does not guarantee that you will be happy with a lender, but it helps weed out the crooks.
6. **A lender who asks you to wire money or pay an individual.** Do not make a payment for a loan or credit card directly to an individual; legitimate lenders do not ask anyone to do that. In addition, do not use a wire transfer service or send money orders for a loan. You have little recourse if there is a problem with a wire transaction, and legitimate lenders do not pressure their customers to wire money.

Finally, just because you have received a slick promotion, seen an advertisement for a loan or credit card in a prominent place in your neighborhood or in your newspaper, on television, or on the Internet, or heard one on the radio, do not assume it is a good deal—or even legitimate. Scam artists work hard to make you think they are legitimate, so it is really important to do your homework.

CHAPTER 27

HOW TO GET A GOOD DEAL ON AUTO LOANS

About This Chapter: This chapter includes text excerpted from "For Young Adults and Teens: Quick Tips for Managing Your Money," Federal Deposit Insurance Corporation (FDIC), 2012.

Strategies for Getting a Good Deal

Many young people look forward to getting their own car but overlook what they may need to do to comfortably afford it, especially if they will be borrowing money. Here are strategies to consider well before you go to the dealership.

Start saving early. "The more money you put down, the less you have to borrow—and that means the less money you will pay in interest on a loan, if you need to borrow at all," said Phyllis Pratt, a Federal Deposit Insurance Corporation (FDIC) Community Affairs Specialist.

Decide how much you can afford to spend each month on a car. In addition to car payments, consider how much you will need for insurance, taxes, registration fees, routine maintenance, and unexpected repairs. Online calculators can help you figure out what you can afford.

Remember that there are alternatives to buying a car. Lease payments may sometimes appear lower than loan payments, but at the end of the lease you will not own the car and you may have to pay more money for excess mileage or body repairs. If you need a car only once in a while, consider using a service that rents cars for periods as short as an hour.

Shop for a loan at your bank and with several other lenders. Compare the offers based on the annual percentage rate (APR) you are quoted by each lender. The APR reflects the total cost of the loan, including interest and certain fees, as a yearly rate. Then consider getting "prequalified" by the lender offering the best deal. That is not the same as a loan approval, but it will expedite the process once you find a car you like. Before you start shopping for a loan, review your credit report to correct wrong information, which can help you qualify for a lower interest rate. In addition, a dealer's

What Is a Buy Rate for an Auto Loan?

A buy rate is the interest rate that a potential lender quotes to your dealer when you apply for dealer-arranged financing.

Your dealer may offer you an interest rate that is higher than the buy rate. The rate the dealer offers you is called the "contract rate." Sometimes the lender pays the dealer a fee for arranging the financing that is based on the difference between these two rates. Dealers may have the discretion to charge you more than the buy rate, so you may be able to negotiate that interest rate.

Ask the dealer if you qualify for a loan with better terms. In general, dealers and lenders are not required to offer the best rates available. You can save money over the life of the loan by getting quotes from multiple lenders, comparing offers, and negotiating for the best interest rate available to you. This could save you hundreds or thousands of dollars over the life of the loan.

(Source: "What Is a Buy Rate for an Auto Loan?" Consumer Financial Protection Bureau (CFPB))

special financing (such as zero-percent interest) may not be the best value if it means foregoing an extra discount on the car. In that situation, you may come out ahead if you borrow from a financial institution, even at a higher interest rate, and save on the purchase price. Also, do not purchase a more expensive car than you feel you can comfortably afford, even if you qualify for a larger loan.

Whether you are buying or leasing, negotiate with the dealer based on the total cost of the car, not the monthly payment. Why? "By extending the length of the loan, a dealer can offer a more expensive vehicle with the same monthly loan payment you were quoted for a less expensive car, but you will pay more in interest costs," said Luke W. Reynolds, Acting Associate Director of the FDIC's Division of Depositor and Consumer Protection (DCP).

CHAPTER 28
KNOW WHAT IS NEGOTIABLE

About This Chapter: This chapter includes text excerpted from "Know What Is Negotiable," Consumer Financial Protection Bureau (CFPB), June 9, 2016.

Did you know that you can negotiate the terms of your auto loan? Negotiating can save you hundreds or even thousands of dollars over the life of your loan.

Decisions to Make at This Step

- Can I get a better loan from a different lender?
- How long do I want this loan to last?
- Is what I am being offered consistent with my research?
- Does this deal work for my budget?

Actions to Take

What Is Negotiable?

In addition to the price of the vehicle, there are the terms and costs of the auto loan that you may be able to negotiate or control. These items, taken together, will influence the amount of your monthly payment and the total loan cost. Later, this chapter will give you tips on how to focus your negotiation to lower your total cost.

Negotiable Loan Terms and Features

- Annual percentage rate (APR) and interest rate
- Length of loan
- Whether or not there will be a prepayment penalty
- Any additional fees associated with the loan

Optional "Add-Ons" That Increase the Amount You Will Borrow

- Optional products for the loan or vehicle, such as extended warranties, guaranteed asset protection (GAP) insurance, and credit insurance
- Optional physical features for the vehicle, such as alarm systems, window tinting, and tire and wheel protection

> **Tip:** Your total loan cost starts with the amount financed. The amount financed is the amount of money you are borrowing. It includes the price of the vehicle, taxes, and other government fees, as well as any add-ons, such as extended warranties and optional credit insurance, minus your down payment and trade-in amount. The amount financed does not include the cost to borrow the money. That cost is known as the "finance charge" and includes interest and certain fees over the life of the loan. Your total loan cost is the amount financed plus the finance charge. By negotiating for better terms on your loan, you can reduce the total amount of money you pay over the life of the loan.

Other Things That Affect the Amount You Will Borrow

- Trade-in amount (if you trade in your vehicle)
- Amount of the down payment
- Fees charged by the dealer, such as dealer preparation fees, origination fees, document fees, and delivery charges

You cannot negotiate taxes or title and registration fees. These are set by your local or state government.

Negotiate to Lower the Total Cost, Not Just the Monthly Payment

Many people think about a loan in terms of the monthly payment. Be careful here. If you reduce the monthly payment by taking out a longer loan, you may pay much more in interest. The total cost of your vehicle financing matters. By negotiating for better terms on your loan, you can reduce the total amount of money you pay over time. For example:

- Getting a lower interest rate and APR means you will pay less to borrow money. The total cost of your loan will be lower.
- A shorter loan term (in which you make monthly payments for fewer months) will reduce your total loan cost. A longer loan can reduce your monthly payment, but you pay more interest over the life of the loan.
- A higher down payment, or a higher price for your trade-in, will reduce the total amount financed because you will have to borrow less money.
- Optional "add-on" products, such as extended warranties, GAP insurance, or credit insurance that are added into your loan amount, will increase your total cost because you will be borrowing more money.

Keep Track of Multiple Factors While Negotiating

When negotiating for your loan, make sure you keep track of all the factors that affect the total cost. If you are negotiating the interest rate, make sure that you also know the length of the loan and other terms. Comparing total loan costs will help you keep an eye on these multiple factors.

Maintain an auto loan worksheet to help keep track of the different factors.

> **Tip:** In general, dealers and lenders are not required to offer the best rates available. When negotiating, ask if you can get a better rate or more favorable terms.

Ask the dealer or lender to tell you the price, trade-in value (if applicable), interest rate, the term of the loan, and estimated monthly payments, and write these numbers down on the auto loan worksheet. It is best to get these numbers early in the process, so you can better compare and negotiate.

Just as the first price you are offered for the vehicle may not be the lowest price available to you, the first rate for a loan that the lender or dealer offers you may not be the lowest rate you qualify for. If the lender or dealer agree to a better loan feature (such as a lower APR or interest rate), check to make sure other factors, such as the length of the loan or the amount financed, have not changed. A lower monthly payment does not necessarily mean a lower interest rate; it might just mean that you are paying for a longer time.

CHAPTER 29
UNDERSTAND HOW TO CLOSE THE DEAL

About This Chapter: This chapter includes text excerpted from "Understand How to Close the Deal," Consumer Financial Protection Bureau (CFPB), June 9, 2016.

By now you have negotiated for your auto and chosen a loan and lender. But, there is still a lot of paperwork to go over and sign. Before you drive off, make sure everything matches what you agreed to when negotiating.

- Does this loan work for my budget?
- Does this match what I agreed to?
- Am I comfortable with this deal?
- Did the lender sign all the paperwork?

Actions to Take for Closing a Deal

Verify That You Get What You Agreed To

Once you have finalized the negotiations, review all of the paperwork before signing the loan documents. The federal Truth in Lending Act (TILA) requires lenders to give you specific disclosures in writing about important terms before you are legally obligated under the loan. One purpose of TILA is to help consumers make apples-to-apples comparisons between loans. The important terms include:

- **Annual percentage rate (APR).** The cost of credit expressed as a yearly rate in a percentage
- **Finance charge.** The cost of credit expressed as a dollar amount (the total amount of interest and certain fees you will pay over the life of the loan if you make every payment when due)
- **Amount financed.** The dollar amount of credit provided to you (this is normally the amount you are borrowing)
- **Total of payments.** The sum of all the payments that you will have made at the end of the loan (this includes repayment of the principal amount of the loan plus all of the finance charges)

ANNUAL PERCENTAGE RATE The cost of your credit as a yearly rate	FINANCE CHARGE The dollar amount the credit will cost you	Amount Financed The amount of credit provided to you or on your behalf	Total of Payments The amount you will have paid after you have made all payments as scheduled	Total Sale Price The total cost of your purchase on credit, including your downpayment of
%	$	$	$	$

Figure 29.1. Terms of Auto Loan

Tip: Walk away if you are not comfortable with any aspect of the loan or the process; you can always leave without completing the deal. Take time to think it over and return another time. No one can make you accept financing or a vehicle that you are not satisfied with.

The TILA disclosure will include other important terms, such as the number of payments, the monthly payment, late fees, whether the loan has a fixed or variable rate, and whether you can prepay your loan without a penalty.

Take time to review the details of your auto loan, and look over the paperwork. If there are things you do not understand, ask questions. You are signing a contract and this is a major purchase; it is important that you understand what you are signing.

Finish the Paperwork before You Drive Away

Before you drive off with your new vehicle, make sure that:

- You have a copy of all documents
- Both you and the dealer have signed
- All blanks are filled in

Some dealers will allow the customer to take possession of the new vehicle before the loan is approved by the lender. This practice, called "spot delivery," could put the deal that you thought you had at risk. Make sure that the financing is nailed down before you sign the contract and drive away with the vehicle.

If you do not have the financing nailed down, the dealer may ask you to come back in and agree to a higher interest rate, add a cosigner, or make some other change different from what you thought was agreed. You do not have to agree to a second deal. If this happens and you do not want to agree to a second deal, you will have to return the vehicle and the dealer will have to unwind the deal and give you back your trade-in and down payment. In some cases, you may want to seek legal assistance and file a complaint with your state Attorney General or consumer protection office.

Pay Attention to the Details after You Drive Away

After you take out a loan, you should receive an introductory message from the lender that provided the financing. This communication will include important information related to your loan, such as where to send your payments and payment due dates. Make sure to make your monthly payments on time to avoid the cost of late fees and the possible repossession of your vehicle, as well as negative entries on your credit report.

Note: Due to the unique challenges of military life, special auto loan and lease protections were established and may be available to you if you are a service member currently on active duty.

CHAPTER 30

CHOOSING BETWEEN DEALER-ARRANGED AND BANK FINANCING

About This Chapter: Text under the heading "Check out the Auto Dealer and Financing—before You Sign" is excerpted from "Check out the Auto Dealer and Financing—before You Sign," Federal Trade Commission (FTC), October 31, 2014; Text under the heading "What Is the Difference between Dealer-Arranged and Bank Financing?" is excerpted from "What Is the Difference between Dealer-Arranged and Bank Financing?" Consumer Financial Protection Bureau (CFPB), November 16, 2016.

Check out the Auto Dealer and Financing before You Sign

You want to buy a car and need financing, but your credit is not so great. Most dealerships have a Finance and Insurance (F&I) Department that will tell you about their financing options. To get the process started, the F&I Department will ask you to complete a credit application, which includes your monthly income and information on current credit accounts, including debt you owe.

At least that is how it is supposed to work. But, there have been reports that some dealers inflate your income information for the financing without your knowledge. That can cause you serious financial harm. You could be saddled with car financing that you cannot afford to repay. That means your car could be repossessed and your credit score could take a hit.

The Federal Trade Commission (FTC) has a few tips to help you avoid unscrupulous finance deals:

- Consider your options for financing. You might be able to arrange financing directly with a credit union or finance company before you pick a car. This will also give you a sense of what credit terms might be available to you so that you can compare them with what a dealer is offering you. If the dealer's offer differs vastly, make sure the offer is based on accurate information about your income and employment.
- Research the dealer before visiting the sales lot. Check the dealer's reputation online by searching for the company's name with words like "scam," "rip-off," or "complaint." Research the dealer with your state

Attorney General and local consumer protection agency (CPA) to make sure there are no unresolved complaints on file. Also, ask family or friends for recommendations.

- If a dealer encourages you to overstate your income, take it as a sign that the dealer is not reputable and leave the dealership.
- Ask to see the credit application—completely filled out—before you sign it. Make sure your income and other personal information are correctly listed.
- Make sure to get a copy of your paperwork before you leave the dealership.
- If you find out your dealer has falsified your income or other personal information, complain to the FTC online or call 877-FTC-HELP (877-382-4357).

What Is the Difference between Dealer-Arranged and Bank Financing?

With dealer-arranged financing, the dealer collects information from you and forwards that information to one or more prospective auto lenders. Alternatively, with bank or other lender financing, you go directly to a bank, credit union, or other lender and apply for a loan.

Bank lenders can "preapprove" you for a loan. If they are willing to make an auto loan to you, the lender will quote you an interest rate, loan term (number of months), and maximum loan amount based on factors such as your credit score(s), the terms of the transaction, and the type of vehicle. This lender will then give you a quote or a conditional commitment letter before you go to the dealership. The bank, credit union, or other lender offers certain terms, and those terms are negotiable.

If the lender(s) chooses to finance your loan, they may authorize or quote an interest rate to the dealer to finance the loan, referred to as the "buy rate." The interest rate that you negotiate with the dealer may be higher than the "buy rate" because it may include an amount that compensates the dealer for handling the financing. Dealers may have the discretion to charge you more than the buy rate they receive from a lender, so you may be able to negotiate the interest rate the dealer quotes to you. Ask or negotiate for a loan with better terms. Be sure to compare the financing offered through the dealership with the rate and terms of any preapproval you received from a bank, credit union, or other lenders. Choose the option that best fits your budget. After the auto purchase is finalized, the dealer-arranged loan may then be sold to the lender, who has already indicated a willingness to extend the credit. That lender may own your loan and collect the monthly payments, or transfer those responsibilities and rights to other companies.

Some types of dealerships finance auto loans "in-house" to borrowers with no credit or poor credit. At "Buy Here Pay Here" dealerships, you might see signs with messages such as "No Credit, No Problem!" The interest rate on loans from these dealerships can be much higher than loans from a bank, credit union, or other types of lenders. You may want to consider whether the cost of the loan outweighs the benefit of buying the vehicle. Even if you have poor or no credit, it may be worth it to see if there is a bank, credit union, or another dealer that is willing to make a loan to you. Another feature of this type of dealership is that your monthly payment is to the dealership. Some Buy Here Pay Here dealerships and some other lenders that lend to people with no credit or poor credit put devices in their vehicles that help them repossess or disable the vehicle if you miss a payment.

> **Tip:** In general, dealers and lenders are not required to offer the best rates available and you can typically negotiate the offered rate. You can save money over the life of the loan by getting quotes from multiple lenders, comparing offers, and negotiating for the best interest rate available to you.

CHAPTER 31
COMMON AUTO LOAN ISSUES

About This Chapter: Text beginning with the heading "Can the Dealer Increase the Interest Rate after You Drive the Vehicle Home?" is excerpted from "Auto Loans Common Issues," Consumer Financial Protection Bureau (CFPB), April 30, 2019; Text under the heading "When Are Late Fees Charged on an Auto Loan?" is excerpted from "When Are Late Fees Charged on an Auto Loan?" Consumer Financial Protection Bureau (CFPB), August 5, 2016.

Can the Dealer Increase the Interest Rate after You Drive the Vehicle Home?

Some dealers will allow the customer to take possession of the new vehicle before the loan is approved by the lender. This practice is sometimes called "spot delivery." In some cases after you drive away with the vehicle but before the sale is finalized, the dealership will later tell you that they could not make the loan at the agreed-upon terms. They then may ask you to bring back the vehicle and renegotiate the loan for a higher interest rate, a longer term, a larger down payment, or a combination of those terms.

If this happens and you do not agree to a second deal, the dealer will have to unwind the sale and give you back your trade-in and down payment. This is sometimes called a "yo-yo sale" and you may be entitled to legal protections in some situations.

Before you drive off with your new vehicle, make sure:

- You reviewed the contract and disclosures before agreeing to the loan and auto sale to make sure you understand the terms of your deal;
- You have a signed copy of all documents that both you and the dealer have signed and that all blanks are filled in;
- The financing and the loan rate is final before you take the vehicle off the dealer's lot.

If the contract did not contain a clear statement that the deal was not final or that the sale was conditional on the dealer being able to find someone to buy your loan within a short duration of time, and if you already signed all of the documents before

What Is the Difference between a Simple Interest Rate and Precomputed Interest in an Auto Loan Contract?

Simple interest and precomputed interest are different ways to calculate your interest due.

The simple interest method uses the amount or actual balance outstanding on the day your payment is due. If you pay more than your monthly payment, this amount should get smaller as you pay down your loan. The precomputed interest method always uses the original payment schedule to figure interest, even if you make payments early.

If you have a contract with precomputed interest and plan to prepay your loan early in full or make larger payments in advance of your regularly scheduled amount, you will not get the same reduction in the interest charges that you would if your contract had a simple interest rate. If you pay on time for each payment over your loan term, there is little difference between simple and precomputed interest.

(Source: "What's the Difference between a Simple Interest Rate and Precomputed Interest in an Auto Loan Contract?" Consumer Financial Protection Bureau (CFPB))

you left with the vehicle, you may have a right to keep it and make the payments as agreed. If you are asked to return to the dealer to discuss your financing and it was not disclosed to you that the deal was not yet final, you may submit a complaint to the Federal Trade Commission (FTC) or, in the case of a Buy Here Pay Here dealer, with the CFPB online or by calling toll-free at 855-411-CFPB (855-411-2372). You can also tell FTC about your experience without submitting a formal complaint. You can also submit a complaint with your state Attorney General or state consumer protection office. If you are in the military, you should report this to your installation Judge Advocate General (JAG) immediately. To find your JAG legal assistance office use the locator. If you need legal assistance, this list of lawyer resources from the American Bar Association (ABA). You can find legal help from your legal aid office or volunteer attorney program.

Does a Creditor Have to Consider Your Part-Time or Retirement Income?

A creditor cannot discount or refuse to consider your (or your cosigner's) income because it comes from part-time employment.

A creditor also cannot discount or refuse to consider the income that is an annuity, pension, or other retirement benefits. Like all other forms of income, however, a creditor can consider the amount of the income and likelihood that it will continue.

When Are Late Fees Charged on an Auto Loan?

Whether a late fee is assessed and the amount of the late fee varies by lender, your contract, and according to state law.

Check your contract to see what it says about late fees. Some contracts will provide a grace period. If you do not pay within that time period, a late fee may be assessed. Late payments may also have a negative impact on your credit score(s).

CHAPTER 32
BEWARE OF ONLINE VEHICLE SALE FRAUD

About This Chapter: Text in this chapter begins with excerpts from "Online Vehicle Sale Fraud," Federal Bureau of Investigation (FBI), January 24, 2018; Text under the heading "Put the Brakes on Phony Online Car Sales" is excerpted from "Put the Brakes on Phony Online Car Sales," Federal Trade Commission (FTC), June 17, 2019.

The Federal Bureau of Investigation (FBI) warns consumers that criminal perpetrators may post fraudulent online classified advertisements offering vehicles for sale that are not, nor have ever been, in their possession.

The fake advertisements usually include photos matching the description of the vehicle and a phone number or e-mail address to contact the supposed seller. Once contact is established, the criminal sends the intended buyer additional photos along with an explanation for the discounted price and the urgency of the transaction. Common reasons provided include:

- The seller is moving or being deployed by the military.
- The seller received the vehicle as part of a divorce settlement.
- The vehicle belonged to a relative who has died.

The criminal makes the fraud appear legitimate by deceptively claiming partnership with a reputable company, such as eBay, and assuring that the transaction will occur through the third party's buyer protection program. They may go so far as to send a fraudulent toll-free number that impersonates the third party. The buyer is told to purchase prepaid gift cards in the sale amount and to share the card codes with the criminal, who then notifies the buyer they will be receiving the vehicle in a number of days. After the transaction is complete, the criminal typically ignores all follow-up calls, text messages, or e-mails from the buyer or may demand additional payments. In the end, the vehicle is not delivered and the buyer is never able to recuperate their losses.

How to Avoid Fraudulent Online Vehicle Sales

You can avoid fraudulent online vehicle sales. The following tips will be helpful to you in this regard.

How You Can Tell If an Online Car Sale Is Fake

- You find bad reviews online. Check out the seller by searching online for the person's name, phone number and email address, plus words such as "review," "complaint," or "scam."
- Sellers try to rush the sale. Resist the pressure. Scammers use high-pressure sales tactics to get you to buy without thinking things through.
- They cannot or will not meet in person or let you inspect the car. Scammers might have an excuse, such as job transfer, military deployment, or divorce, for why you cannot see them or the car. But, experts agree that you should have an independent mechanic inspect a used car before you buy it.
- They want you to pay with gift cards or by wire transfer. If anyone tells you to pay that way, it is a scam. Every time.
- The sellers demand more money after the sale of "shipping" or "transportation" costs.

- If it appears too good to be true, it probably is.
- Use the Internet to research the advertised item and the seller's name, e-mail addresses, telephone numbers, and other unique identifiers.
- Use the Internet to research the company's contact information and its shipping and payment policies before completing a transaction. Ensure the legitimacy of the contact information and that the company accepts the requested payment option.
- Avoid sellers who refuse to meet in person, or who refuse to allow the buyer to physically inspect the vehicle before the purchase.
- Ask for the vehicle identification number (VIN), license plate (if possible), and the name of the individual to whom the car is currently registered.
- Criminals take extra effort to disguise themselves and may have recognizable words in their e-mail name or domain. If you are suspicious or unsure about an e-mail that claims to be from a legitimate business, locate the business online and contact them directly.

If you believe you have been a victim of this scam, please file a complaint with the FBI's Internet Crime Complaint Center (IC3) at www.ic3.gov.

Put the Brakes on Phony Online Car Sales

You can buy practically anything online, including used cars. But, before you shell out any hard-earned cash, here is a warning about scammers trying to sell cars they do not have or own.

How the Scam Works

Criminals post advertisements on online auction and sales websites, such as eBay Motors, for inexpensive used cars (that they do not really own). They offer to chat online, share photos, and answer questions. They may even tell you the sale will go through a well-known retailer's buyer protection program. Sellers have been sending fake invoices that appear to come from eBay Motors and demanding payment in eBay gift cards. If you call the number on the invoice, the scammer pretends to work for eBay Motors. Trusting buyers have lost hundreds of thousands of dollars over the past year alone.

The VIN does not match the VIN for the car you are interested in. A vehicle history report can help you spot such discrepancies.

CHAPTER 33

PROTECT YOURSELF FROM DECEPTIVE AUTO SCAMS

About This Chapter: This chapter includes text excerpted from "Are Car Ads Taking You for a Ride?" Federal Trade Commission (FTC), January 2014.

Whether you are buying or leasing, shopping for a car can be fun and exciting. But, wading through advertisements and promotions offered by car dealers also can be stressful. Some advertise unusually low prices, low or no upfront payments, low- or no-interest loans, or low monthly payments. Others promise high trade-in allowances, free or low-cost options, or rebates. And if you are looking to lease a vehicle, advertisements for very low—or no payment—at signing may be especially enticing.

But, the Federal Trade Commission (FTC), the nation's consumer protection agency (CPA), says Beware: Not all dealers play by the rules. Details about special offers and promotions may be buried in the fine print, clicks away from online claims, may not be disclosed at all, or may not be disclosed until you get to the showroom or the finance office. But, the law requires that if a dealer advertises discounts, prices, or special low payments, the advertisements must clearly explain the important details of the offers and how a buyer may qualify for them.

Deceptive Car Advertisements

Here are some claims that may be deceptive and why.

Vehicles Are Available at a Specific Low Price or for a Specific Discount

What may be missing: The low price is after a down payment, often thousands of dollars, plus other fees, such as taxes, licensing and document fees, on approved credit.
Other pitches: The discount is only for a pricy, fully-loaded model, or the reduced price or discount offered might depend on qualifications such as the buyer being a recent college graduate or having an account at a particular bank.

Tip: When you are shopping for a vehicle, you should ask for quotes that include the vehicle and all of the options that you want to purchase. You should shop around for the best deal on the price, the interest rate on your loan, and any trade-in. Shopping at multiple dealers can help you get a better price. Shopping around with multiple lenders before you purchase can help you get the best interest rate available to you on your auto loan.

(Source: "What I a Manufacturer Suggested Retail Price (MSRP)?" Consumer Financial Protection Bureau (CFPB))

"Only $99/Month"

What may be missing: The advertised payments are temporary "teaser" payments. Payments for the rest of the loan term are much higher. A variation on this pitch: You will owe a balloon payment—usually thousands of dollars—at the end of the term.

Zero or Low-Rate Loans

What may be missing: The low advertised annual percentage rate (APR) may apply only to loans up to a certain amount—which may be a lot less than the purchase price. You will pay a higher APR for loans financing higher amounts. A variation on this pitch: rates may not be stated as "APR," meaning the advertised rate may not reflect the true "annual" cost of financing and may exclude certain costs required to be included in the APR.

"$0 Due at Lease Signing"

What may be missing: The fine print indicates that additional fees—sometimes several thousand dollars—are due at lease signing.

You Have Won!

What may be missing: The prize. This is just a tactic to get you into the showroom.

Questions to Ask about Discounts, Low Prices, and Special Offers

To find your best deal, ask the right questions. The answers should help you determine whether the special promotions offer genuine value—or are simply smoke and mirrors:

- Do you have to pay sizeable amounts—say, a downpayment or taxes—that are not included in the advertised low price?
- Does the advertised discount apply only to certain models of the vehicle? Is it available if you order a car instead of buying one off the lot?
- Do you need to have certain qualifications to get the advertised discount, low price, or credit terms?
- To get the advertised low rate financing:
    - Do you have to repay the loan in a short time period, say 36 months?

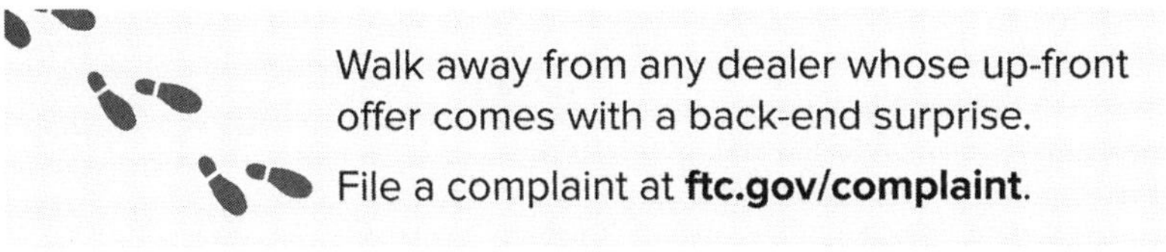

Figure 33.1. Deceptive Car Advertisements: What You Should Do ***(Source: "Deceptive Car Ads," Federal Trade Commission (FTC))***

    - Does the loan need to be for a certain amount? If so, what are the financing terms for loans with higher amounts?
    - Do you have to buy special merchandise, such as an extended warranty, a service contract, or rustproofing?
    - Will you be charged a higher vehicle price? The price may be lower if you pay cash or supply your own financing from a bank or credit union.
- Do the advertised low monthly payments apply for the entire term of the loan? Do they instead increase after only a few months? Is a balloon payment—possibly thousands of dollars—due at the end of the loan?
- If the advertisement offers $0 due at lease signing, do you still have to pay something before you drive off the lot—say, fees, taxes, a security deposit, or the first month's payment?
- Does the dealer's prize promotion mean you have won something substantial? What is it?

Before You Sign

Once you decide which dealer offers the car you want, be sure all the terms, including the price—and the financing if you get credit through the dealer—are what you agreed to. If you lease from the dealer, check that the terms are what you negotiated, too. Read the documents you get very carefully, especially the credit or lease contract. Be sure you understand the terms before you sign. If the deal is not what you negotiated, ask questions. Do not sign, and do not leave the dealership with a new vehicle until the terms you and the dealer negotiated are on the contract, and you are clear about your obligation, including all your payments.

PART 3 | ADD-ON EXPENSES: CAR MAINTENANCE AND INSURANCE

CHAPTER 34

SAVING MONEY ON GAS

About This Chapter: Text in this chapter begins with excerpts from "Saving Money on Gas," Federal Trade Commission (FTC), May 2011; Text under the heading "'Gas-Saving' Products" is excerpted from "'Gas-Saving' Products," Federal Trade Commission (FTC), August 2012.

Whether driving crosstown or cross-country, everybody wants to save money at the pump. Regardless of the make and model, your car's estimated gas mileage is just that—an estimate. An important variable is how you fuel, drive, and maintain your car. The Federal Trade Commission (FTC), the nation's consumer protection agency (CPA), offers these bumper-to-bumper tips to help you get the most mileage out of your gas purchases.

At the Pump

Check your owner's manual for the most effective octane level for your car. For most cars, the recommended gasoline is regular octane. In most cases, using a higher octane gas than the manufacturer recommends offers no benefit—and costs you at the pump. Some cars do require premium fuel, so before you fill up, check your owner's manual to find out if the higher-priced gas is required or just recommended.

Shop around. Specialized phone apps and websites can help you find the cheapest gas prices in your area. Also, many gas stations advertise regular weekly specials at their locations.

Charge it. Consider a credit card that offers cash back for gas purchases. Some offer two- to five-percent rebates, but it is wise to read the fine print. Fees, charges, interest rates, and benefits can vary among credit card issuers.

On the Road

Start driving as soon as the engine is started. Modern engines do not need much time to warm up. The engine actually warms up more quickly once the car is operating, and will stay warm after stopping.

Do not speed. Gas mileage decreases rapidly at speeds above 60 miles per hour. According to Fueleconomy.gov, each 5 mph you drive over 60 mph is like paying an additional 24 cents per gallon for gas.

Avoid unnecessary idling. It wastes fuel, costs you money, and pollutes the air. Turn off the engine if you anticipate a wait.

Use overdrive gears and cruise control when appropriate. They improve fuel economy when you are driving on the highway.

Minimize the need to brake by anticipating traffic conditions. Be alert for slowdowns and red lights. Anticipate bends and turns on familiar roads. Letting up on the gas often eliminates the need for braking.

Avoid jackrabbit starts and stops. Avoiding these can increase your mpg and prolong the life of your brakes.

Use the air conditioner only when you absolutely need it. Air conditioning dramatically reduces fuel economy. Most air conditioners have an "economy" setting that allows the circulation of unchilled air. Many also have a "maximum" or "recirculation" setting that reduces the amount of hot outside air that must be chilled. Both settings can reduce the air conditioning load—and save gas.

Combine errands. Several short trips taken from a cold start can use twice as much fuel as one trip covering the same distance when the engine is warm.

Remove excess weight from the trunk. An extra 100 pounds in the trunk can reduce a typical car's fuel economy by up to two percent.

Avoid packing items on top of your car. A loaded roof rack or carrier creates wind resistance and can decrease fuel economy by five percent.

At the Garage

Keep your engine tuned. Tuning your engine according to your owner's manual can increase gas mileage by an average of four percent.

Keep your tires properly inflated and aligned. This can increase gas mileage up to three percent, improve handling, and prolong the life of your tires. Check your owner's manual or the door jamb for the proper level of inflation (not the tire itself, which shows the maximum tire inflation pressure); check the tire pressure when the tires are cold because internal pressure increases when the car has been on the road for a while and the tires heat up.

Change your oil. According to the U.S. Department of Energy (DOE) and U.S. Environmental Protection Agency (EPA), you can improve your gas mileage by using the manufacturer's recommended grade of motor oil. Motor oil that says "Energy Conserving" on the performance symbol of the American Petroleum Institute (API) contains friction-reducing additives that can improve fuel economy.

When Shopping

Be skeptical about any gizmo that promises to improve your gas mileage. The EPA has tested supposed gas-saving devices—including "mixture enhancers" and fuel-line magnets—and found that very few provided any fuel economy benefits. Those devices that did work provided only a slight improvement in gas mileage. In fact, some products may even damage your car's engine or cause a substantial increase in exhaust emissions.

Gas-Saving Products

When gas prices go up, it seems like the number of advertisements for gas-saving products does, too. Although there are practical steps you can take to increase your gas mileage, be on the lookout for gas-saving claims for automotive devices or oil and gas additives. Even for the few gas-saving products that have been found to work, the savings are small.

Gas-Saving Claims

When gas prices climb, products that claim they will save gas might look good. But, it is a smart idea to be skeptical of any gas-saving claims for automotive devices or oil and gas additives.

Here are some examples of claims you might see:

"Improves fuel economy by 20 percent."

Advertisements typically tout savings from 12 to 25 percent. However, despite evaluating or testing more than 100 alleged gas-saving devices, the EPA has not found any product that significantly improves gas mileage. In fact, some "gas-saving" products may damage a car's engine or substantially increase exhaust emissions.

"After installing this product, my car gets an extra 4 miles per gallon."

Advertisements may feature glowing testimonials from satisfied customers. But, few people have the ability or the equipment to test for precise changes in gas mileage after installing a product that claims to save gas. Many variables affect fuel consumption, including traffic, road and weather conditions, and the car's condition.

For example, a letter to a company praised its "gas-saving" product. But, the product was installed at the same time the car owner got a complete engine tune-up—a fact not mentioned in the letter. The bump in gas mileage attributed to the product may well have been the result of the tune-up.

"It's approved by the federal government."

No government agency endorses gas-saving products for cars. The most an advertisement could claim is that the EPA has reached certain conclusions about possible gas savings by testing the product or by evaluating the manufacturer's own test data. If the seller claims that its product has been evaluated by EPA, ask for a copy of the EPA report, or check epa.gov for information.

The Effect on Your Car

While the EPA evaluates or tests some products to determine whether they will significantly improve or hurt fuel economy, the agency does not conduct durability tests: it cannot say what effect the products will have on a vehicle over time. It is possible

Gas-Saving Tips

Combine errands into one trip. Combining trips can reduce the distance you drive, and it allows you to travel more miles when your engine is warm. Your engine runs more efficiently when it is warmed up.

- Stagger your work hours to avoid peak rush hours so that you spend less time in stop-and-go traffic.
- Drive your most fuel-efficient vehicle.
- Telecommute (work from home) if your employer permits it.
- Participate in carpools and ride-share programs.
- Walk or cycle short distances when possible.
- Use public transit if it is available and convenient for you.

(Source: "Gas-Saving Tips," U.S. Department of Energy (DOE))

that some products may harm the car or negatively affect its performance. In fact, the emission control systems in today's cars are very sophisticated and complex with features that alert drivers to problems. Retrofit products may have a negative effect on these systems.

Real Money-Saving Steps

You can take many free or low-cost steps to save on gas, including buying only the octane level you need, watching your speed, properly maintaining the vehicle, and checking tire pressure.

If you are in the market for a car, you also might consider getting one that is fuel-efficient. In fact, deciding which vehicle to buy may be the most important fuel economy choice you make. The difference between a car that gets 20 MPG (miles per gallon) and one that gets 30 MPG amounts to $4,375 over 5 years, assuming gas costs $3.50 per gallon and you drive 15,000 miles a year.

Devices Tested by the U.S. Environmental Protection Agency

In the past, the EPA tested many types of "gas-saving" products as part of its Voluntary Aftermarket Retrofit Device Evaluation Program. Most devices tested had little to no effect on fuel economy or exhaust emissions; some even had a negative effect.

EPA testing also has received no credible data showing a positive effect on fuel economy from:

- Devices that turn water into fuel
- Fuel line devices
- Mixture enhancers

CHAPTER 35

PAYING A PREMIUM FOR HIGH-OCTANE GASOLINE?

About This Chapter: This chapter includes text excerpted from "Paying a Premium for High-Octane Gasoline?" Federal Trade Commission (FTC), August 2012.

Unless it is recommended by your owner's manual, do not spend the money on high-octane gas. In most cases, there is no benefit. Higher octane helps only if you have problems with your engine "knocking."

Read Your Owner's Manual

Unless your engine is knocking, buying higher-octane gasoline is a waste of money. Premium gas costs 15 to 20 cents per gallon more than regular. That can add up to $100 or more a year in extra costs. Studies indicate that altogether, drivers may be spending hundreds of millions of dollars each year for higher-octane gas than they need.

It may seem like buying higher-octane "premium" gas is like giving your car a treat, or boosting its performance. But take note: the recommended gasoline for most cars is regular octane. In fact, in most cases, using higher-octane gasoline than your owner's manual recommends offers absolutely no benefit. It will not make your car perform better, go faster, get better mileage, or run cleaner. Your best bet: listen to your owner's manual.

The only time you might need to switch to a higher octane level is if your car engine knocks when you use the recommended fuel. This happens to a small percentage of cars.

About Octane Ratings

What Are Octane Ratings?

Octane ratings measure a gasoline's ability to resist engine knock—a rattling or pinging sound that results from premature ignition of the compressed fuel-air mixture in one or more cylinders. Most gas stations offer three octane grades: regular (usually 87 octanes), mid-grade (usually 89 octanes), and premium (usually 92 or 93). The ratings are posted on bright yellow stickers on each gas pump.

What Is the Right Octane Level for Your Car?

Check your owner's manual. Regular octane is recommended for most cars. However, some cars with high compression engines, such as sports cars and certain luxury cars, need mid-grade or premium gasoline to prevent knocking.

How can you tell if you are using the right octane level? Listen to your car's engine. If it does not knock when you use the recommended octane, you are using the right grade of gasoline.

Will High-Octane Gasoline Clean Your Engine Better?

No, as a rule, high-octane gasoline does not outperform regular octane in preventing engine deposits from forming, in removing them, or in cleaning your car's engine. In fact, the U.S. Environmental Protection Agency (EPA) requires that all octane grades of all brands of gasoline contain engine-cleaning detergent additives to protect against the build-up of harmful levels of engine deposits during the expected life of your car.

Should You Ever Switch to a Higher-Octane Gasoline?

A few car engines may knock or ping even if you use the recommended octane. If this happens, try switching to the next highest octane grade. In many cases, switching to the mid-grade or premium-grade gasoline will eliminate the knock. If the knocking or pinging continues after one or two fill-ups, you may need a tune-up or some other repair. After that work is done, go back to the lowest octane grade at which your engine runs without knocking.

Will Knocking Harm My Engine?

Occasional light knocking or pinging will not harm your engine and does not mean you need higher octane. But, a heavy or persistent knock can lead to engine damage.

Is All "Premium" or "Regular" Gasoline the Same?

The octane rating of gas labeled "premium" or "regular" is not the same across the country. One state may require a minimum octane rating of 92 for all premium gasoline, while another may allow 90 octanes to be called "premium." To make sure you know what you are buying, check the octane rating on the yellow sticker on the gas pump.

Report Labeling Problems

If you do not see a yellow octane sticker on a gasoline pump, file a complaint with the Federal Trade Commission (FTC). The FTC enforces the Fuel Rating Rule, designed to ensure producers and marketers give you the information you need at the pump.

CHAPTER 36
AUTO REPAIR BASICS

About This Chapter: This chapter includes text excerpted from "Auto Repair Basics," Federal Trade Commission (FTC), August 2012.

The best way to avoid auto repair rip-offs is to be prepared. Knowing how your vehicle works and how to identify common car problems is a good beginning. It is also important to know how to choose a good mechanic, the kinds of questions to ask, and your consumer rights. This kind of information may help you keep a lid on mechanical mistakes.

Repair Information

How to Choose a Repair Shop

- Ask for recommendations from friends, family, and other people you trust. Look for a repair shop before you need one to avoid being rushed into a last-minute decision.
- Shop around by phone and online for the best deal, and compare warranty policies on repairs.
- Ask to see current licenses if state or local law requires repair shops to be licensed or registered. Also, your state Attorney General's office or local consumer protection agency (CPA) may know whether there is a record of complaints about a particular repair shop.
- Make sure the shop will honor your vehicle's warranty.

How to Choose a Technician

- Look for shops that display various certifications—such as an automotive service excellence (ASE) seal. Certification indicates that some or all of the technicians meet basic standards of knowledge and competence in specific technical areas. Make sure the certifications are current but remember that certification alone is no guarantee of good or honest work.
- Ask if the technician or shop has experience working on the same make or model vehicle as yours.

Repair Charges: Unlocking the Mystery

Before you arrange to have any work performed, ask how the shop prices its work. Some shops charge a flat rate for labor on auto repairs. This published rate is based on an independent or manufacturer's estimate of the time required to complete repairs. Others charge on the basis of the actual time the technician worked on the repair.

If you need expensive or complicated repairs, or if you have questions about recommended work, consider getting a second opinion.

Find out if there will be a diagnostic charge if you decide to have the work performed elsewhere. Many repair shops charge for diagnostic time.

Shops that do only diagnostic work and do not sell parts or repairs may be able to give you an objective opinion about which repairs are necessary.

If you decide to get the work done, ask for a written estimate.

What Should a Written Estimate Include?

- It should identify the condition to be repaired, the parts needed, and the anticipated labor charge. Make sure you get a signed copy.
- It should state that the shop will contact you for approval before they do any work exceeding a specified amount of time or money. State law may require this.

What Should I Know about the Parts to Be Repaired or Replaced?

Parts are classified as:

- **New**—These parts generally are made to original manufacturer's specifications, either by the vehicle manufacturer or an independent company. Your state may require repair shops to tell you if nonoriginal equipment will be used in the repair. Prices and quality of these parts vary.
- **Remanufactured, rebuilt, and reconditioned**—These terms generally mean the same thing: parts have been restored to a sound working condition. Many manufacturers offer a warranty covering replacement parts, but not the labor to install them.
- **Salvage**—These are used parts taken from another vehicle without alteration. Salvage parts may be the only source for certain items, though their reliability is seldom guaranteed.

What Do I Need after the Work Is Done?

Get a completed repair order describing the work done. It should list each repair, parts supplied, the cost of each part, labor charges, and the vehicle's odometer reading when you brought the vehicle in as well as when the repair order was completed. Ask for all replaced parts. State law may require this.

Preventive Maintenance

What Are the Consequences of Postponing Maintenance?

Many parts of your vehicle are interrelated. Ignoring maintenance can lead to trouble: specific parts—or an entire system—can fail. Neglecting even simple routine maintenance, such as changing the oil or checking the coolant, can lead to poor fuel economy, unreliability, or costly breakdowns. It also may invalidate your warranty.

What Maintenance Guidelines Should I Follow to Avoid Costly Repairs?

Follow the manufacturer's maintenance schedule in your owner's manual for your type of driving. Some repair shops create their own maintenance schedules, which call for more frequent servicing than the manufacturer's recommendations. Compare shop maintenance schedules with those recommended in your owner's manual. Ask the repair shop to explain—and make sure you understand—why it recommends service beyond the recommended schedule.

Protecting Your Auto Repair Investment

What Warranties and Service Contracts Apply to Vehicle Repairs?

Warranties

There is no "standard warranty" on repairs. Make sure you understand what is covered under your warranty and get it in writing.

Warranties may be subject to limitations, including time, mileage, deductibles, businesses authorized to perform warranty work or special procedures required to obtain reimbursement.

Service Contracts

Many automobile dealers and others sell optional contracts—service contracts—issued by vehicle manufacturers or independent companies. Not all service contracts are the same; prices vary and usually are negotiable. To help decide whether to purchase a service contract, consider:

- Its cost
- The repairs to be covered
- Whether coverage overlaps coverage provided by any other warranty
- The deductible
- Where the repairs are to be performed
- Procedures required to file a claim, such as prior authorization for specific repairs or meeting required vehicle maintenance schedules
- Whether repair costs are paid directly by the company to the repair shop or whether you will have to pay first and get reimbursed

How Do I Resolve a Dispute Regarding Billing, Quality of Repairs or Warranties?

Document all transactions as well as your experiences with dates, times, expenses, and the names of people you dealt with.

Talk to the shop manager or owner first. If that does not work, contact your Attorney General or local CPA for help. These offices may have information on alternative dispute resolution programs in your community. Another option is to file a claim in small claims court. You do not need an attorney to do this.

Heading Off Problems

The more you know about your vehicle, the more likely you will be able to head off repair problems. You can detect many common vehicle problems by using your senses: eyeballing the area around your vehicle, listening for strange noises, sensing a difference in the way your vehicle handles, or even noticing unusual odors.

Looks Like Trouble

Small stains or an occasional drop of fluid under your vehicle may not mean much, but wet spots deserve attention. Check puddles immediately.

You can identify fluids by their color and consistency:

- Yellowish green, pastel blue, or fluorescent orange colors indicate an overheated engine or an antifreeze leak caused by a bad hose, water pump, or leaking radiator.
- A dark brown or black oily fluid means the engine is leaking oil. A bad seal or gasket could cause the leak.
- A red oily spot indicates a transmission or power-steering fluid leak.
- A puddle of clear water usually is no problem. It may be normal condensation from your vehicle's air conditioner.

Smells Like Trouble

Some problems are under your nose. You can detect them by their odor:

- The smell of burned toast—a light, sharp odor—often signals an electrical short and burning insulation. To be safe, try not to drive the vehicle until the problem is diagnosed.
- The smell of rotten eggs—a continuous burning-sulfur smell—usually indicates a problem in the catalytic converter or other emission-control devices. Do not delay diagnosis and repair.
- A thick acrid odor usually means burning oil. Look for the sign of a leak.
- The smell of gasoline vapors after a failed start may mean you have flooded the engine. Wait a few minutes before trying again. If the odor persists, chances are there is a leak in the fuel system—a potentially dangerous problem that needs immediate attention.
- Burning resin or an acrid chemical odor may signal overheated brakes or clutch. Check the parking brake. Stop. Allow the brakes to cool after repeated hard braking on mountain roads. Light smoke coming from a wheel indicates a stuck brake. The vehicle should be towed for repair.
- A sweet, steamy odor indicates a coolant leak. If the temperature gauge or warning light does not indicate overheating, drive carefully to the nearest service station, keeping an eye on your gauges. If the odor is accompanied by a hot, metallic scent and steam from under the hood, your engine has overheated. Pull over immediately. Continued driving could cause severe engine damage. The vehicle should be towed for repair.

Sounds Like Trouble

Squeaks, squeals, rattles, rumbles, and other sounds provide valuable clues about problems and maintenance needs. Here are some common noises and what they mean:

Squeal—A shrill, sharp noise, usually related to engine speed:

- Loose or worn power steering, fan, or air-conditioning belt

Click—A slight sharp noise, related to either engine speed or vehicle speed:

- Loose wheel cover
- Loose or bent fan blade
- Stuck valve lifter or low engine oil

Screech—A high-pitched, piercing metallic sound that usually occurs while the vehicle is in motion:

- Caused by brake wear indicators that let you know it is time for maintenance

Rumble—a low-pitched rhythmic sound

- Defective exhaust pipe, converter or muffler
- Worn universal joint or other drive-line components

Ping—A high-pitched metallic tapping sound, related to engine speed:

- Usually caused by using gas with a lower octane rating than recommended. Check your owner's manual for the proper octane rating. If the problem persists, engine ignition timing could be at fault

Heavy Knock—A rhythmic pounding sound:

- Worn crankshaft or connecting rod bearings
- Loose transmission torque converter

Clunk—A random thumping sound:

- Loose shock absorber or other suspension components
- Loose exhaust pipe or muffler

Feels Like Trouble

Difficult handling, a rough ride, vibration, and poor performance are symptoms you can feel. They almost always indicate a problem.

Steering

- Misaligned front wheels and/or worn steering components, such as the idler arm or ball joint, can cause wandering or difficulty steering in a straight line.
- Pulling—the vehicle's tendency to steer to the left or right—can be caused by something as routine as under-inflated tires, or as serious as a damaged or misaligned front end.

Ride and Handling

- Worn shock absorbers or other suspension components—or improper tire inflation—can contribute to poor cornering.
- While there is no hard and fast rule about when to replace shock absorbers or struts, try this test: bounce the vehicle up and down hard at each wheel and then let go. See how many times the vehicle bounces. Weak shocks will allow the vehicle to bounce twice or more.
- Springs do not normally wear out and do not need replacement unless one corner of the vehicle is lower than the others. Overloading your vehicle can damage the springs.
- Balance tires properly. An unbalanced or improperly balanced tire causes a vehicle to vibrate and may wear steering and suspension components prematurely.

Brakes

Brake problems have several symptoms. Schedule diagnosis and repair if:

- The vehicle pulls to one side when the brakes are applied
- The brake pedal sinks to the floor when pressure is maintained
- You hear or feel scraping or grinding during braking
- The "brake" light on the instrument panel is lit

Engine

The following symptoms indicate engine trouble. Get a diagnosis and schedule the repair.

- Difficulty starting the engine
- The "check engine" light on the instrument panel is lit
- Rough idling or stalling
- Poor acceleration
- Poor fuel economy
- Excessive oil use (more than one quart between changes)
- Engine continues running after the key is removed

Transmission

Poor transmission performance may come from actual component failure or a simple disconnected hose or plugged filter. Make sure the technician checks the simple items first; transmission repairs normally are expensive. Some of the most common symptoms of transmission problems are:

- Abrupt or hard shifts between gears
- Delayed or no response when shifting from neutral to drive or reverse
- Failure to shift during normal acceleration
- Slippage during acceleration. The engine speeds up, but the vehicle does not respond

What Is an Extended Warranty or Vehicle Service Contract?

An extended warranty or vehicle service contract covers the costs of some types of repairs in addition to or after the manufacturer's warranty ends.

Extended warranties and vehicle service contracts typically exclude routine maintenance such as oil changes and tire replacement. Consider the cost of the warranty and what is covered and excluded, as well as how you plan to use the vehicle before purchasing an extended warranty or vehicle service contract. You may find that the additional warranty coverage is not worth the additional cost.

(Source: "What Is an Extended Warranty or Vehicle Service Contract?" Consumer Financial Protection Bureau (CFPB))

Troubleshooting

Car trouble does not always mean major repairs. Here are some common causes of trouble and techniques to help you and your technician find and fix problems:

- Alternator—Loose wiring can make your alternator appear defective. Your technician should check for loose connections and perform an output test before replacing the alternator.
- Battery—Corroded or loose battery terminals can make the battery appear dead or defective. Your technician should clean the terminals and test battery function before replacing the battery.
- Starter—What appears to be a defective starter actually may be a dead battery or poor connection. Ask your technician to check all connections and test the battery before repairing the starter.
- Tune-up—the old-fashioned "tune-up" may not be relevant to your vehicle. Fewer parts, other than belts, spark plugs, hoses, and filters, need to be replaced on newer vehicles.

CHAPTER 37

AUTO WARRANTIES, ROUTINE MAINTENANCE, AND SERVICE CONTRACTS

About This Chapter: Text in this chapter begins with excerpts from "Auto Service Contracts and Warranties," Federal Trade Commission (FTC), August 2012; Text beginning with the heading "Do You Have to Use the Dealer for Repairs and Maintenance to Keep Your Warranty in Effect?" is excerpted from "Auto Warranties & Routine Maintenance," Federal Trade Commission (FTC), May 2015; Text under the heading "What Is the Difference between a Manufacturer's Warranty and an Extended Vehicle Warranty or Service Contract?" is excerpted from "What Is the Difference between a Manufacturer's Warranty and an Extended Vehicle Warranty or Service Contract?" Consumer Financial Protection Bureau (CFPB), May 2015.

If you are shopping for a new or used car, the salesperson may encourage you to buy an auto service contract to help protect against unexpected or costly repairs. While a service contract may sound like a good idea, it may overlap with the vehicle's existing manufacturer's warranty. So before you spend the extra money, do some research to see if an auto service contract makes sense. Coverage varies widely.

Auto Service Contracts 101

A service contract is a promise to perform (or pay for) certain repairs or services. Sometimes called an "extended warranty," a service contract is not a warranty as defined by federal law. A service contract may be arranged at any time and always costs extra; a warranty comes with a new car and is included in the purchase price. Used cars also may come with some type of warranty coverage.

Research Your Options

Auto service contracts are sold by vehicle manufacturers, auto dealers, and independent providers. If you are considering a service contract, shop around so you understand exactly what you are buying.

Do I Have to Buy a Service Contract?

You are generally not required to buy an auto service contract when you buy a car. You also are generally not required to buy a service contract to get financing. If the dealer tells you that you have to buy a service contract to qualify for financing, contact the lender to find out if this is true. Some people have had trouble canceling their service contract after learning that the lender did not require one.

Also, beware unscrupulous dealers who may try to include an auto-service contract in your loan without your consent. If you see a charge for a service contract that you did not agree to, tell the dealer to take it out before you sign the loan agreement.

Does the Service Contract Duplicate Any Warranty Coverage?

Compare service contracts with the manufacturer's warranty. New cars come with a manufacturer's warranty, which usually offers coverage for at least three years or 36,000 miles, whichever comes first. A service contract likely will not provide benefits until the manufacturer's warranty expires. Check over the documents to make sure this is true before you agree to buy a service contract.

What Is the Length of the Service Contract?

If the service contract lasts longer than you expect to own the car, ask if it can be transferred when you sell the car and whether there is a fee, or if a shorter contract is available. If you are buying a "demonstrator"—a new car that has not been owned, leased, or used as a rental, but has been driven by dealer staff—ask when the warranty coverage begins and ends. It may have begun when the dealer put the car into service.

Who Backs the Service Contract?

Find out who performs or pays for repairs under the terms of the service contract. It may be the manufacturer, the dealer, or an independent company. Many service contracts are handled by companies called "administrators," that authorize the payment of claims to any dealers under the contract. If you have a dispute over whether a claim should be paid, deal with the administrator. If the administrator goes out of business, the dealership still may be obligated to perform under the contract. The reverse may also be true: If the dealer goes out of business, the administrator may be required to fulfill the terms of the contract. Whether you have any legal remedies depends on your contract's terms and/or your state's laws.

Find out if the auto service contract is underwritten by an insurance company. This is required in some states. If the contract is backed by an insurance company, contact your state insurance commission to ask about the solvency of the company and whether any complaints are on file.

Insurance regulations generally require companies to:

- Maintain an adequate financial reserve to pay claims
- Base their contract fees on expected claims. Some service contract providers have been known to make huge profits because the cost of their contracts far exceeds the cost of repairs or services they provide.
- Seek approval from the state insurance office for premiums or contract fees.

Check out the dealer and the administrator with your local or state consumer protection office or local automobile dealers association to see if any complaints are on file against the company. You also can search online for complaints.

If you decide to buy a service contract through a dealership—and the contract is backed by an administrator or a third party—make sure the dealer forwards your payment and you get written confirmation. Some people discovered too late that the dealer failed to forward their payment, leaving them with no coverage months after they signed a contract. Contact your local or state consumer protection office if you have reason to believe that your contract was not put into effect as agreed.

How Much Does a Service Contract Cost?

Usually, the price of the service contract is based on the car make, model, condition (new or used), coverage, and length of the contract. The upfront cost can range from one to several thousand dollars. In addition, you may need to pay a deductible. Find out if the deductible is charged on a per-visit or per-repair basis. This can make a big difference. For example, assume you have a $100 deductible and your car needs three parts repaired. With the deductible per visit, you pay $100. If you have a deductible per repair, you pay $300.

Service contracts often limit how much they will pay for towing or related rental car expenses—meaning you have to cover the remaining cost. There also may be transfer or cancellation fees if you sell your car or end the contract early.

What Do Service Contracts Cover?

Few service contracts cover all repairs. Common repairs for parts, such as brakes and clutches, generally are not included in auto service contracts. The best advice: If an item is not listed, assume it is not covered. Watch out for absolute exclusions that deny coverage for any reason. For example: If a covered part is damaged by a noncovered part, the claim may be denied. Or if the contract specifies that only "mechanical breakdowns" will be covered, problems caused by "normal wear and tear" may be excluded. If the engine has to be taken apart to diagnose a problem and during the process, the mechanic discovers noncovered parts that need to be repaired or replaced, you may have to pay for the labor involved in the tear-down and reassembling of the engine.

You may not have full protection even for parts that are covered in the contract. Some companies use a "depreciation factor" in calculating coverage: the company may pay only partial repair or replacement costs based on your car's mileage.

How Are Claims Handled?

When your car needs to be repaired or serviced, you may be able to choose among several service dealers or authorized repair centers. Or, you may have to take it to the dealer you bought it from. That could be inconvenient if you bought the car from a dealership in another town. Find out if your car will be covered if it breaks down while you are using it on a trip or if you take it when you move out of town.

Some auto service contract companies and dealers offer service only in specific geographical areas. Find out if you need prior authorization from the contract provider for any repair work or towing services. Be sure to ask how long it takes to get authorization, whether you can get authorization outside of normal business hours, and whether the company has a toll-free number for authorization. Test the toll-free number before you buy the contract to see if you can get through easily.

You may have to pay for covered repairs and then wait for the service company to reimburse you. If the auto service contract does not specify how long reimbursement usually takes, ask. Find out who settles claims in case you have a dispute with the service contract provider and need to use a dispute resolution program.

Are New or Reconditioned Parts Authorized for Use in Covered Repairs?

If this concerns you, you will want to know whether the authorized repair facility maintains an adequate stock of parts. Repair delays may occur if authorized parts are not readily available and must be ordered.

What Are My Responsibilities?

Under the service contract, you may have to follow all the manufacturer's recommendations for routine maintenance, such as oil changes. If you do not, it could void the contract. To prove you have maintained the car properly, keep detailed records, including receipts. Find out if the contract prohibits you from taking the car to an independent station for routine maintenance or performing the work yourself. The contract may specify that the dealer that sold you the car is the only authorized facility for servicing the car.

Beware of Auto Warranty Scams

Be skeptical of mail and phone calls warning that the warranty on your car is about to expire. The companies behind the letters and calls may give the impression they represent your car dealer or manufacturer. With phrases, such as "Motor Vehicle Notification," "Final Warranty Notice," or "Notice of Interruption," they are trying to make the offer seem urgent—and to get you to call a toll-free number. Investigate before you buy it.

More than likely, these pitches are from unrelated businesses that want to sell you extended warranties—more accurately known as "service contracts"—that often sell for hundreds or thousands of dollars. If you respond to a call from a business pitching so-called extended warranties, you are likely to hear high-pressure sales tactics, as well as demands for personal financial information and down payment, before you get any details about the service contract. And if you buy a service contract, you may find that the company behind it will not be in business long enough to fulfill its commitments.

Steer Clear of Auto Warranty Scams

If you get a mail or phone calls about renewing your vehicle warranty, do not take the information at face value. Your vehicle's warranty may be far from expiring—or it may have expired already. If you have a question about your warranty, check your owner's manual, call the dealer who sold you the car, or contact the vehicle manufacturer.

Be alert to fast talkers. Telemarketers pitching auto warranties often use high-pressure tactics to hide their true motives. Take your time. Most legitimate businesses will give you time and written information about an offer before asking you to commit to a purchase.

Never give out personal financial or other sensitive information, such as your bank account, credit card, Social Security number (SSN), driver's license number, or Vehicle Identification Number (VIN) unless you know who you are dealing with. Scam artists often ask for this information during an unsolicited sales pitch and then use it to commit other frauds against you.

Be skeptical of any unsolicited sales calls and recorded messages. If your phone number is on the National Do Not Call (NDNC) Registry, you should not get a live or recorded sales pitches unless you have specifically agreed to accept such calls, bought something from the company within the last 18 months, or asked the company for information within the last 3 months. To report violations of the NDNC or to register a phone number, visit DoNotCall.gov or call 888-382-1222.

Used Cars: Warranty Protection

When shopping for a used car, look for the Buyer's Guide posted on the side window. The Federal Trade Commission (FTC) requires the Guide on all used cars sold by dealers. It tells whether a service contract is available. It also indicates whether the vehicle is being sold with a warranty, with implied warranties only, or "as is."

Warranty

If the manufacturer's warranty is still in effect on the used car, you may have to pay a fee to get coverage, making it a service contract. However, if the dealer absorbs the cost of the manufacturer's fee, the coverage is considered a warranty.

Implied Warranties Only

There are two common types of implied warranties. Both are unspoken and unwritten, and based on the principle that the seller stands behind the product. Under a "warranty of merchantability," the seller promises the product will do what it is supposed to do. For example, a toaster will toast, or a car will run. If the car does not run, implied-warranties law says that the dealer must fix it (unless it was sold "as is") so that the buyer gets a working car. A "warranty of fitness for a particular purpose" applies when you buy a vehicle on a dealer's advice that it is suitable for a certain use, such as hauling a trailer. Used cars usually are covered by implied warranties under state law.

As-Is—No Warranty

If you buy a car "as is," you must pay for all repairs, even if the car breaks down on the way home from the dealership. However, if you buy a dealer-service contract within

90 days of buying the used car, state law "implied warranties" may give you additional rights.

Some states prohibit "as is" sales on most or all used cars. Other states require the use of specific words to disclaim implied warranties. In addition, some states have used car "lemon laws" under which a consumer can receive a refund or replacement if the vehicle is seriously defective. To find out about your state laws, check with your local or state consumer protection office (CPA) or Attorney General.

Complaints

If you have a problem with an auto service contract, first try to resolve the dispute with the provider. If that does not work, contact your state Attorney General, state insurance commission, or local CPA. You also may file a complaint with the FTC.

If you think you have been victimized by an auto warranty scam, file a complaint with the FTC. Although the FTC does not intervene in individual disputes, the information you provide may indicate a pattern of possible law violations requiring action by the Commission.

Do You Have to Use the Dealer for Repairs and Maintenance to Keep Your Warranty in Effect?

No. An independent mechanic, a retail chain shop, or even you can do routine maintenance and repairs on your vehicle. In fact, the Magnuson-Moss Warranty Act, which is enforced by the FTC, makes it illegal for manufacturers or dealers to claim that your warranty is void or to deny coverage under your warranty simply because someone other than the dealer did the work. The manufacturer or dealer can, however, require consumers to use select repair facilities if the repair services are provided to consumers free of charge under the warranty.

That said, there may be certain situations in which a repair may not be covered. For example, if you or your mechanic replaced a belt improperly and your engine is damaged as a result, your manufacturer or dealer may deny responsibility for fixing the engine under the warranty. However, according to the FTC, the manufacturer or dealer must be able to demonstrate that it was the improper belt replacement—rather than some other defect—that caused the damage to your engine. The warranty would still be in effect for other parts of your car.

Will Using "Aftermarket" or Recycled Parts Void Your Warranty?

No. An "aftermarket" part is a part made by a company other than the vehicle manufacturer or the original equipment manufacturer. A "recycled" part is a part that was made for and installed in a new vehicle by the manufacturer or the original equipment manufacturer, and later removed from the vehicle and made available for resale or reuse. Simply using an aftermarket or recycled part does not void your warranty. The Magnuson-Moss Warranty Act makes it illegal for companies to void your warranty or deny coverage under the warranty simply because you used an aftermarket or recycled part. The manufacturer or dealer can, however, require consumers to use select parts if those parts are provided to consumers free of charge under the warranty.

Still, if it turns out that the aftermarket or recycled part was itself defective or was not installed correctly, and it causes damage to another part that is covered under the warranty, the manufacturer or dealer has the right to deny coverage for that part and charge you for any repairs. The FTC says the manufacturer or dealer must show that the aftermarket or recycled part caused the need for repairs before denying warranty coverage.

What Is the Difference between a Manufacturer's Warranty and an Extended Vehicle Warranty or Service Contract?

Warranties provided by the manufacturer as part of the vehicle cost typically cover only certain problems with the vehicle. Extended warranties or service contracts sold for an additional charge typically cover problems with mechanical and electrical parts not covered by the manufacturers' warranty.

Warranties are typically provided by auto manufacturers as part of the overall cost of a new vehicle. These warranties will cover certain problems and last for a certain period of time or miles of driving.

Extended warranties or service contracts are offered or sold at an additional charge by auto dealerships. These provide protection on certain mechanical and electrical components not covered by the manufacturer's warranty. Extended warranties typically exclude routine maintenance such as oil changes and tire replacement. They can be very expensive for you. However, you do not have to buy an extended warranty when you purchase a vehicle or at any time. They are completely optional.

When deciding whether to purchase an extended warranty, you should review the contract carefully and consider the following:

- The cost of the extended warranty (You can negotiate the price.)
- What types of problems or repairs are covered
- What problems are not covered
- How long the extended warranty lasts
- Whether or not the extended warranty coverage overlaps with the manufacturer's warranty
- How you plan to use your vehicle

You should also check whether the coverage of the service contract overlaps with the problems and time periods the manufacturer's warranty covers to avoid paying for unneeded coverage. You may find that any additional coverage is not worth the additional cost.

CHAPTER 38

AUTOMOBILE, GAP, AND CREDIT INSURANCE

About This Chapter: Text under the heading "Auto Insurance" is excerpted from "Car Repairs and Auto Insurance," USA.gov, December 13, 2019; Text under the heading " What Is Guaranteed Auto Protection (GAP) Insurance?" is excerpted from "What Is Guaranteed Auto Protection (GAP) Insurance?" Consumer Financial Protection Bureau (CFPB), June 8, 2016; Text under the heading "What Is Credit Insurance for an Auto Loan?" is excerpted from "What Is Credit Insurance for an Auto Loan?" Consumer Financial Protection Bureau (CFPB), June 7, 2016; Text under the heading "Should You Have Car Insurance Lined up before You Purchase a Vehicle?" is excerpted from "Should I Have Car Insurance Lined up before I Purchase a Vehicle?" Consumer Financial Protection Bureau (CFPB), June 8, 2016.

Auto Insurance

Auto insurance protects you from paying the full cost for vehicle repairs and medical expenses due to a collision. Some factors that affect the premiums you pay for this protection, include your:

- Gender
- Age
- Marital status
- Credit history
- Car's make and model
- City and neighborhood

Types of Auto Insurance

Every state requires drivers to have auto insurance. If you do not have insurance, you must have financial responsibility waivers. These waivers ensure that you can pay for property damages or medical expenses. There are several components that can make up your insurance policy:

- **Liability coverage** protects you if you are at fault for a collision. It pays for medical expenses and vehicle damage for the other driver and passengers.

- **Uninsured motorist coverage** pays for damages to your car and medical expenses if an uninsured driver hits your car.
- **Collision coverage** pays to repair your vehicle if you were at fault for the damage.
- **Under-insured motorist coverage** pays damages for your car if someone hits it, but their insurance cannot pay for your car damages.
- **Comprehensive coverage** pays for damage to your car due to theft, fire, or falling objects.

Auto insurance requirements vary from state to state. Most states require drivers to have liability coverage. You may choose to opt-out of certain types of coverage, depending on your budget and your car's age. Check with your state insurance regulator to learn more about its requirements.

Be sure to read the declarations page of your auto insurance policy. This is a summary of your policy. It includes:

- The length of coverage
- Annual premium
- The largest amount your insurance company will pay for each type of claim, and
- How your insurance company splits your premium payment between each part of your coverage

What Is Guaranteed Auto Protection Insurance?

Guaranteed Auto Protection (GAP) insurance may be offered to you when you buy a vehicle. GAP insurance covers the difference (or gap) between the amount you owe on your auto loan and what your insurance pays if your vehicle is stolen, damaged, or totaled.

You do not have to buy this insurance, but if you decide you want it, shop around. Lenders may set varying prices for this product.

It is highly unusual for a lender to require that you buy GAP insurance. If you are told that you are required to purchase a product such as GAP insurance, ask to see where your sales contract says it is required. If the contract does not explicitly state that it is required, then you cannot be required to purchase it.

If you are told you must purchase a GAP plan to qualify for financing, contact the lender yourself to find out if that is true. If it is true, the cost of the GAP insurance must be included in the finance charge and reflected in the disclosed annual percentage rate (APR). GAP insurance can be excluded from the finance charge and APR if it is optional. If you have a complaint or a concern about this insurance product, you can contact your state insurance department or commissioner.

What Is Credit Insurance for an Auto Loan?

Credit insurance is optional insurance that cover your auto payments to your lender in certain situations, such as if you die or become disabled. When you are applying for your auto loan, you may be asked if you want to buy credit insurance.

> **Tip:** Remember, any add-on product that you finance costs you not just the upfront cost but also the cost of the interest when you pay for this product over the life of the loan.

Before deciding to buy credit insurance, think about your choices and about the cost of this insurance. If you add credit insurance to your loan, this increases your loan amount and you will pay additional interest.

If you are considering credit insurance, make sure you understand the terms of the policy being offered. There are four main types of credit insurance:

- **Credit life insurance**, which pays off all or some of your loan if you die
- **Credit disability insurance**, also known as "accident and health insurance," which makes payments on the loan if you become ill or injured and cannot work
- **Involuntary unemployment insurance**, also known as "involuntary loss of income insurance," which makes your loan payments if you lose your job due to no fault of your own, such as from a layoff
- **Credit property insurance**, which protects personal property used to secure the loan—in the case of an auto loan this would be your car—if it is destroyed by events such as theft, accident, or natural disasters

If a lender tells you that you will only get the loan if you buy the optional credit insurance, you can submit a complaint to your state Attorney General, your state insurance commissioner, or the Federal Trade Commission (FTC).

Should You Have Car Insurance Lined up before You Purchase a Vehicle?

If you do not already have auto insurance, you should shop for insurance before you purchase a vehicle. If you already have insurance, your current insurer can tell you how to add any new vehicle to your policy and how much it will cost.

All lenders require that you have insurance for damage to the vehicle. If you do not have the required insurance, the lender may take out "force-placed" insurance to cover your vehicle. Force-placed insurance protects only the lender, not you, and will add to the cost of your loan. Force-placed insurance is usually a lot more expensive than what you can obtain by finding an insurance policy yourself. Force-placed insurance does not cover you if you injure someone or damage property with your vehicle.

Automobile insurance costs can vary widely, so it can pay to shop around. It is very important to know the cost of insurance when deciding whether you can afford a new vehicle. You should budget for insurance as you are deciding what level of monthly payments you can afford.

CHAPTER 39

GETTING A GOOD DEAL WHEN BUYING A USED CAR

About This Chapter: This chapter includes text excerpted from "Buying a Used Car," Federal Trade Commission (FTC), November 2016.

Before you start shopping for a used car, do some homework. It may save you serious money. Consider your driving habits, what the car will be used for, and your budget. Research models, options, costs, repair records, safety tests, and mileage online and through libraries and bookstores.

Before You Buy a Used Car

Whether you buy a used car from a dealer or an individual:

- Test drive the car under varied road conditions—on hills, highways, and in stop-and-go traffic.
- Ask for the car's maintenance record from the owner, dealer, or repair shop.
- Determine the value of the vehicle before you negotiate the purchase. Check the National Automobile Dealers Association's (NADA) Guides, Edmunds, Kelley Blue Book, and Consumer Reports. Some of these organizations charge for this information.
- Research the upkeep costs for models you are interested in, including the frequency of repairs and maintenance costs.
- Examine the car using an inspection checklist that deal with used cars. You can find checklists in magazines, books, and on websites.
- Check whether there are any unrepaired recalls on a vehicle. Start by asking the dealer if the vehicle you are considering has a recall. You also can check yourself by entering the vehicle identification number (VIN) at safercar.gov, or by calling the National Highway Traffic Safety Administration's (NHTSA) Vehicle Safety Hotline at 888-327-4236. If there

is a recall, ask the dealer to fix it, or to give you information showing it was fixed. Keep in mind that federal law does not require dealers to fix recalls on used cars, so you might need to get the repair done yourself. But, do not wait—according to NHTSA, all safety recalls pose safety risks and, left unrepaired, might lead to accidents.

- Get an independent review of a vehicle's history. Check a trusted database service that gathers information from state and local authorities, salvage yards, and insurance companies. For example, the U.S. Department of Justice's (DOJ) National Motor Vehicle Title Information System (NMVTIS) offers information about a vehicle's title, odometer data, and certain damage history. Expect to pay a small fee for each report. The National Insurance Crime Bureau (NICB) maintains a free database that includes flood damage and other information. You can investigate a car's history by its VIN. You also can search online for companies that sell vehicle history reports. If the report is not recent or you suspect that it has missing or fabricated information, verify it with the reporting company. The information in the reports may not be complete, so you may want to get a second report from a different reporting company. Some dealer websites have links to free reports.
- Consider hiring a mechanic to inspect the car.

Payment in Full versus Financing

You have two choices: pay in full or finance over time. Financing increases the total cost of the car because you are also paying for the cost of credit, including interest and other costs. Consider how much you can put down, the monthly payment, the financing term (such as 48 months), and the annual percentage rate (APR). Rates usually are higher and financing periods shorter on used cars than on new ones.

Dealers and other finance sources (such as finance companies, credit unions, and banks) offer a variety of financing terms. Shop around, compare offers, and negotiate the best deal you can. If you are a first-time buyer—or if your credit is not great—be cautious about special financing offers. They can require a big down payment and a high APR. If you agree to finance that carries a high APR, you may be taking a big risk.

- If you decide to sell the car before the end of the financing period, the amount you get from the sale may be less than the amount you need to pay off the financing agreement.
- If the car is repossessed or declared a total loss because of an accident, you may have to pay a considerable amount to repay the loan even after the proceeds from the sale of the car or the insurance payment have been deducted.
- If money is tight, you might consider paying cash for a less expensive car.
- If you decide to finance, make sure you understand the financing agreement before you sign any documents.

- What is the exact price you are paying for the vehicle?
- How much are you financing?
- What is the finance charge (the dollar amount the credit will cost you)?
- What is the APR (a measure of the cost of credit, expressed as a yearly rate)?
- How many payments will you make—and how much is each one?
- What is the total sales price—the sum of the monthly payments plus the down payment?

Dealer Sales and the Buyers Guide

Used cars are sold through a variety of outlets: franchised and independent dealers, rental car companies, leasing companies, used car superstores, and online. Ask friends, relatives, and coworkers for recommendations. Contact your local consumer protection agency (CPA) and state Attorney General to find out if any unresolved complaints are on file about a particular dealer. You also can search online for reviews or complaints. Enter the name of the seller and the word "review" or "complaint" into a search engine.

Some dealers attract customers with "no-haggle prices," "factory certified" used cars, and better warranties. Consider the dealer's reputation when you evaluate its advertisements.

Dealers are not required by federal law to give used car buyers a three-day right to cancel. In some states, dealers are required to give a right to cancel. In other states, the right to return the car in a few days for a refund exists only if the dealer chooses to offer this privilege. Dealers may describe the right to cancel as a "cooling-off" period, a money-back guarantee, or a "no questions asked" return policy. Before you buy from a dealer, ask about the dealer's return policy, get it in writing, and read it carefully.

The Federal Trade Commission's (FTC) Used Car Rule requires dealers to display a Buyers Guide in every used car they offer for sale, and to give it to buyers after the sale. This includes light-duty vans, light-duty trucks, demonstrators, and program cars. Demonstrators are new cars that have not been owned, leased, or used as rentals but have been driven by dealer staff. Program cars are low-mileage, current-model-year vehicles returned from short-term leases or rentals. Buyers Guides do not have to be posted on motorcycles and most recreational vehicles. Anyone who sells, or offers for sale, fewer than six cars in a year does not have to post a Buyers Guide.

The Buyers Guide tells you:

- The major mechanical and electrical systems on the car, including some of the major problems you should look out for
- Whether the vehicle is being sold "as is" or with a warranty
- What percentage of the repair costs a dealer will pay under the warranty
- To get all promises in writing
- To ask to have the car inspected by an independent mechanic before you buy

- To get a vehicle history report and to visit ftc.gov/usedcars for information on how to get a vehicle history report, how to check for safety recalls, and other topics
- To ask for Spanish buyers guide if the sale is conducted in Spanish
- The dealer's contact information, including the contact for complaints
- To remember: spoken promises are difficult to enforce

Keep the Buyers Guide for reference after the sale. Maine and Wisconsin are exempt from the FTC's Used Car Rule. Those states require dealers to display a different version of the Buyers Guide.

An Independent Inspection before You Buy

It is best to have any used car inspected by an independent mechanic before you buy it. For about $100, you will get a general indication of the mechanical condition of the vehicle. An inspection is a good idea even if the car has been "certified" and inspected by the dealer and is being sold with a warranty or service contract. A mechanical inspection is different from a safety inspection. Safety inspections usually focus on conditions that make a car unsafe to drive. They are not designed to determine the overall reliability or mechanical condition of a vehicle.

To find a prepurchase inspection facility, check the phone book under "Automotive Diagnostic Service," go online, or ask friends, relatives, and co-workers for referrals. Look for facilities that display certifications, such as an Automotive Service Excellence (ASE) seal, and search online for comments.

Ask what the inspection includes, how long it takes, and how much it costs.

If the dealer would not let you take the car off the lot, perhaps because of insurance restrictions, you may be able to find a mobile inspection service that will go to the dealer. If that is not an option, ask the dealer to have the car inspected at a facility you designate. You will have to pay the inspection fee. If a dealer would not allow an independent inspection, you might want to consider doing business elsewhere.

Once the vehicle has been inspected, ask the mechanic for a written report with a cost estimate for all necessary repairs. Be sure the report includes the vehicle's make, model, and VIN. If you decide to make a purchase offer to the dealer after considering the inspection's results, you can use the estimated repair costs to negotiate the price of the vehicle.

Private Sales

Buying a car from a private individual is different from buying from a dealer.

- Private sellers generally are not covered by the Used Car Rule and do not have to use the Buyers Guide. However, you can use the Guide's list of an automobile's major systems as a shopping tool, and you can ask the seller if you can have the vehicle inspected by a mechanic.

Used Car Rule

The Used Car Rule, formally known as the "Used Motor Vehicle Trade Regulation Rule," has been in effect since 1985. It requires car dealers to display a window sticker, known as a "Buyers Guide," on the used cars they offer for sale. The Buyers Guide discloses whether the dealer offers a warranty and, if so, its terms and conditions, including the duration of the coverage, the percentage of total repair costs the dealer will pay, and which vehicle systems the warranty covers. In states that do not permit sales of used cars "as is," or without warranties, dealers must display an alternative version of the Buyers Guide.

(Source: "Used Car Rule," Federal Trade Commission (FTC))

- Private sales usually are not covered by the "implied warranties" of state law. That means a private sale will probably be on an "as is" basis unless your purchase agreement with the seller specifically states otherwise. If you have a written contract, the seller must live up to the promises stated in the contract.
- The car may be covered by a manufacturer's warranty or a separately purchased service contract. However, warranties and service contracts may not be transferable, and other limits or costs may apply. Before you buy the car, ask to review its warranty or service contract. Many states do not require individuals to ensure that their vehicles will pass state inspection or carry a minimum warranty before they offer them for sale. You can ask your state Attorney General's office or local CPA about the requirements in your state.

Problems after Buying a Used Car

If you have a problem that you think is covered by a warranty or service contract, follow the instructions to get service. If a dispute arises, try to work it out with the dealer. Talk with the salesperson or, if necessary, the owner of the dealership. Many problems can be resolved at this level. However, if you believe you are entitled to service, but the dealer disagrees, you have some options:

- If your warranty is backed by a car manufacturer, contact the local representative of the manufacturer. The local or zone representative is authorized to decide issues of warranty service and repairs to satisfy customers. Some manufacturers are willing to repair certain problems in specific models for free, even if the manufacturer's warranty does not cover the problem. Ask the manufacturer's zone representative or the service department of a franchised dealership that sells your car model whether there is such a policy.
- Contact your state Attorney General or the American Association of Motor Vehicle Administrators (AAMVA).
- You might consider using a dispute-resolution organization if you and the dealer are willing. Under the terms of many warranties, this may be

a required first step before you can sue the dealer or manufacturer. If you bought your car from a franchised dealer, you may be able to seek mediation through the Automotive Consumer Action Program (AUTOCAP), a dispute resolution program coordinated nationally by the NADA and sponsored through state and local dealer associations in many cities. Check with the dealer association in your area to see if they operate a mediation program.

If none of these steps is successful, small claims court is an option. Here, you can resolve disputes involving small amounts of money, often without an attorney. The clerk at your local small claims court can tell you how to file a suit and the dollar limit in your state.

The Magnuson-Moss Warranty Act also may be helpful. Under this federal law, you can sue based on breach of express warranties, implied warranties, or service contracts. If successful, consumers can recover reasonable attorneys' fees and other court costs. A lawyer can advise you if this law applies.

CHAPTER 40
WARRANTIES AND SERVICE CONTRACTS FOR USED CARS

About This Chapter: This chapter includes text excerpted from "Buying a Used Car," Federal Trade Commission (FTC), November 2016.

Warranties

When you buy a used car from a dealer, the Buyers Guide must reflect any negotiated changes in warranty coverage. It becomes part of your sales contract and overrides any contrary provisions. For example, if the Buyers Guide says the car comes with a warranty and the contract says the car is sold "as is," the dealer must give you the warranty described in the Guide.

As-Is—No Dealer Warranty

When the dealer offers a vehicle "as is," the box next to the "As-Is—No Dealer Warranty" disclosure on the Buyers Guide must be checked. If the box is checked but the dealer promises to repair the vehicle or cancel the sale if you are not satisfied, make sure the promise is written on the Buyers Guide. Otherwise, you may have a hard time getting the dealer to make good on this promise. Some states—Connecticut, Hawaii, Kansas, Maine, Maryland, Massachusetts, Minnesota, Mississippi, New Jersey, New Mexico, New York, Rhode Island, Vermont, West Virginia, and the District of Columbia—do not allow "as is" sales for many used vehicles.

Louisiana, New Hampshire, and Washington require different disclosures from those on the Buyers Guide to create a valid "as is" sale. If the dealer fails to provide proper state disclosures, the sale is not "as is." To find out what disclosures are required for "as is" sales in your state, contact your state Attorney General.

Implied Warranties

State laws hold dealers responsible if cars they sell do not meet reasonable quality standards. These obligations are called "implied warranties"—unspoken, unwritten promises from the seller to the buyer. However, dealers in most states can use the words "as is" or "with all faults" in a written notice to buyers to eliminate implied warranties. There is no specified time period for implied warranties.

If you have a written warranty that does not cover your problems, you still may have coverage through implied warranties. That is because when a dealer sells a vehicle with a written warranty or service contract, implied warranties are included automatically. Dealers cannot delete this protection if they provide a written warranty. Any limit on an implied warranty's time must be included in the written warranty.

Implied Warranty of Merchantability

The most common type of implied warranty is the warranty of merchantability: The seller promises that the product offered for sale will do what it is supposed to. That a car will run is an example of a warranty of merchantability. This promise applies to the basic functions of a car. It does not cover everything that could go wrong.

Breakdowns and other problems after the sale do not prove the seller breached the warranty of merchantability. A breach occurs only if the buyer can prove that a defect existed at the time of sale. A problem that occurs after the sale may be the result of a defect that existed at the time of sale or not. As a result, a dealer's liability is judged on a case-by-case basis.

Implied Warranty of Fitness for a Particular Purpose

A warranty of fitness for a particular purpose applies when you buy a vehicle based on the dealer's advice that it is suitable for a particular use. For example, a dealer who suggests you buy a specific vehicle for hauling a trailer is promising that the vehicle will be suitable for that purpose.

Full and Limited Warranties

Dealers may offer a full or limited warranty on all or some of a vehicle's systems or components. Most used car warranties are limited and their coverage varies. A full warranty includes the following terms and conditions:

- Anyone who owns the vehicle during the warranty period is entitled to warranty service.
- Warranty service will be provided free of charge, including removing and reinstalling a covered system.
- You have the choice of a replacement or a full refund if the dealer cannot repair the vehicle or covered system after a reasonable number of tries.
- You only have to tell the dealer that warranty service is needed to get it unless the dealer can prove that it is reasonable to require you to do more.
- Implied warranties have no time limits.

If any of these statements does not apply, the warranty is limited.

The Federal Trade Commission (FTC), working jointly with 12 partner agencies in seven states, conducted the first compliance sweep of car dealerships since the amended Used Car Rule took effect in 2018. Under the amended Rule, dealers must display a revised window sticker called a "Buyers Guide," which contains warranty and other important information for consumers, on each used car they offer for sale.

The compliance sweep was conducted between April and June 2018, in 20 cities nationwide. The inspectors found Buyers Guides on 70 percent of the more than 2,300 vehicles inspected, with almost half of those displaying the revised Buyers Guide. Of the 94 dealerships inspected, 33 had the revised Buyers Guide on more than half of their vehicles, and 14 had revised Buyers Guides on all of their used cars.

Following the sweep, the FTC sent letters to each dealership detailing the results of the inspections and providing material to help them come into full compliance with the amended Rule. Over the coming weeks, dealerships that were not displaying the revised Buyers Guide can expect follow-up inspections to ensure they have brought themselves into compliance with the amended Rule. Under the FTC Act, dealers who fail to comply face penalties of up to $41,484 per violation. State and local law-enforcement agencies also enforce the recently amended Rule.

(Source: "FTC, Partners Conduct First Compliance Sweep under Newly Amended Used Car Rule," Federal Trade Commission (FTC))

A full or limited warranty does not have to cover the entire vehicle. The dealer may specify that only certain systems are covered. Some parts or systems may be covered by a full warranty.

Warranty Documents

Make sure you get a copy of the dealer's warranty document if you buy a car that is offered with a warranty. Review it carefully to determine what is covered. The warranty gives detailed information, such as how to get repairs for a covered system or part. It also tells who is legally responsible for fulfilling the terms of the warranty. If it is a third party, investigate their reputation. Look up reviews online.

Unexpired Manufacturer's Warranties

If the manufacturer's warranty still is in effect, the dealer may note that in the "systems covered/duration" section of the Buyers Guide. To make sure you can take advantage of the coverage, ask the dealer for the car's warranty documents. Verify the information (what is covered, expiration date/miles, and necessary paperwork) by calling the manufacturer's zone office. Make sure you have the vehicle identification number (VIN) when you call.

Service Contracts

A service contract is a promise to perform (or pay for) certain repairs or services. Although a service contract is sometimes called an "extended warranty," it is not a warranty as defined by federal law. A service contract may be arranged at any time and always costs extra; a warranty comes with a new car and is included in the original price. Used cars also may come with some type of warranty coverage included in the sales price. The separate and additional cost distinguishes a service contract from a warranty.

To decide if you need a service contract, consider:

- Whether the service contract duplicates warranty coverage or offers protection that begins after the warranty runs out. Does the service contract extend beyond the time you expect to own the car? If so, is the service contract transferable or is a shorter contract available?
- Whether the vehicle is likely to need repairs and how much they are going to cost. You can determine the value of a service contract by figuring whether the cost of repairs is likely to exceed the price of the contract.
- Whether the service contract covers all parts and systems. Check out all claims carefully. For example, "bumper to bumper" coverage may not mean what you think.
- Whether a deductible is required and, if so, the amount and terms.
- Whether the contract covers incidental expenses, such as towing and rental car charges while your car is being serviced
- Whether repairs and routine maintenance have to be done at the dealer
- Whether there is a cancellation and refund policy for the service contract, and if it has cancellation fees
- Whether the dealer or company offering the service contract is reputable. Some dealers sell third-party service contracts.

If you buy a service contract from the dealer within 90 days of buying a used vehicle, federal law prohibits the dealer from eliminating implied warranties on the systems covered in the contract. For example, if you buy a car "as is," the car normally is not covered by implied warranties. But, if you buy a service contract covering the engine, you automatically get implied warranties on the engine. These may give you protection beyond the scope of the service contract. Make sure you get written confirmation that your service contract is in effect.

CHAPTER 41

DO NOT GET SWAMPED BUYING A FLOOD-DAMAGED CAR

About This Chapter: This chapter includes text excerpted from "Don't Get Swamped Buying a Flood-Damaged Car," Federal Trade Commission (FTC), October 30, 2018.

In the wake of the recent hurricanes, used car buyers should use caution: Storm-damaged vehicles are sometimes cleaned up and taken out of state for sale. You might not know a vehicle is damaged until you take a closer look or have a mechanic check it out.

Here is what to do:

- **Look for** water stains, mildew, sand, or silt under the carpet, floor mats, and dashboard, and for fogging inside headlights and taillights. New carpet or upholstery in an older vehicle may be another red flag.
- **Check for** a heavy aroma of cleaners and disinfectants, which is a sign that someone's trying to mask a mold or odor problem.
- **Get a vehicle history report**. Before you buy any car, you always want to check the car's history. Start at vehiclehistory.gov, which is run by the National Motor Vehicle Title Information System (NMVTIS). But, to get flood-damage information, go to the National Insurance Crime Bureau's (NICB) free database, which lists flood damage and other information for cars that were insured. (If the car you are buying did not have insurance, it would not be in that database.) Of course, there are other reports that have additional information, such as accident and repair history.
- **Understand the difference between titles**. A "salvage title" means the car was declared a total loss by an insurance company because of a serious accident or some other problems. A "flood title" means the car has damage from sitting in water deep enough to fill the engine compartment. The title status is part of a vehicle history report.
- **Have your mechanic inspect the car** for water contamination.

The National Motor Vehicle Title Information System (NMVTIS) serves as a repository of information related to vehicles that have been in the possession of auto recyclers, junkyards, and salvage yards. This repository is then used by states and consumers to ensure that junk or salvage vehicles are not later re-sold and ensures that the vehicle identification numbers (VINs) from destroyed vehicles can never be used for a stolen auto. Thieves use the VINs from destroyed vehicles because they know that the true VIN will never appear again on the road and because they know that if the VINs are reported to state motor vehicle titling agencies, there is a strong likelihood that the reporting may not result in a flagged or retired record (also known as a "kill title" report). Because NMVTIS reporting is mandated and because consumers and states can access the information, the system makes it much easier to detect attempts to use VINs from destroyed or salvage vehicles in cloning operations.

Although not required, NMVTIS can also serve as a tool for junk and salvage yards to check vehicle history for any reason before accepting the vehicle into inventory.

(Source: "For Auto Recyclers, Salvage Yards, and Junk Yards," National Motor Vehicle Title Information System (NMVTIS))

- **Report fraud**. If you suspect a dealer is knowingly selling a storm-damaged car or a salvaged vehicle as a good-condition used car, contact the National Insurance Crime Bureau (NICB).

PART 4 | YOUR LEGAL RIGHTS AS A CONSUMER

CHAPTER 42
CREDIT AND YOUR CONSUMER RIGHTS

About This Chapter: This chapter includes text excerpted from "Credit and Your Consumer Rights," Federal Trade Commission (FTC), June 2017.

A good credit rating is very important. Businesses inspect your credit history when they evaluate your applications for credit, insurance, employment, and even leases. They can use it when they choose to give or deny you credit or insurance, provided you receive fair and equal treatment. Sometimes, things happen that can cause credit problems: a temporary loss of income, an illness, even a computer error. Solving credit problems may take time and patience, but it does not have to be an ordeal.

The Federal Trade Commission (FTC) enforces the credit laws that protect your right to get, use, and maintain credit. These laws do not guarantee that everyone will receive credit. Instead, the credit laws protect your rights by requiring businesses to give all consumers a fair and equal opportunity to get credit and to resolve disputes over credit errors. This chapter explains your rights under these laws and offers practical tips to help you solve credit problems.

Your Credit Report

Your credit report contains information about where you live, how you pay your bills, and whether you have been sued or filed for bankruptcy. Credit reporting companies sell the information in your report to businesses that use it to evaluate your applications for credit, insurance, employment, or renting a home.

The federal Fair Credit Reporting Act (FCRA) promotes the accuracy and privacy of information in the files of the nation's credit reporting companies.

Under the FCRA:

- You have the right to receive a copy of your credit report. A copy of your report must contain all the information in your file at the time of your request.
- Each of the nationwide credit reporting companies—Equifax, Experian, and TransUnion—is required to provide you with a free copy of your credit report, at your request, once every 12 months

Fair Credit Reporting Act

The Act (Title VI of the Consumer Credit Protection Act) protects information collected by consumer reporting agencies such as credit bureaus, medical information companies, and tenant-screening services. Information in a consumer report cannot be provided to anyone who does not have a purpose specified in the Act. Companies that provide information to consumer-reporting agencies also have specific legal obligations, including the duty to investigate disputed information. In addition, users of the information for credit, insurance, or employment purposes must notify the consumer when an adverse action is taken on the basis of such reports. The Fair and Accurate Credit Transactions Act added many provisions to this Act primarily relating to record accuracy and identity theft. The Dodd-Frank Act transferred to the Consumer Financial Protection Bureau most of the rulemaking responsibilities added to this Act by the Fair and Accurate Credit Transactions Act and the Credit CARD Act, but the Commission retains all its enforcement authority.

(Source: "Fair Credit Reporting Act," Federal Trade Commission (FTC))

- Under federal law, you are also entitled to a free report if a company takes adverse action against you, such as denying your application for credit, insurance, or employment, and you ask for your report within 60 days of receiving notice of the action. The notice will give you the name, address, and phone number of the credit reporting company. You are also entitled to one free report a year if you are unemployed and plan to look for a job within 60 days; if you are on welfare; or if your report is inaccurate because of fraud, including identity theft.

Your Credit Application

When creditors evaluate a credit application, they cannot engage in discriminatory practices.

The Equal Credit Opportunity Act (ECOA) prohibits credit discrimination on the basis of sex, race, marital status, religion, national origin, age, or receipt of public assistance. Creditors may ask for this information (except religion) in certain situations, but they may not use it to discriminate against you when deciding whether to grant you credit.

The ECOA protects consumers who deal with companies that regularly extend credit, including banks, small loan and finance companies, retail and department stores, credit card companies, and credit unions. Everyone who participates in the decision to grant credit, including real estate brokers who arrange financing, must follow this law. Businesses applying for credit also are protected by this law.

Under the ECOA:

- You cannot be denied credit based on your race, sex, marital status, religion, age, national origin, or receipt of public assistance.
- You have the right to have reliable public assistance considered in the same manner as other income.
- If you are denied credit, you have a legal right to know why.

Your Credit Billing and Electronic Fund Transfer Statements

It is important to check credit billing and electronic fund transfer account statements regularly because these documents may contain mistakes that could damage your credit status or reflect improper charges or transfers. If you find an error or discrepancy, notify the company and dispute the error immediately. The Fair Credit Billing Act (FCBA) and Electronic Fund Transfer Act (EFTA) establish procedures for resolving mistakes on credit billing and electronic fund transfer account statements, including:

- Charges or electronic fund transfers (EFTs) that you—or anyone you have authorized to use your account—have not made
- Charges or EFTs that are incorrectly identified or show the wrong date or amount
- Math errors
- Failure to post payments, credits, or EFTs properly
- Failure to send bills to your current address—provided the creditor receives your change of address, in writing, at least 20 days before the billing period ends
- Charges or EFTs for which you ask for an explanation or written proof of purchase along with a claimed error or request for clarification

The FCBA generally applies only to "open-end" credit accounts—credit cards and revolving charge accounts, such as department store accounts. It does not apply to loans or credit sales that are paid according to a fixed schedule until the entire amount is paid back, such as an automobile loan. The EFTA applies to EFTs, such as those involving automatic teller machines (ATMs), point-of-sale (POS) debit transactions, and other electronic banking transactions.

Your Debts and Debt Collectors

You are responsible for your debts. If you fall behind in paying your creditors, or if an error is made on your account, you may be contacted by a "debt collector." A debt collector is any person, other than the creditor, who regularly collects debts owed to others, including lawyers who collect debts on a regular basis. You have the right to be treated fairly by debt collectors.

The Fair Debt Collection Practices Act (FDCPA) applies to personal, family, and household debts. This includes money you owe for the purchase of a car, for medical care, or for charge accounts. The FDCPA prohibits debt collectors from engaging in unfair, deceptive, or abusive practices while collecting these debts. Under the FDCPA:

- Debt collectors may contact you only between 8 a.m. and 9 p.m.
- Debt collectors may not contact you at work if they know your employer disapproves.
- Debt collectors may not harass, oppress, or abuse you.

- Debt collectors may not lie when collecting debts, such as falsely implying that you have committed a crime.
- Debt collectors must identify themselves to you on the phone.
- Debt collectors must stop contacting you if you ask them to do so in writing.

Solving Your Credit Problems

Your credit report can influence your purchasing power, as well as your opportunity to get a job, rent or buy an apartment or a house, and buy insurance. When negative information in your report is accurate, only the passage of time can assure its removal. A credit reporting company can report most accurate negative information for 7 years and bankruptcy information for 10 years. Information about an unpaid judgment against you can be reported for 7 years or until the statute of limitations runs out, whichever is longer. There is no time limit on reporting information about criminal convictions, information reported in response to your application for a job that pays more than $75,000 a year, and information reported because you have applied for more than $150,000 worth of credit or life insurance. There is a standard method for calculating the 7-year reporting period. Generally, the period runs from the date that the event took place.

If you are having problems paying your bills, contact your creditors immediately. Try to work out a modified payment plan with them that reduces your payments to a more manageable level. Do not wait until your account has been turned over to a debt collector.

Here are some additional tips for solving credit problems:

- If you want to dispute a credit report, bill, or credit denial, write to the appropriate company and send your letter "return receipt requested."
- When you dispute a billing error, include your name, account number, the dollar amount in question, and the reason you believe the bill is wrong.
- If in doubt, request written verification of a debt.
- Keep all your original documents, especially receipts, sales slips, and billing statements. You will need them if you dispute a credit bill or report. Send copies only. It may take more than one letter to correct a problem.
- Be skeptical of businesses that offer instant solutions to credit problems. There are not any.
- Be persistent. Resolving credit problems can take time and patience.
- There is nothing that a credit-repair company can charge you for that you cannot do for yourself for little or no cost.

If you are not disciplined enough to create a workable budget and stick to it, work out a repayment plan with your creditors, or keep track of mounting bills, or consider contacting a credit-counseling organization. Many credit-counseling organizations are nonprofits and work with you to solve your financial problems. But, not all are reputable. For example, just because an organization says it is "nonprofit," there is no guarantee that its services are free, affordable, or even legitimate. In fact, some credit-counseling organizations charge high fees, or hide their fees by pressuring consumers to make "voluntary" contributions that only cause more debt.

Most credit counselors offer services through local offices, the Internet, or on the telephone. If possible, find an organization that offers in-person counseling. Many universities, military bases, credit unions, housing authorities, and branches of the U.S. Cooperative Extension Service operate nonprofit credit-counseling programs. Your financial institution, local consumer protection agency (CPA), and friends and family also may be good sources of information and referrals.

Reputable credit-counseling organizations can advise you on managing your money and debts, help you develop a budget, and offer free educational materials and workshops. Their counselors are certified and trained in the areas of consumer credit, money and debt management, and budgeting. Counselors discuss your entire financial situation with you and help you develop a personalized plan to solve your money problems. An initial counseling session typically lasts an hour, with an offer of follow-up sessions.

CHAPTER 43

YOUR EQUAL CREDIT OPPORTUNITY RIGHTS

About This Chapter: This chapter includes text excerpted from "Your Equal Credit Opportunity Rights," Federal Trade Commission (FTC), January 2013.

People often use credit to pay for education or a house, a remodeling job or a car, or to finance a loan to keep their business operating.

The Federal Trade Commission (FTC), the nation's consumer protection agency (CPA), enforces the Equal Credit Opportunity Act (ECOA), which prohibits credit discrimination on the basis of race, color, religion, national origin, sex, marital status, age, or because you get public assistance. Creditors may ask you for most of this information in certain situations, but they may not use it when deciding whether to give you credit or when setting the terms of your credit. Not everyone who applies for credit gets it or gets the same terms. Factors, such as income, expenses, debts, and credit history are among the considerations lenders use to determine your creditworthiness.

The law provides protections when you deal with any organizations or people who regularly extend credit, including banks, small loans, and finance companies, retail and department stores, credit-card companies, and credit unions. Everyone who participates in the decision to grant credit or in setting the terms of that credit, including real-estate brokers who arrange financing, must comply with the ECOA.

What Creditors May Not Tell You While You Are Seeking Credit

When you apply for credit, creditors may not:

- Discourage you from applying or reject your application because of your race, color, religion, national origin, sex, marital status, age, or because you receive public assistance
- Consider your race, sex, or national origin, although you may be asked to disclose this information if you choose to. (It helps federal agencies enforce antidiscrimination laws.) A creditor may consider your immigration status

Because the Justice Department's authority to prosecute matters extends only to those instances of a pattern or practice of discrimination on a prohibited basis, individuals who believe that they are the victims of unfair discrimination in a credit transaction should contact the appropriate regulatory agency. The agencies and the types of creditors that they regulate for purposes of compliance with ECOA are as follows:

- **Consumer Financial Protection Bureau (CFPB).** Banks, savings associations, and credit unions with total assets of over $10 billion and their affiliates. Also shares enforcement authority with the FTC over mortgage brokers, mortgage originators, mortgage servicers, lenders offering private educational loans, and payday lenders regardless of size.
- **Office of the Comptroller of the Currency (OCC).** National banks, federal savings associations and federal branches/agencies of foreign banks with total assets of under $10 billion (the words "National" or "Federal" or the initials "N.A." or "F.S.B." appear in or after the bank's name).
- **Federal Reserve Board (FRB).** Financial institutions with total assets of under $10 billion that are members of the Federal Reserve System (FRS), except national banks and federal branches/ agencies of foreign banks.
- **Federal Deposit Insurance Corporation (FDIC).** State-chartered banks with total assets of under $10 billion that are not members of the FRS.
- **National Credit Union Association (NCUA).** Federal credit unions (the words "Federal credit union" appear in the institution's name).

(Source: "The Equal Credit Opportunity Act," U.S. Department of Justice (DOJ))

and whether you have the right to stay in the country long enough to repay the debt.

- Impose different terms or conditions, such as higher interest rate or higher fees, on a loan based on your race, color, religion, national origin, sex, marital status, age, or because you receive public assistance
- Ask if you are widowed or divorced. A creditor may use only the terms "married," "unmarried," or "separated."
- Ask about your marital status if you are applying for a separate, unsecured account. A creditor may ask you to provide this information if you live in "community property" states: Arizona, California, Idaho, Louisiana, Nevada, New Mexico, Texas, Washington, and Wisconsin. A creditor in any state may ask for this information if you apply for a joint account or one secured by the property.
- Ask for information about your spouse, except:
  - If your spouse is applying with you
  - If your spouse will be allowed to use the account
  - If you are relying on your spouse's income or on alimony or child support income from a former spouse
  - If you live in a community property state
- Ask about your plans for having or raising children, but they can ask questions about expenses related to your dependents

- Ask if you get alimony, child support, or separate maintenance payments unless they tell you first that you do not have to provide this information if you are not relying on these payments to get credit. A creditor may ask if you have to pay alimony, child support, or separate maintenance payments.

What Creditors May Not Tell You While Granting or Setting the Terms of Credit

When deciding to grant you credit or when setting the terms of credit, creditors may not:

- Consider your race, color, religion, national origin, sex, marital status or whether you get public assistance
- Consider your age, unless:
  - You are too young to sign contracts, generally under 18
  - You are at least 62, and the creditor will favor you because of your age
  - It is used to determine the meaning of other factors important to creditworthiness. For example, a creditor could use your age to determine if your income might drop because you are about to retire.
  - It is used in a valid credit scoring system that favors applicants 62 and older. A credit scoring system assigns points to answers you give on credit applications. For example, your length of employment might be scored differently depending on your age.
- Consider whether you have a telephone account in your name. A creditor may consider whether you have a phone.
- Consider the racial composition of the neighborhood where you want to buy, refinance, or improve a house with money you are borrowing

Evaluating Your Income

When evaluating your income, creditors may not:

- Refuse to consider reliable public-assistance income the same way as other income
- Discount income because of your sex or marital status. For example, a creditor cannot count a man's salary at 100 percent and a woman's at 75 percent. A creditor may not assume a woman of childbearing age will stop working to raise children.
- Discount or refuse to consider income because it comes from part-time employment, Social Security, pensions, or annuities
- Refuse to consider reliable alimony, child support, or separate maintenance payments. A creditor may ask you for proof that you receive this income consistently.

Your Rights

You also have the right to:

- Have credit in your birth name (Mary Smith), your first and your spouse's last name (Mary Jones), or your first name and a combined last name (Mary Smith-Jones)
- Get credit without a cosigner, if you meet the creditor's standards
- Have a cosigner other than your spouse, if one is necessary
- Keep your own accounts after you change your name, marital status, reach a certain age, or retire, unless the creditor has evidence that you are not willing or able to pay
- Know whether your application was accepted or rejected within 30 days of filing a complete application
- Know why your application was rejected. The creditor must tell you the specific reason for the rejection or that you are entitled to learn the reason if you ask within 60 days. An acceptable reason might be "your income was too low" or "you haven't been employed long enough." An unacceptable reason might be "you didn't meet our minimum standards." That information is not specific enough.
- Learn the specific reason you were offered less favorable terms than you applied for, but only if you reject these terms. For example, if the lender offers you a smaller loan or a higher interest rate, and you do not accept the offer, you have the right to know why those terms were offered.
- Find out why your account was closed or why the terms of the account were made less favorable unless the account was inactive or you failed to make payments as agreed

A Special Note to Women

A good credit history—a record of your bill payments—often is necessary to get credit. This can hurt many married, separated, divorced, and widowed women. Typically, there are two reasons women do not have credit histories in their own names: either they lost their credit histories when they married and changed their names, or creditors reported accounts shared by married couples in the husband's name only.

If you are married, separated, divorced, or widowed, contact your local credit-reporting companies to make sure all relevant bill-payment information is in a file under your own name. Your credit report includes information on where you live, how you pay your bills, and whether you have been sued, arrested, or filed for bankruptcy. National credit-reporting companies sell the information in your report to creditors, insurers, employers, and other businesses that, in turn, use it to evaluate your applications for credit, insurance, employment, or renting a home.

The Fair Credit Reporting Act (FCRA) requires each of the three nationwide credit reporting companies—Equifax, Experian, and TransUnion—to give you a free copy of your credit report, at your request, once every 12 months. To order your report, visit annualcreditreport.com or call 877-322-8228.

Are You Being Discriminated Against?

If you suspect a creditor has discriminated against you, take action!

- Complain to the creditor. Sometimes you can persuade the creditor to reconsider your application.
- Check with your state Attorney General's office to see if the creditor violated state equal credit opportunity laws.
- Consider suing the creditor in federal district court. If you win, you can recover your actual damages and be awarded punitive damages if the court finds that the creditor's conduct was willful. You also may recover reasonable lawyers' fees and court costs. Or you might consider finding others with the same claim and getting together to file a class-action suit. An attorney can advise you on how to proceed.
- Report violations to the appropriate government agency. If you have been denied credit, the creditor must give you the name and address of the agency to contact.

A number of federal agencies, including the FTC, share enforcement responsibility for the ECOA.

CHAPTER 44

AUTOMOBILE LOANS AND YOUR RIGHTS FAQS

About This Chapter: Text beginning with the heading "My Lender or Dealer Said That My Spouse Had to Cosign My Auto Loan. Is This Right?" is excerpted from "Auto Loans Know Your Rights," Consumer Financial Protection Bureau (CFPB), June 12, 2016; Text under the heading "What You Should Do If You Think an Auto Dealer or Lender Is Violating the Law" is excerpted from "What Should I Do If I Think an Auto Dealer or Lender Is Violating the Law?" Consumer Financial Protection Bureau (CFPB), April 18, 2016.

My Lender or Dealer Said That My Spouse Had to Cosign My Auto Loan. Is This Right?

In general, a creditor such as a lender or a dealer cannot require your spouse's (or another person's) signature for individual credit if you qualify on your own for the amount and terms requested.

If you are applying for joint credit, however, a lender or dealer may require your spouse's signature (or the signature of the person with whom you are applying).

What Happens If I Left Some of My Personal Possessions in My Vehicle When It Was Repossessed?

Your rights vary depending on your state, but most states require repossessing companies to make any of your possessions left in the vehicle available to you.

You will have to go get them at a time that is convenient for the repossessing company. It is important to document what items you left in the vehicle and their estimated value. If your vehicle has been repossessed and you left the property in your vehicle, contact your lender immediately to arrange to get your belongings. If the lender or repossessing company is demanding payment for the return of your property, you should consult an attorney. You could also file a complaint with your state Attorney General or consumer protection office.

Am I Required to Purchase Credit Insurance from a Lender or Dealer to Get an Auto Loan?

No, generally you cannot be required to buy credit insurance. Lenders cannot deny you credit if you refuse to buy optional credit insurance. If you feel pressured to buy credit insurance, walk away and consider looking for a different dealer or lender.

If a lender or dealer denies you credit because you refuse to buy any optional products such as credit insurance you may want to submit a complaint with the Consumer Financial Protection Bureau (CFPB). In addition to filing a complaint with the CFPB, you can also file a complaint with the Federal Trade Commission (FTC). You can also file a complaint with your state Attorney General or state consumer protection office.

Credit insurance is usually expensive and you may be able to accomplish the same goal by obtaining other insurance coverage, such as life insurance. Other coverage may be cheaper and provide you with more flexibility by allowing you to pay off more than just the amount of your auto loan. Before you sign any loan papers, ask the lender whether the loan includes any charges for credit insurance.

Can a Lender or Dealer Consider My Sex, Marital Status, or Dependents When Deciding Whether to Give Me an Auto Loan?

A creditor, such as a lender or a dealer, cannot discriminate on the basis of sex or marital status.

If you are applying for individual credit in your own name, a creditor such as a lender or a dealer may not deny you credit on the basis of sex or marital status. If your credit is sufficient to qualify you for your own auto loan, a lender or dealer generally may not require that your spouse cosign. Generally, a lender or dealer must evaluate married and unmarried applicants by the same standards.

If you are applying for joint credit or credit secured by collateral (such as a vehicle), the lender or dealer may not deny you on the basis of sex but may ask if you are married, unmarried, or separated. The lender or dealer may explain that the "unmarried" category includes single, divorced, and widowed persons. A lender or dealer may not treat married joint applicants differently from unmarried joint applicants based on the existence, absence, or likelihood of a marital relationship.

A lender or dealer may consider your marital status as it affects the lender's ability to reach the property in the event of nonpayment. For example, for auto loans, a lender or dealer could consider whether your spouse has an interest in the property that is being offered as collateral for the loan.

A lender or dealer may request information about your spouse or former spouse only if:

You May Have a Right to "Cure" or Reinstate the Lease

Defaulting on a lease or voluntarily returning your vehicle to the lessor can trigger a substantial early termination fee. Check your lease agreement. Under the federal Consumer Leasing Act (CLA), the method for calculating the early termination fee must be disclosed in the lease. The early termination fee is generally the difference between the early termination payoff and the amount credited to you for the vehicle. Suppose, for example, that your early termination payoff amount is $16,000 and the amount credited for the vehicle is $14,000. The early termination charge would be $16,000 minus $14,000, or $2,000. The earlier your lease is terminated, the greater this charge is likely to be. If you are unable to pay the early termination fee and default, the lessor can report the amount of delinquent fees to the credit bureau.

If you are charged an early termination fee, be sure you understand how it is being calculated and consult an attorney if you think it has been done incorrectly.

If you have a problem with your auto lease, you can submit a complaint online with the CFPB or call 855-411-CFPB (855-411-2372).

- Your spouse or former spouse will be responsible for paying debts on the account
- You are relying on your spouse's income or former spouse's income to repay the credit requested
- You are relying on alimony, child support, or separate maintenance payments from a spouse or former spouse to repay the credit requested
- You reside in a "community property" state. The community property states are Alaska (if you sign a special agreement), Arizona, California, Idaho, Louisiana, Nevada, New Mexico, Texas, Washington, and Wisconsin.
- You are relying on property located in a "community property" state to repay the credit requested

A creditor such as a lender or a dealer may ask about the number and ages of your dependents. A lender or dealer may also ask about dependent-related financial obligations or expenses. However, a lender or dealer may do so only if they ask for this information without regard to sex or marital status or any other prohibited basis. A lender or dealer cannot ask you about your birth-control practices, your intentions concerning having or raising children, or your capability to have children.

What Happens If I Do Not Make the Payments on My Auto Lease?

If you miss payments, the dealership or finance company you lease your vehicle from, known as the "lessor," may be entitled to repossess the vehicle.

Your lease agreement will state what constitutes a default of the lease as well as if there is any "grace period" in making lease payments. Not making a contractually required monthly payment will normally be a breach of the lease and the lessor can then repossess the vehicle from you. You should contact your lender if you are unable to make your monthly payment on its due date. Servicemembers may have additional protections under the Servicemember's Civil Relief Act (SCRA). You should contact your local JAG to find out if these protections apply.

I Bought a Used Car and Financed It at the Dealership. They Told Me That the Car Was in Good Shape, but It Turned out to Have Serious Mechanical Problems. The Dealer Says the Warranty Does Not Cover Any of the Problems. I Cannot Afford to Pay My Loan Payment and Get the Car Fixed. What Can I Do?

Federal and state laws exist that may protect you in this situation. For example, some states have lemon laws that may provide a way for you to get paid back for a car that repeatedly fails to meet standards of quality and performance.

Am I Required to Purchase an Extended Warranty or Guaranteed Auto Protection Insurance from a Lender or Dealer to Get an Auto Loan?

It is highly unusual for a lender or dealer to require an extended warranty or GAP insurance.

If your lender or dealer says you are required to purchase a product, such as GAP insurance or an extended warranty, ask them to show you where your sales contract says it is required. If the contract does not explicitly state that it is required, you cannot be required to purchase it.

Can a Lender or Dealer Consider the Fact That I Am Not a Citizen of the United States?

A creditor such as a lender or a dealer cannot discriminate on the basis of national origin. However, a lender or dealer may ask about your permanent residency and immigration status.

A lender or dealer may consider this information or any additional information that may affect its rights and remedies regarding repayment.

A lender or dealer may also take into account any law, regulation, or executive order that limits dealings with citizens of certain countries.

Can a Lender or Dealer Ask Me about My Race, Color, Religion, National Origin, or Sex?

For nonmortgage transactions, generally, a creditor cannot ask about your race, color, religion, national origin, or sex.

What Should I Do If I Think That a Lender or Auto Dealer Discriminated against Me in My Auto Loan Application, Such as by Denying My Application or Charging Me a Higher Interest Rate?

If you are denied an auto loan, you should receive information about why you were denied. If you believe that your lender or dealer discriminated against you, you can file a complaint with the FTC, CFPB, or with your state Attorney General or state consumer protection office.

The Equal Credit Opportunity Act (ECOA) makes it illegal for a creditor such as a lender or a dealer to discriminate against any applicant in any aspect of a credit transaction, including auto loans, because of:

- Race
- Color
- Religion
- National origin
- Sex (including gender)
- Marital status
- Age (if the applicant is old enough to enter into a contract)
- Receipt of income from any public-assistance program. This includes, but is not limited to, Social Security and Supplemental Security Income (SSI), unemployment compensation, Temporary Assistance to Needy Families (TANF), and the Supplemental Nutrition Assistance Program (SNAP).
- Exercising in good faith a right under the Consumer Credit Protection Act (CCPA), which includes consumer protection statutes relating to credit

This means that a lender or dealer may not use any of the above grounds as a reason to:

- Refuse you an auto loan if you qualify for it
- Discourage you from applying for an auto loan
- Provide you an auto loan on terms that are different from the terms given to someone else who is similarly situated to you, such as having similar creditworthiness
- Close your account

If you are denied an auto loan, you should receive information about why you were denied. This is called an "adverse action notice." This notice includes a statement of the specific reasons for the denial or a notice that you may request a statement of specific reasons within 60 days.

If you believe that your lender or dealer discriminated against you on any of these grounds, you can submit a complaint with the FTC or with the CFPB online or by calling

> **Watch for Warning Signs**
> Credit discrimination is often hidden or even unintentional, which makes it hard to spot. Look for red flags, such as:
> - You are treated differently in person than on the phone.
> - You are discouraged from applying for credit.
> - You hear the lender make negative comments about race, national origin, sex, or other protected characteristics.
> - You are refused credit even though you qualify for it.
> - You are offered credit at a higher rate than the one you applied for, even though you qualify for the lower rate.
> - You are denied credit, but not given a reason why or told how to find out why.
> - Your deal sounds too good to be true.
> - You feel pushed or pressured to sign.

us toll-free at 855-411-CFPB (855-411-2372). You can also tell us about your experience without submitting a formal complaint.

You can also file a complaint with your state Attorney General or state consumer protection office. If you are in the military, you should report this to your installation JAG immediately. To find your JAG Legal Assistance Office, use the locator.

In addition, state or local laws may prohibit discrimination on additional grounds.

If I Cannot Make My Auto Loan Payments, Will My Vehicle Be Repossessed?

If you are late on your payments, a lender may repossess your vehicle.

Your credit will be affected, you may still owe on any "deficiency balance" on the auto loan, and you will be responsible for repossession costs.

To try to avoid the repossession:

- **Contact your lender as soon as possible.** Your lender may be willing to work with you to come up with an affordable payment plan, especially if you have made timely payments in the past. If you do reach an agreement, get it in writing so there is not a dispute later.
- **Refinance.** You may be able to get a lower interest rate or spread out the payments over more time. Generally, a longer-term loan means you will pay more in interest. Shop around.
- **Sell your vehicle.** Figure out how much you owe on the auto loan and then check the approximate market value of your vehicle. If you owe less than the value of the vehicle, you can sell it and use the proceeds to pay off the loan. Check your auto loan contract to see if you have a prepayment penalty for paying off early.

Repossession Methods

Besides physically removing the vehicle, some lenders may also use a starter interrupt device (SID) in place of repossession or to help facilitate repossession. A SID is a device that allows a lender or lessor to remotely deactivate a vehicle's ignition system if a borrower/lessee misses payments or defaults. The shutdown can be temporary until payment is made, or it can be done to make repossession easier. The rules on SIDs vary from state to state, so ask your lender before signing the contract if your vehicle is equipped with a SID. If it is, you should ask how this process will work—for example, will you get any warning before the vehicle is shutdown? Is there a way for the vehicle to be restarted in case of an emergency?

You may have other rights and obligations under your state's law. You may be able to get more information about your state law from your state Attorney General, your state consumer protection office, a private attorney, or your local legal services office.

If you do not pay, the lender can repossess your vehicle. In many states, as soon as you have missed a payment on the vehicle, your lender has the right to take back or repossess the vehicle without warning you or getting a court order. Some states have laws that require notice before repossession, alerting you to what payments have been missed, while also providing a short time period in which you can make up payments to prevent repossession. Servicemembers have additional repossession protections under the SCRA for auto loans and leases taken out before entering military service.

The lender may not "breach the peace" in repossessing. Under state law, a lender may not repossess a vehicle unless it can do so without a breach of peace. The definition of breach of the peace varies depending on your state law. Typically, it includes things like threatening or using physical force, removing a vehicle from a closed garage without permission, or continuing with repossession after you have resisted or refused to allow the repossession. If the lender commits a breach of the peace, you may contact law enforcement. A breach of the peace may also give you a claim for damages or a defense, which may lessen the amount you eventually owe after the sale of the vehicle.

Can a Lender or Dealer Consider My Age, My Receipt of Part-Time Income, or My Retirement Income When Deciding Whether to Give Me an Auto Loan?

Generally, a creditor such as a lender or a dealer cannot use your age to make credit decisions.

There are exceptions to this rule, such as:

- If the applicant is too young to enter into a contract. State law governs the age at which you can enter into a legally binding contract
- Age can be considered in a valid credit scoring system. The credit scoring system may not disfavor applicants 62 years old or older. It may favor applicants 62 years or older.

- A lender or dealer may relate your age to other information about you that the lender or dealer considers in evaluating creditworthiness. For example, a lender or dealer may consider your job and length of time to retirement to determine whether your income, including your retirement income, will be adequate for the life of the loan.

A lender or dealer cannot discount or refuse to consider the income that comes from:

- Part-time employment
- An annuity, pension, or other retirement benefits
- A public-assistance program. This includes, but is not limited to, Social Security and Supplemental Security Income (SSI), unemployment compensation, Temporary Assistance to Needy Families (TANF), and Supplemental Nutrition Assistance Program (SNAP).

Like all other forms of income, however, a creditor such as a lender or a dealer can consider the amount of the income and the likelihood that it will continue.

If I Need to Have a Cosigner, Can a Lender or Dealer Require That It Be My Spouse?

No. If you do not individually qualify, a creditor such as a lender or dealer may request a cosigner, guarantor, endorser, or similar party.

Your spouse may function as this additional party. But, a lender or dealer cannot require that it be your spouse.

Can a Lender or Dealer Ask Me about Alimony, Child Support, or Separate Maintenance Payments That I Receive When I Apply for an Auto Loan?

Yes, but only if you want the lender or dealer to consider such payments as part of your application for credit.

A lender or dealer may ask whether income stated in your application comes from alimony, child support, or separate maintenance payments. However, the lender or dealer must first tell you that you do not have to reveal such income if you do not want it considered.

If you do want to have the dealer or lender consider your alimony, child support, or maintenance payments, the lender or dealer may consider the amount of such income and the likelihood that it will continue. In determining this, a lender or dealer may consider factors such as whether there is a written agreement or court decree, how long and how regularly you have been receiving payments, the availability of court or other procedures to compel payment, and the creditworthiness of the payor when that information is available.

I Am a Member of the Military or a Spouse/Family Member of a Servicemember and I Think I Have a Loan That Exceeds What I Can Be Charged by Law. What Should I Do?

If you think you have been overcharged for a loan, you should seek legal assistance.

It is possible that you will not have to pay the charges that exceed the legal limit. Check with your local JAG office for more information.

My Auto Loan Paperwork Said the Extended Warranty Was Optional but I Was Told That I Was Required to Purchase an Extended Warranty to Get the Promotional Interest Rate. Do I Have to Purchase It?

If the paperwork says the warranty is optional, the dealer cannot require you to purchase it.

If you believe that your dealer has misrepresented the terms of an agreement, you may file a complaint with the FTC and your state Attorney General or state consumer protection office. Also, you may want to consider contacting a private attorney for assistance.

What You Should Do If You Think an Auto Dealer or Lender Is Violating the Law

If your problem is with a lender or a Buy Here Pay Here dealer, you may file a complaint with the CFPB and your state Attorney General. If your problem is with a traditional dealer, you may file a complaint with the FTC and your state Attorney General.

Keep all the documents, voicemails, and records of your interactions with the dealer or lender.

Also, you may want to consider contacting a private attorney for assistance.

CHAPTER 45

UNDERSTANDING AUTO TRADE-INS AND NEGATIVE EQUITY

About This Chapter: This chapter includes text excerpted from "Auto Trade-Ins and Negative Equity," Federal Trade Commission (FTC), March 2012.

Some car dealers advertise that when you trade in one vehicle to buy another, they will pay off the balance of your loan—no matter how much you owe. But, some people owe more on their car than the car is worth. They have "negative equity," and for them, the dealer's promises to pay off their entire loan may be misleading.

The Federal Trade Commission (FTC), the nation's consumer protection agency, says that people with negative equity should pay special attention to vehicle trade-in offers. That is because, although the advertisement claims that they will have no further responsibility for any amount of their old loan, the advertisement may be untrue. Dealers may include the negative equity in consumers' new car loans. That would increase their monthly payments by adding principal and interest.

Here is how that might play out: Say you want to trade in your car for a newer model. Your loan payoff is \$18,000, but your car is worth \$15,000. You have a negative equity of \$3,000, which must be paid if you want to trade-in your vehicle. If the dealer promises to pay off this \$3,000, it should not be included in your new loan. Nevertheless, some dealers add the \$3,000 to the loan for your new car, deduct the amount from your down payment, or do both. In either case, this would increase your monthly payments; not only would the \$3,000 be added to the principal, but you would be financing it, too.

The FTC says that understanding how negative equity works in a vehicle trade-in can help you make a better-informed choice about purchasing and financing a car, and help you identify whether the claims in car advertisements that promise to pay off your loan are misleading.

Federal law requires that before you sign a contract to finance the purchase of a car, the dealer must give you certain disclosures about the cost of that credit. Read them,

Tip: If you do roll the balance of the old loan into a new loan for a new vehicle, ask questions. Make sure that you understand the total cost of the new loan. You need to know the amount borrowed, the APR and interest rate, the loan term (in months), and the monthly payment—before you agree to anything. If your new loan does not cover the amount you still owe on your old vehicle then you could have two loans and two monthly payments to make. If your new loan does cover what you still owe on your old vehicle, you could be borrowing a lot more than the price of the new vehicle. Either way, you may want to carefully consider whether it makes sense to go through with the transaction and purchase the next vehicle if you still owe money on your trade-in. *(Source: "What Is Negative Equity in an Auto Loan?" Consumer Financial Protection Bureau (CFPB))*

and look for the details about the down payment and the amount financed. Make sure you understand how your negative equity is being treated before you sign the contract. Otherwise, you may wind up paying a lot more than you expect.

Dealing with Negative Automobile Equity

Here are some tips to help you avoid the snowball effect of negative equity:

- Find out what your current vehicle is worth before you negotiate the purchase of a new car. Check the National Automobile Dealers Association's (NADA) Guides, Edmunds, and Kelley Blue Book.
- If you have negative equity, either because of your current car loan or a rollover from a previous loan:
  - Think about postponing your purchase until you are in a positive equity position. For example, consider paying down your loan faster by making additional, principal-only payments.
  - Think about selling your car yourself to try getting more for it than its wholesale value.
  - If you decide to go ahead with a trade-in, ask how the negative equity is being treated in the trade-in. Read the contract carefully, making sure that any promises made orally are included. Do not sign the contract until you understand all the terms and the amount you will be paying every month.
  - Keep the length of your new loan term as short as you can manage. If the negative equity amount is rolled into the new loan, the longer your loan, the longer you will take to reach positive equity in the vehicle.

Where to Complain

To report problems with dealer advertising and sales and finance contracts, including advertisements that falsely promise to pay off the negative equity in your car loan, contact:

- The Federal Trade Commission (www.ftccomplaintassistant.gov)
- Your state Attorney General (www.consumer.ftc.gov/now-leaving)

CHAPTER 46
COPING WITH DEBT

About This Chapter: This chapter includes text excerpted from "Coping with Debt," Federal Trade Commission (FTC), November 2012.

Having trouble paying your bills? Getting notices from creditors? Are your accounts being turned over to debt collectors? Are you worried about losing your home or your car? You are not alone. Many people face a financial crisis at some point in their lives. Whether the crisis is caused by personal or family illness, the loss of a job, or overspending, it can seem overwhelming. But, often, it can be overcome. Your financial situation does not have to go from bad to worse.

If you or someone you know is in financial hot water, consider these options: self-help using realistic budgeting and other techniques; debt-relief services, such as credit counseling or debt settlement from a reputable organization; debt consolidation; or bankruptcy. How do you know which will work best for you? It depends on your level of debt, your level of discipline, and your prospects for the future.

Self-Help

Developing a Budget

The first step toward taking control of your financial situation is to do a realistic assessment of how much money you take in and how much money you spend. Start by listing your income from all sources. Then, list your "fixed" expenses—those that are the same each month—such as mortgage payments or rent, car payments, and insurance premiums. Next, list the expenses that vary—such as groceries, entertainment, and clothing. Writing down all your expenses, even those that seem insignificant, is a helpful way to track your spending patterns, identify necessary expenses, and prioritize the rest. The goal is to make sure you can make ends meet on the basics: housing, food, healthcare, insurance, and education. You can find information about budgeting and money-management techniques online, at your public library, and in bookstores. Computer software programs can be useful tools for developing and maintaining a budget, balancing your checkbook, and creating plans to save money and pay down your debt.

Contacting Your Creditors

Contact your creditors immediately if you are having trouble making ends meet. Tell them why it is difficult for you, and try to work out a modified payment plan that reduces your payments to a more manageable level. Do not wait until your accounts have been turned over to a debt collector. At that point, your creditors have given up on you.

Dealing with Debt Collectors

Federal law dictates how and when a debt collector may contact you: not before 8 a.m. or after 9 p.m. or while you are at work if the collector knows that your employer does not approve of the calls. Collectors may not harass you, lie, or use unfair practices when they try to collect a debt. And they must honor a written request from you to stop further contact.

Managing Your Auto and Home Loans

Your debts can be unsecured or secured. Secured debts usually are tied to an asset, such as your car for a car loan or your house for a mortgage. If you stop making payments, lenders can repossess your car or foreclose on your house. Unsecured debts are not tied to any particular asset, and include most credit-card debt, bills for medical care, and signature loans.

Most automobile-financing agreements allow a creditor to repossess your car any time you are in default. No notice is required. If your car is repossessed, you may have to pay the balance due on the loan, as well as towing and storage costs, to get it back. If you cannot do this, the creditor may sell the car. If you see default approaching, you may be better off selling the car yourself and paying off the debt: You will avoid the added costs of repossession and a negative entry on your credit report.

If you fall behind on your mortgage, contact your lender immediately to avoid foreclosure. Most lenders are willing to work with you if they believe you are acting in good faith and the situation is temporary. Some lenders may reduce or suspend your payments for a short time. When you resume regular payments, though, you may have to pay an additional amount toward the past-due total. Other lenders may agree to change the terms of the mortgage by extending the repayment period to reduce the monthly debt. Ask whether additional fees would be assessed for these changes, and calculate how much they total in the long term.

If you and your lender cannot work out a plan, contact a housing counseling agency. Some agencies limit their counseling services to homeowners with Federal Housing Administration (FHA) mortgages, but many offer free help to any homeowner who is having trouble making mortgage payments. Call the local office of the U.S. Department of Housing and Urban Development (HUD) or the housing authority in your state, city, or county for help in finding a legitimate housing counseling agency near you.

Debt-Relief Services

If you are struggling with significant credit-card debt and cannot work out a repayment plan with your creditors on your own, consider contacting a debt-relief service, such as credit counseling or debt settlement. Depending on the type of service, you might get advice on how to deal with your mounting bills or create a plan for repaying your creditors.

Before you do business with any debt-relief service, check it out with your state Attorney General and local consumer protection agency (CPA). They can tell you if any consumer complaints are on file about the firm you are considering doing business with. Ask your state Attorney General if the company is required to be licensed to work in your state and, if so, whether it is.

If you are thinking about getting help to stabilize your financial situation, do some homework first. Find out what services a business provides, how much it costs, and how long it may take to get the results they promised. Do not rely on verbal promises. Get everything in writing, and read your contracts carefully.

Credit Counseling

Reputable credit-counseling organizations can advise you on managing your money and debts, help you develop a budget, and offer free educational materials and workshops. Their counselors are certified and trained in consumer credit, money and debt management, and budgeting. Counselors discuss your entire financial situation with you, and help you develop a personalized plan to solve your money problems. An initial counseling session typically lasts an hour, with an offer of follow-up sessions.

Most reputable credit counselors are nonprofits and offer services through local offices, online, or on the phone. If possible, find an organization that offers in-person counseling. Many universities, military bases, credit unions, housing authorities, and branches of the U.S. Cooperative Extension Service (CES) operate nonprofit credit-counseling programs. Your financial institution, local consumer protection agency (CPA), and friends and family also may be good sources of information and referrals.

But, be aware that "nonprofit" status does not guarantee that services are free, affordable, or even legitimate. In fact, some credit counseling organizations charge high fees, which they may hide, or urge their clients to make "voluntary" contributions that can cause more debt.

Debt-Management Plans

If your financial problems stem from too much debt or your inability to repay your debts, a credit-counseling agency may recommend that you enroll in a debt-management plan (DMP). A DMP alone is not credit counseling, and DMPs are not for everyone. Do not sign up for one of these plans unless and until a certified credit counselor has spent time thoroughly reviewing your financial situation, and has offered you customized advice on managing your money. Even if a DMP is appropriate for you, a reputable-credit counseling organization still can help you create a budget and teach you money-management skills.

In a DMP, you deposit money each month with the credit-counseling organization. It uses your deposits to pay your unsecured debts, such as your credit-card bills, student loans, and medical bills, according to a payment schedule the counselor develops with you and your creditors. Your creditors may agree to lower your interest rates or waive certain fees. But, it is a good idea to check with all your creditors to be sure they offer the concessions that a credit-counseling organization describes to you. A successful DMP requires you to make regular, timely payments; it could take 48 months or more to complete your DMP. Ask the credit counselor to estimate how long it will take for you to complete the plan. You may have to agree not to apply for—or use—any additional credit while you are participating in the plan.

Debt-Settlement Programs

Debt-settlement programs typically are offered by for-profit companies, and involve them negotiating with your creditors to allow you to pay a "settlement" to resolve your debt—a lump sum that is less than the full amount that you owe. To make that lump-sum payment, the program asks that you set aside a specific amount of money every month in savings. Debt-settlement companies usually ask that you transfer this amount every month into an escrow-like account to accumulate enough savings to pay off any settlement that is eventually reached. Further, these programs often encourage or instruct their clients to stop making any monthly payments to their creditors.

Debt-Settlement Has Risks

Although a debt-settlement company may be able to settle one or more of your debts, there are risks associated with these programs to consider before enrolling:

- These programs often require that you deposit money in a special savings account for 36 months or more before all your debts will be settled. Many people have trouble making these payments long enough to get all (or even some) of their debts settled, and end up dropping out of the programs as a result. Before you sign up for a debt-settlement program, review your budget carefully to make sure you are financially capable of setting aside the required monthly amounts for the full length of the program.
- Your creditors have no obligation to agree to negotiate a settlement of the amount you owe. So there is a possibility that your debt-settlement company will not be able to settle some of your debts—even if you set aside the monthly amounts required by the program. Also, debt-settlement companies often try to negotiate smaller debts first, leaving interest and fees on large debts to continue to mount.
- Because debt-settlement programs often ask or encourage you to stop sending payments directly to your creditors, they may have a negative impact on your credit report and other serious consequences. For example,

your debts may continue to accrue late fees and penalties that can put you further in the hole. You also may get calls from your creditors or debt collectors requesting repayment. You could even be sued for repayment. In some instances, when creditors win a lawsuit, they have the right to garnish your wages or put a lien on your home.

Debt-Settlement and Debt-Elimination Scams

Some companies offering debt-settlement programs may not deliver on their promises, such as their "guarantees" to settle all your credit-card debts for 30 to 60 percent of the amount you owe. Other companies may try to collect their fees from you before they settle any of your debts. The FTC's Telemarketing Sales Rule (TSR) prohibits companies that sell debt-settlement and other debt-relief services on the phone from charging a fee before they settle or reduce your debt. Some companies may not explain the risks associated with their programs, including that many (or most) of their clients drop out without settling their debts, that their clients' credit reports may suffer, or that debt collectors may continue to call them.

Before you enroll in a debt-settlement program, do your homework. You are making a big decision that involves spending a lot of your money that could go toward paying down your debt. Enter the name of the company with the word "complaints" into a search engine. Read what others have said about the companies you are considering, including whether they are involved in a lawsuit with any state or federal regulators for engaging in deceptive or unfair practices.

Fees

If you do business with a debt-settlement company, you may have to put money in a dedicated bank account, which will be administered by an independent third party. The funds are yours and you are entitled to the interest that accrues. The account administrator may charge you a reasonable fee for account maintenance, and is responsible for transferring funds from your account to pay your creditors and the debt-settlement company when settlements occur.

Disclosure Requirements

Before you sign up for the service, the debt-relief company must give you information about the program:

- **Price and terms.** The company must explain its fees and any conditions on its services.
- **Results.** The company must tell you how long it will take to get results—how many months or years before it will make an offer to each creditor for a settlement.
- **Offers.** The company must tell you how much money or what percentage of each outstanding debt you must save before it will make an offer to each creditor on your behalf.

- **Nonpayment.** If the company asks you to stop making payments to your creditors—or if the program relies on your not making payments—it must tell you about the possible negative consequences of your action.

The debt-relief company also must tell you:

- That the funds are yours and you are entitled to the interest earned
- The account administrator is not affiliated with the debt-relief provider and does not get referral fees, and
- That you may withdraw your money at any time without penalty

Tax Consequences

Depending on your financial condition, any savings you get from debt-relief services can be considered income and taxable. Credit-card companies and others may report settled debt, which the IRS considers income to the IRS, unless you are "insolvent." Insolvency is when your total debts are more than the fair market value of your total assets. Insolvency can be complex to determine. Talk to a tax professional if you are not sure whether you qualify for this exception.

Use Caution When Shopping for Debt-Relief Services

Avoid any debt-relief organization—whether it is credit counseling, debt settlement, or any other service—that:

- Charges any fees before it settles your debts or enters you into a DMP plan
- Pressures you to make "voluntary contributions," which is really another name for fees
- Touts a "new government program" to bail out personal credit-card debt
- Guarantees it can make your unsecured debt go away
- Tells you to stop communicating with your creditors, but does not explain the serious consequences
- Tells you it can stop all debt-collection calls and lawsuits
- Guarantees that your unsecured debts can be paid off for pennies on the dollar
- Will not send you free information about the services it provides without requiring you to provide personal financial information, such as your credit-card account numbers and balances
- Tries to enroll you in a DMP without reviewing your financial situation with you
- Offers to enroll you in a DMP without teaching you budgeting and money-management skills
- Demands that you make payments into a DMP before your creditors have accepted you into the program

Avoiding Debt Traps

If you are considering loan products that meet an immediate need, it is important to avoid debt traps on your path to achieving your financial goals.

A debt trap is a situation in which people take out a loan and then have to take out new loans to make the payment on the first loan. It is called a "trap" because, for many people, it becomes difficult to escape the cycle of borrowing and taking on more debt to cover the loan payment and still be able to pay for other expenses such as food, rent, and transportation.

A debt trap can happen when people use short-term loans that have to be paid back in just a couple of payments such as payday loans. Signature loans and deposit advance loans are other examples of short-term loans.

These loans have many things in common. They:

- Are small dollar loans— generally under $500
- Must be repaid quickly—14 days is the median term of payday loans
- Require the borrower to give creditors access to repayment through an authorization to present a check or debit a borrower's deposit account

(Source: "Your Money, Your Goals," Consumer Financial Protection Bureau (CFPB))

Debt Consolidation

You may be able to lower your cost of credit by consolidating your debt through a second mortgage or a home equity line of credit. But, these loans require you to put up your home as collateral. If you cannot make the payments—or if your payments are late—you could lose your home.

What is more, consolidation loans have costs. In addition to interest, you may have to pay "points," with one point equal to one percent of the amount you borrow. Still, these loans may provide certain tax advantages that are not available with other kinds of credit.

Bankruptcy

Personal bankruptcy also may be an option, although its consequences are long-lasting and far-reaching. People who follow the bankruptcy rules receive a discharge—a court order that says they do not have to repay certain debts. However, bankruptcy information (both the date of the filing and the later date of discharge) stays on a credit report for 10 years and can make it difficult to get credit, buy a home, get life insurance, or sometimes get a job. Still, bankruptcy is a legal procedure that offers a fresh start for people who have gotten into financial difficulty and can't satisfy their debts.

There are two main types of personal bankruptcy: Chapter 13 and Chapter 7. Each must be filed in a federal bankruptcy court. Filing fees are several hundred dollars.

Chapter 13 allows people with a steady income to keep property, such as a mortgaged house or a car, that they might otherwise lose through the bankruptcy process. In Chapter 13, the court approves a repayment plan that allows you to use your future income to pay off your debts during three to five years, rather than surrender any property. After you make all the payments under the plan, you receive a discharge of your debts.

Chapter 7 is known as "straight bankruptcy;" it involves liquidating all assets that are not exempt. Exempt property may include automobiles, work-related tools, and basic household furnishings. Some of your property may be sold by a court-appointed official, called a "trustee," or turned over to your creditors.

Both types of bankruptcy may get rid of unsecured debts and stop foreclosures, repossessions, garnishments, and utility shut-offs, as well as debt-collection activities. Both also provide exemptions that let you keep certain assets, although exemption amounts vary by state. Personal bankruptcy usually does not erase child support, alimony, fines, taxes, and some student-loan obligations. And, unless you have an acceptable plan to catch up on your debt under Chapter 13, bankruptcy usually does not allow you to keep property when your creditor has an unpaid mortgage or security lien on it.

You must get credit counseling from a government-approved organization within six months before you file for any bankruptcy relief. You can find a state-by-state list of government-approved organizations at the U.S. Trustee Program, the organization within the U.S. Department of Justice (DOJ) that supervises bankruptcy cases and trustees. Also, before you file a Chapter 7 bankruptcy case, you must satisfy a "means test." This test requires you to confirm that your income does not exceed a certain amount. The amount varies by state and is publicized by the U.S. Trustee Program.

Debt Scams

Advance-Fee Loans

Some companies guarantee you a loan if you pay them a fee in advance. The fee may range from $100 to several hundred dollars. Resist the temptation to follow-up on these advance-fee loan guarantees. They may be illegal. It is true that many legitimate creditors offer extensions of credit through telemarketing and require an application or appraisal fee in advance. But, legitimate creditors never guarantee that you will get the loan—or even represent that a loan is likely. Under the FTC's TSR, a seller or telemarketer who guarantees or represents a high likelihood of your getting a loan or some other extension of credit may not ask for—or accept—payment until you get the loan.

Credit Repair

Be suspicious of claims from so-called credit-repair clinics. Many companies appeal to people with poor credit histories, promising to clean up their credit reports for a fee. But, anything these companies can do for you for a fee, you can do yourself—for free. You have the right to correct inaccurate information in your file, but no one—regardless of their claims—can remove accurate negative information from your credit report. Only time and a conscientious effort to repay your debts will improve your credit report. Federal—and some state—laws ban these companies from charging you a fee until the services are fully performed.

CHAPTER 47

DEBT COLLECTION FAQS

About This Chapter: This chapter includes text excerpted from "Debt Collection FAQs," Federal Trade Commission (FTC), March 2018.

When a debt collector calls, it is important to know your rights and what you need to do. The Federal Trade Commission (FTC) enforces the Fair Debt Collection Practices Act (FDCPA), which makes it illegal for debt collectors to use abusive, unfair, or deceptive practices when they collect debts.

What Types of Debts Are Covered?

Your credit-card debt, auto loans, medical bills, student loans, mortgage, and other household debts are covered. Business debts are not.

Can Debt Collectors Contact Me Any Time or Any Place?

No. Debt collectors cannot contact you at inconvenient times or places. They cannot contact you before 8 a.m. or after 9 p.m., unless you agree to it. They also cannot contact you at work if they are told you are not allowed to get calls there.

How Can a Debt Collector Contact Me?

Debt collectors can call you or send letters, emails, or text messages to collect a debt.

How Can I Stop a Debt Collector from Contacting Me?

Send a letter by mail asking for contact to stop. (Make yourself a copy before you do.) You might want to send it by certified mail and pay for a "return receipt" so you have a record the collector received it. Once the collector gets your letter, it can only contact you to confirm it will stop contacting you or to tell you a specific action, such as filing a lawsuit, will be taken. If you are represented by an attorney and inform the collector, the collector must communicate with your attorney, not you, unless the attorney fails to respond within a reasonable period of time to the communication from the debt collector.

You might want to talk to the collector at least once, even if you do not think you owe the debt or cannot repay it immediately. That way you can confirm whether it is really your debt. If it is your debt, you can find out from the collector more information about it. In talking with a debt collector, be careful about sharing your personal or financial information, especially if you are not already familiar with the collector.

Can a Debt Collector Contact Anyone Else about My Debt?

A debt collector generally cannot discuss your debt with anyone but you or your spouse. If an attorney is representing you, the debt collector has to contact the attorney. A collector can contact other people to find out your address, your home phone number, and where you work, but usually cannot contact them more than once.

What Does the Debt Collector Have to Tell Me about the Debt?

A collector has to send you a written "validation notice" within five days of first contacting you. The notice has to say:

- How much money you owe
- The name of the creditor you owe it to
- What to do if you do not think it is your debt

What If I Do Not Think I Owe the Debt?

You can send the debt collector a letter saying you do not owe any or all of the money or asking for verification of the debt. If you send the letter within 30 days of getting the validation notice, the collector has to send you written verification of the debt, like a copy of a bill for the amount you owe, before they can start trying to collect the debt again. You also can get a collector to stop contacting you, at any time, by sending a letter by mail asking for contact to stop.

What Are Debt Collectors Not Allowed to Do?

They cannot harass you. For example, they cannot:

- Threaten you with violence or harm
- Use obscene or profane language
- Repeatedly use the phone to annoy you

They cannot lie. For example, they cannot:

- Misrepresent the amount you owe
- Lie about being attorneys or government representatives
- Falsely claim you will be arrested, or claim legal action will be taken against you if it is not true

They cannot engage in unfair practices. For example, they cannot:

- Try to collect interest, fees, or other charges on top of the amount you owe, unless the original contract or your state law allows it
- Deposit a postdated check early
- Take or threaten to take your property unless it can be done legally

Can I Control Which Debts My Payments Apply To?

Yes. If a debt collector is trying to collect more than one debt from you, it must apply any payment you make to the debt you choose. A debt collector may not apply a payment to a debt you say you do not owe.

What Should I Do If a Debt Collector Sues Me?

If a debt collector files a lawsuit against you to collect a debt, respond, either personally or through your attorney, by the date specified in the court papers. That will preserve your rights.

Can a Debt Collector Take Money from My Paycheck?

Yes, but the collector must first sue you to get a court order—called a "garnishment"—that says it can take money from your paycheck to pay your debts. A collector also can seek a court order to take money from your bank account. Do not ignore a lawsuit, or you could lose the opportunity to fight a court order.

Can My Federal Benefits Be Garnished?

Many federal benefits are generally exempt from garnishment, though they might still be garnished to pay delinquent taxes, alimony, child support, or student loans. States have their own laws about which state benefits can be garnished.

What If My Debt Is Old?

Debt collectors have a certain number of years they can sue you and win to collect a debt. It is called the "statute of limitations," and usually begins when you fail to make a payment on a debt. Once it is over, your unpaid debt is considered "time-barred," but in some states, you have to raise the age of the debt as a defense to win.

How long the statute of limitations on a debt lasts depends on what kind of debt it is, and the law in your state or the state specified in your credit contract.

Also, under the laws of some states, if you make a payment or provide written acknowledgment of your debt, the clock may start ticking again.

Can a Debt Collector Contact Me about a Time-Barred Debt?

Yes. Even if a debt collector cannot successfully sue you over a time-barred debt, you may still owe it.

What If I Am Not Sure Whether My Debt Is Time-Barred?

Ask the collector when its records show you made your last payment. You also can send the collector a letter within 30 days of receiving a written notice of the debt. Explain why you are disputing the debt and that you want to verify it. A collector must stop trying to collect until it gives you verification.

Does a Time-Barred Debt Stay on My Credit Report?

Maybe. The statute of limitations for a debt is usually different from the reporting period for a debt on your credit report. In general, negative information stays on your credit report for seven years.

Do I Have to Pay a Debt That Is Considered Time-Barred?

It is up to you. Consider talking to an attorney before you decide. You can:

- Pay nothing. The collector cannot sue you, but can continue to contact you unless you send a letter by mail asking for contact to stop.
- Make a partial payment. In some states, if you pay any amount on a time-barred debt or even promise to pay, the debt is "revived," and the statute of limitations resets. The collector might be able to sue you to collect the full amount of the debt, which may include extra interest and fees.
- Pay off the debt. Some collectors will accept less than what you owe to settle a debt. Before you make any payment to settle a debt, get a signed form or letter from the collector that says the amount you are paying settles the entire debt and releases you from any further obligation. Also, keep a record of the payments you make to pay off the debt.

What Should I Do If I Am Sued for a Time-Barred Debt?

You still need to respond. Consider talking to an attorney. If you ignore a lawsuit, the collector could get a court judgment and garnishment against you. Tell the judge the debt is time-barred, and show a copy of the verification notice from the collector or any information that shows the date of your last payment.

Where Do I Report a Debt Collector for an Alleged Violation?

Report any problems you have with a debt collector to:

- Your state Attorney General's office
- The Federal Trade Commission
- The Consumer Financial Protection Bureau

Many states have their own debt-collection laws that are different from the federal Fair Debt Collection Practices Act (FDCPA). Your Attorney General's office can help you determine your rights under your state's law.

If You Think That a Caller May Be a Fake Debt Collector

- **Ask the caller for his or her name, company, street address, and telephone number.** Tell the caller that you refuse to discuss any debt until you get a written "validation notice." The notice must include the amount of the debt, the name of the creditor you owe, and your rights under the FDCPA. If a caller refuses to give you all of this information, do not pay! Paying a fake debt collector will not always make them go away. They may make up another debt to try to get more money from you.
- **Stop speaking with the caller.** If you have the caller's address, send a letter demanding that the caller stop contacting you, and keep a copy of your files. By law, real debt collectors must stop calling you if you ask them to in writing.
- **Do not give the caller personal, financial, or other sensitive information.** Never give out or confirm personal, financial, or other sensitive information, such as your bank account, credit card, or Social Security number, unless you know whom you are dealing with. Scam artists, like fake debt collectors, can use your information to commit identity theft—charging your existing credit cards, opening a new credit card, checking, or savings accounts, writing fraudulent checks, or taking out loans in your name.
- **Contact your creditor.** If the debt is legitimate—but you think the collector may not be—contact your creditor about the calls. Share the information you have about the suspicious calls and find out who, if anyone, the creditor has authorized to collect the debt.
- **Report the call.** Contact the FTC and your state Attorney General's office with information about suspicious callers. Many states have their own debt collection laws in addition to the federal FDCPA. Your Attorney General's office can help you determine your rights under your state's law.

What Else Can I Do If I Think a Debt Collector Has Broken the Law?

You can sue a collector in a state or federal court within one year of the date the law was violated. You can sue for damages, such as lost wages and medical bills. If you cannot prove damages, you can still be awarded up to $1,000, plus reimbursement for attorney's fees and court costs. A group of people suing as part of a class-action lawsuit can recover money for damages up to $500,000, or one percent of the collector's net worth, whichever amount is lower.

Even if a court finds a debt collector violated the FDCPA in trying to collect a debt, you still owe the debt.

CHAPTER 48
PREPAYMENT PENALTY

About This Chapter: Text in this chapter begins with excerpts from "What Is a Prepayment Penalty?" Consumer Financial Protection Bureau (CFPB), September 25, 2017; Text under the heading "Can I Be Charged a Penalty for Paying Off My Mortgage Early?" is excerpted from "Can I Be Charged a Penalty for Paying Off My Mortgage Early?" Consumer Financial Protection Bureau (CFPB), March 18, 2016; Text under the heading "Can I Prepay My Loan at Any Time without Penalty?" is excerpted from "Can I Prepay My Loan at Any Time without Penalty?" Consumer Financial Protection Bureau (CFPB), June 8, 2016; Text under the heading "Financing a Car? Ask about Prepayment Penalties" is excerpted from "Financing a Car? Ask about Pre-Payment Penalties," Federal Trade Commission (FTC), April 4, 2014.

A prepayment penalty is a fee that some lenders charge if you pay off all or part of your loan early. If you have a prepayment penalty, you would have agreed to this when you closed on your home. Not all mortgages have a prepayment penalty.

Typically, a prepayment penalty only applies if you pay off the entire loan balance—for example, because you sold your home, or are refinancing your loan—within a specific number of years (usually 3 or 5 years). In some cases, a prepayment penalty could apply if you pay off a large amount of your loan all at once. Prepayment penalties do not normally apply if you pay extra principal on your loan in small chunks at a time—but it is always a good idea to double-check with the lender.

If you have a problem with your loan, you can submit a complaint to the Consumer Financial Protection Bureau (CFPB) online or by calling 855-411-CFPB (855-411-2372).

If you are behind on your loan, or having a hard time making payments, you can use the CFPB's "Find a Counselor" tool to get a list of housing counseling agencies in your area that are approved by the U.S. Department of Housing and Urban Development (HUD). You can also call the HOPE™ Hotline, open 24 hours a day, 7 days a week, at 888-995-HOPE (888-995-4673).

Can I Be Charged a Penalty for Paying off My Loan Early?

Whether you can be charged a penalty for paying off your loan early depends on what type of loan you have and the specific terms of your loan.

Tip: If a loan you are considering has a prepayment penalty, make sure to read the fine print carefully. Make sure you understand exactly the circumstances under which you will have to pay, and how much. Ask your lender for a quote for a similar loan without a prepayment penalty so you can compare total costs and make an informed decision.

Tip: When you receive your Truth in Lending Act (TILA) disclosure, review it along with your contract before signing. Look for information about your loan amount, your interest rate, annual percentage rate (APR), payment amount and any prepayment penalties. If what is on paper does not match what the lender or dealer told you, ask for an explanation and new paperwork. Remember, many aspects of the loan are negotiable. Ask for a loan that does not have a prepayment penalty if that is important to you. If you do not like the terms of a loan and the lender will not negotiate, you can always shop around for a different lender with terms that better suit your needs.

Some loans have prepayment penalties during the first years of the loan. These fees may impose substantial costs on homeowners with adjustable-rate mortgage loans who want to refinance before their rates increase, and some fixed mortgages have prepayment penalties as well.

Many states have laws that limit the amount or duration of these penalties. Whether your loan carries a prepayment penalty must have been disclosed in your loan documents. Sometimes it is only disclosed in something called the "Addendum to the Note"—look at the Note and anything with "Addendum" in the title.

Can I Prepay My Loan at Any Time without Penalty?

Whether you can pay off your loan early without a penalty depends on your contract and on your state's law.

If the lender wants to charge you a penalty or fee to pay off the loan early, the contract has to contain a prepayment penalty clause. Review your Truth in Lending disclosures and the contract before you sign the agreement. These documents will tell you whether there is a penalty for paying early. You should also ask your lender, or the auto dealer if you are getting dealer financing, if there is a prepayment penalty. If there is, you can negotiate to have the penalty removed from the contract or ask for a different loan.

Why it matters: If your loan has a high-interest rate, you may later be able to refinance at a lower interest rate and payment. When you refinance, you prepay the original loan in full. Ask your bank, credit union, or other lenders about interest rates.

Financing a Car? Ask about Prepayment Penalties

If you are in the market for a new or used car, you may be considering financing options. For example, you might get a loan from a bank or use dealership financing. In either case, you will have to sign a contract that specifies the terms, including how much money you owe and what your payments are.

Remember that the terms of this contract have a big impact on the total cost of the car. For example, a five-year contract may have lower monthly payments than a three-year contract. But, your total cost will be higher. Use the worksheet at www.consumer.ftc.gov/articles/0056-financing-or-leasing-car#shop to compare offers with different terms.

When considering a contract, here is one question that is well worth asking: Can I pay off the debt early without paying a penalty? The answer depends on how the contract is structured. Before signing any paperwork, it is important to know if the terms call for simple interest or precomputed interest.

- Simple interest is calculated based on the amount you owe. The quicker you pay it off, the less interest you will pay.
- Precomputed interest is a fixed amount, calculated and added at the beginning of the contract. Even if you pay it off early, you still pay the interest in full. If a refund or rebate of interest is included in your agreement, you may get back some of the interest you paid—but not all of it.

The "prepayment penalty" is another term to watch for. Banks and finance companies sometimes require borrowers who pay off a debt early to pay a fee.

When negotiating terms, ask about a simple interest contract with no prepayment penalties. Shop around and compare offers from dealerships with offers from banks or credit unions.

And remember that even if your contract allows you to make extra payments, there may be a special process to do so. Before sending any extra money, contact the company's customer-service department and ask about the process for making a principal-only payment. Otherwise, your extra payment might not be credited properly to your account.

Be sure to make your scheduled payments on time until you have paid for the loan in full. Making payments late has consequences: late fees add up, and late payments can affect your credit. When you believe you have paid every dollar you owe, ask for a written statement that says so.

CHAPTER 49
VEHICLE REPOSSESSION

About This Chapter: This chapter includes text excerpted from "Vehicle Repossession," Federal Trade Commission (FTC), November 2008.

Chances are you rely on your vehicle to get you where you need to go—and when you need to go—whether it is to work, school, the grocery store, or the soccer field. But, if you are late with your car payments, or in some states, if you do not have adequate auto insurance, your vehicle could be taken away from you.

When you finance or lease a vehicle, your creditor or lessor has important rights that end once you have paid off your loan or lease obligation. These rights are established by the contract you signed and the law of your state. For example, if you do not make timely payments on the vehicle, your creditor may have the right to "repossess"—or take back–your car without going to court or warning you in advance. Your creditor also may be able to sell your contract to a third party, called an "assignee," who may have the same right to seize the car as the original creditor.

The Federal Trade Commission (FTC), the nation's consumer protection agency, wants you to know that your creditor's rights may be limited. Some states impose rules about how your creditor may repossess the vehicle and resell it to reduce or eliminate your debt. Creditors that violate any rules may lose other rights against you or have to pay you damages.

Seizing the Vehicle

In many states, your creditor can seize your vehicle as soon as you default on your loan or lease. Your contract should state what constitutes a default, but failure to make a payment on time is a typical example.

However, if your creditor agrees to change your payment date, the terms of your original contract may not apply any longer. If your creditor agrees to such a change, make sure you have it in writing. Oral agreements are difficult to prove.

Once you are in default, the laws of most states permit the creditor to repossess your car at any time, without notice, and to come onto your property to do so. But, when seizing the vehicle, your creditor may not commit a "breach of the peace." In some states, that means using physical force, threats of force, or even removing your car from a closed garage without your permission.

Should there be a breach of the peace in seizing your car, your creditor may be required to pay a penalty or to compensate you if any harm is done to you or your property. A breach of peace also may give you a legal defense if your creditor sues you to collect a "deficiency judgment"—that is, the difference between what you owe on the contract (plus repossession and sale expenses) and what your creditor gets from the resale of your vehicle.

Selling the Vehicle

Once your vehicle has been repossessed, your creditor may decide to either keep it as compensation for your debt or resell it in a public or private sale. In some states, your creditor must let you know what will happen to the car. For example, if the car will be sold at public auction, state law may require that the creditor tell you the time and place of the sale so that you can attend and participate in the bidding. If the vehicle will be sold privately, you may have a right to know the date of the sale.

In any of these circumstances, you may be entitled to "redeem"—or buy back—the vehicle by paying the full amount you owe (usually, that includes your past-due payments and the entire remaining debt), in addition to the expenses connected with the repossession, such as storage, preparation for sale, and attorney fees. Or you could try to buy back the vehicle by bidding on it at the repossession sale.

Some states have consumer protection laws that allow you to "reinstate" your loan. This means you can reclaim your car by paying the amount you are behind on your loan, together with your creditor's repossession expenses. Of course, if you reclaim your car, your future payments must be made on time, and you must meet the terms of your reinstated contract to avoid another repossession.

Any resale of a repossessed vehicle must be conducted in a "commercially reasonable manner." Your creditor does not have to get the highest possible price for the vehicle—or even a good price. But, a resale price that is below fair market value may indicate that the sale was not commercially reasonable. "Commercially reasonable" may depend on the standard sales practices in your area. A creditor's failure to resell your car in a commercially reasonable manner may give you a claim against that creditor for damages or a defense against a deficiency judgment.

Personal Property in the Vehicle

Regardless of the method used to dispose of a repossessed car, a creditor may not keep or sell any personal property found inside. In some states, your creditor must tell you what personal items were found in your car and how you can retrieve them. Your creditor also may be required to use reasonable care to prevent anyone else from removing your property from the car. If your creditor cannot account for articles left in your vehicle, you may want to speak to an attorney about your right to compensation.

What If the Lender Offers to Just Take the Vehicle Back and Forgive the Loan? Will It Affect My Credit Report?

You must get the lender to state in writing that returning the vehicle fully satisfies your loan; otherwise, you may still be liable on the loan and for any deficiency.

Additionally, you must ask the lender to confirm in writing that it will not report your return of the vehicle to the credit reporting agencies as a "repossession." Get a full release from the lender if you turn over the vehicle and the keys voluntarily. Unless you take these steps, your returning the vehicle and turning in the keys does not stop the lender from claiming that you owe more money on your auto loan or a deficiency. A loan delinquency and a repossession will stay on your credit report for seven years from the date of the delinquency or repossession.

(Source: "What If the Lender Offers to Just Take the Vehicle Back and Forgive the Loan? Will It Affect My Credit Report?" Consumer Financial Protection Bureau (CFPB))

Paying the Deficiency

Any difference between what you owe on your contract (plus certain expenses) and what your creditor gets for reselling the vehicle is called a "deficiency." For example, if you owe $10,000 on the car and your creditor sells it for $7,500 the deficiency is $2,500 plus any other fees you owe under the contract. Those might include fees related to the repossession and early termination of your lease or early payoff of your financing. In most states, your creditor is allowed to sue you for a deficiency judgment to collect the remaining amount owed as long as it followed the proper procedures for repossession and sale. Similarly, your creditor must pay you if there are surplus funds after the sale proceeds are applied to the outstanding contract obligation and related expenses, but this situation is less common.

You may have a legal defense against a deficiency judgment if, for example, your creditor breached the peace when seizing the vehicle, failed to sell the car in a commercially reasonable manner, or waited too long before suing you. An attorney will be able to tell you whether you have grounds to contest a deficiency judgment.

Electronic Disabling Devices

Some creditors might not provide you with financing unless you agree to the installation of an electronic device that prevents your car from starting if you do not make your payments on time. Depending on your contract with the lender and your state's laws, using that sort of device may be considered the same as a repossession or a breach of the peace. How your state treats the use of these devices could affect your rights. Contact your state consumer protection agency or an attorney if you have questions about the use of these devices in your state.

Talking with Your Creditor or Lessor

It is easier to try to prevent a vehicle repossession from taking place than to dispute it after the fact. Contact your creditor as soon as you realize you will be late with a payment. Many creditors work with consumers they believe will be able to pay soon, even if slightly late. You may be able to negotiate a delay in your payment or a revised schedule of payments. If you can reach an agreement to change your original contract, get it in writing to avoid questions later.

However, your creditor or lessor may refuse to accept late payments or make other changes in your contract—and may demand that you return the car. If you agree to a "voluntary repossession," you may reduce your creditor's expenses, which you would be responsible for paying. But, even if you return the car voluntarily, you still are responsible for paying any deficiency on your contract, and your creditor may still enter the late payments or repossession on your credit report.

Finally, if you are facing, or already in, bankruptcy, ask an attorney for information about your rights to the vehicle during that process.

CHAPTER 50
FILING CAR COMPLAINTS

About This Chapter: This chapter includes text excerpted from "Car Complaints," USA.gov, December 13, 2019.

If you have a complaint about your car, file it with the dealer, lender, or manufacturer. If you do not get results, you can contact a state or federal government agency. If your complaint is about:

- **Deceptive car advertisements or dealers**—File a complaint with your state consumer protection agency (CPA) and the Federal Trade Commission (FTC).
- **Terms of your auto loan agreement or payments**—File a complaint with the Consumer Financial Protection Bureau (CFPB).
- **Car warranty**—Contact your state's Attorney General. But, if you bought a used car from a private owner, the warranty may not be valid.
- **Safety of your car, child car seats, or tires**—File a complaint with the Department of Transportation (DOT).

Some agencies will investigate your complaint. Others accept complaints so that they can file a case against the company in the future.

Lemon Laws

A car is called a "lemon" when it is determined that the vehicle is defective beyond repair. Most states have some form of a lemon law to protect car buyers. These laws tend to only apply to new cars. Check with your state's consumer protection office to see if they also cover used cars. Each state has its own requirements, but common factors to qualify as a lemon include:

- **The number of miles driven**—The defects had to happen within a certain number of months or miles driven.
- **Major defects**—Defects have to involve the actual operation of the car. Examples include the ignition, brakes, engine, or transmission.

Learn How the Complaint Process Works

When you submit a complaint to the CFPB, your complaint goes through several steps that help you get a response about your issue and help us identify problems in the marketplace.

1. **Complaint submitted.** You submit a complaint about an issue you have with a company about a consumer financial product or service, or another government agency forwards your complaint to the CFPB. You will receive email updates and can log in to track the status of your complaint.
2. **Review and route.** The CFPB will forward your complaint and any documents you provide to the company and work to get a response from them. If CFPB finds that another government agency would be better able to assist, it will forward your complaint to them and let you know.
3. **Company response.** The company reviews your complaint, communicates with you as needed, and reports back about the steps taken or that will be taken on the issue you identify in your complaint.
4. **Complaint published.** The CFPB publishes information about your complaint—such as the subject and date of the complaint—on their public Consumer Complaint Database. With your consent, it will also publish your description of what happened, after taking steps to remove personal information.
5. **Consumer review.** The CFPB will let you know when the company responds. You will be able to review the company's response and will have 60 days to provide feedback about the company's response.

(Source: "Learn How the Complaint Process Works," Consumer Financial Protection Bureau (CFPB))

- **Reasonable repair attempts**—You have to give mechanics multiple chances to repair the problems.
- **The number of days in the shop**—Your car has to have been in the mechanic's shop for a significant number of days, (generally 30 days or more) within a year.

To get your problem resolved, first contact the car manufacturer. Send the manufacturer a complaint letter by certified mail detailing the problems. Include copies of work orders and invoices, and your request for a refund or other solution. If the manufacturer does not help, you still may be able to resolve the problem. Many car contracts have mandatory arbitration clauses to settle disputes so that maybe your next step. Get the rules specific to where you live from your state Attorney General or consumer protection office.

Also, contact the Better Business Bureau (BBB) auto line at www.bbbprograms.org/programs/bbb-autoline. This lemon law complaint program covers car warranty issues against participating manufacturers.

Mandatory Arbitration Clauses

Mandatory arbitration clauses are phrases written into contracts that state that if you have a dispute with a company, you must resolve it through arbitration. These clauses can prevent you from filing a lawsuit against a company. Arbitration clauses are fairly common in automotive, credit card, and cell phone contracts. But now, they are appearing in website terms and conditions statements, coupons, or corporate social media profiles. While arbitration can be less expensive, it is sometimes seen as unfair to make arbitration a requirement before a negative incident has happened or knowing how serious the problem is. Also, the decisions are binding, so you cannot appeal the decision, even if the company was severely negligent.

Before you sign a contract or even use a website, read the contract or terms of service for mentions of "arbitration," "binding arbitration," or "resolution programs." This language is often in the fine print of the contract and can be easily missed. Also, note that some companies may let you opt-out of these clauses if you do so within 30 days.

CHAPTER 51

NATIONAL MOTOR VEHICLE TITLE INFORMATION SYSTEM

About This Chapter: This chapter includes text excerpted from "For Consumers—What Is NMVTIS?" National Motor Vehicle Title Information System (NMVTIS), U.S. Department of Justice (DOJ), January 29, 2009.

The National Motor Vehicle Title Information System (NMVTIS) is an electronic system that provides consumers with valuable information about a vehicle's condition and history. Prior to purchasing a vehicle, the NMVTIS allows consumers to find information on the vehicle's title, most recent odometer reading, brand history, and, in some cases, historical theft data.

A "brand" is a descriptive label that states assign to a vehicle to identify the vehicle's current or prior condition, such as "junk," "salvage," "flood," or another designation. By capturing into one system specific information from multiple entities (state motor vehicle titling agencies, automobile recyclers, junk and salvage yards, and insurance carriers), the NMVTIS offers states and consumers protection from title fraud, offers detection of stolen vehicles from being retitled, and makes it more difficult for criminals to use stolen vehicles for criminal purposes. For example:

- After Hurricane Katrina, authorities reported truckloads of flooded vehicles being taken out of Louisiana to other states as far away as the upper Midwest, where they were dried out, cleaned, and readied for sale to unsuspecting consumers in states that do not brand flood vehicles. Prospective purchasers of these vehicles may not have known that the vehicles had been subjected to a saltwater flood that made the vehicles' electrical systems (including their airbag sensors) more prone to failure. The NMVTIS is designed to prevent vehicle histories such as these from being "washed," or concealed, because it is designed to serve as a national repository of vehicle brand information. Fully implemented, the NMVTIS will have data from every state and will be queried before any state issues a

Tips on How to Steer Clear of Car Cloning

- If you think your car was cloned (for instance, you receive notice of unpaid parking tickets that are not yours), contact your local police.
- If you are car shopping, beware of a car being sold for substantially less than comparable makes and models.
- Get a copy of the car's vehicle history report.
- Check out the VIN plate on the dashboard for any evidence of tampering (scratches, etc.).
- Look for incorrect spellings on paperwork, such as vehicle titles.
- Trust your intuition—if it sounds too good to be true, it probably is!

(Source: "Steering Clear of Car Cloning," Federal Bureau of Investigation (FBI))

vehicle a new title, making it extremely difficult (if not impossible) to wash a "flood" designation from a vehicle.

- South Florida law enforcement involved in "Operation Roadrunner" recovered approximately 250 cloned, stolen vehicles across the U.S. and expressed their belief that had the NMVTIS been fully implemented, much of this criminal activity would have been prevented. In this multistate investigation, it was discovered that a criminal enterprise based in South Florida was stealing vehicles and replacing the vehicle identification numbers (VINs) on the stolen vehicles with VINs removed from other vehicles of the same make, model, and year. These "cloned" vehicles were then used for criminal purposes or sold to unsuspecting consumers. Because the stolen cars and their fraudulent title paperwork displayed legitimate VINs taken from other automobiles (i.e., they were "clones"), consumers, state's motor vehicle titling agencies, and law enforcement could not detect the vehicles' true stolen status. The criminal enterprise that was taken down in this investigation was linked to many other types of criminal activity, including major violent crimes.
- In one Western state, Department of Motor Vehicles (DMV) clerks checking the NMVTIS prior to issuing a new title have identified vehicles suspected of being stolen and vehicles with potentially fraudulent documentation and have been able to notify law enforcement instantly, before a new title was issued and while the suspects were still in the DMV offices. This has prevented crimes (e.g., fraud) and assisted law enforcement in investigating other crimes (e.g., theft).

The NMVTIS was created to:

- Prevent the introduction or reintroduction of stolen motor vehicles into interstate commerce

- Protect states and consumers (individual and commercial) from fraud
- Reduce the use of stolen vehicles for illicit purposes, including the funding of criminal enterprises
- Provide consumers protection from unsafe vehicles

In addition, the system provides law enforcement with an important tool to reduce auto theft and vehicle-related crimes.

National Motor Vehicle Title Information System: Consumer Benefits

The law requires the NMVTIS information to be made available to prospective purchasers, including businesses that purchase used automobiles or commercial consumers. Commercial consumers include lenders who are financing the purchase of automobiles (and in many cases actually own them as the lien holders) and automobile dealers. Lenders and dealers are integral components of the automobile purchasing and titling process, and their ability to avoid fraud also protects individual consumers.

Prior to purchasing a vehicle, consumers can search the NMVTIS to discover:

- Information from a vehicle's current title, including the vehicle's brand history. "Brands" are descriptive labels regarding the status of a motor vehicle, such as "junk," "salvage," and "flood" vehicles.
- The latest reported odometer readings
- Any determination that the vehicle is "salvage" by an insurance company or a self-insuring organization (including those vehicles determined to be a "total loss")
- Any reports of the vehicle being transferred or sold to an auto recycler, junkyard, or salvage yard

Through the NMVTIS, once a vehicle is branded by a state motor vehicle titling agency, that brand becomes a permanent part of the vehicle's NMVTIS record. Vehicles that incur significant damage are often branded "junk" or "salvage." Motor vehicles with brands on their titles can without much difficulty have their brands "washed" (i.e., removed) from the titles. Brand washing can occur if the motor vehicle is retitled in another state that does not check with the originating state or does not check with all states that previously issued a title on that vehicle to determine whether the vehicle has any existing brands that may not be shown on the current paper title. Fraud can occur when these vehicles are presented for sale to unsuspecting consumers without disclosure of their true condition, including brand history. These consumers may pay more than the vehicle's fair market value and may purchase an unsafe vehicle.

Experian Automotive reported that in just the first 6 months of 2008 there were more than 185,000 titles that were initially branded in one state, and then transferred and retitled in a second state in a way that resulted in the issuance of a purportedly clean title. The NMVTIS is effective in greatly reducing (if not eliminating) this type of fraud, preventing a significant number of crimes, and potentially saving the lives of consumers who might otherwise unknowingly purchase unsafe vehicles.

Understanding State Differences

The National Motor Vehicle Title Information System (NMVTIS) is designed to collect information from states, but not to change the nomenclature used in, or standards created by, state motor vehicle laws or by state motor vehicle titling agencies. Each state has its own laws, standards, and terminology that are unaffected by the NMVTIS. For example, one state may examine and brand a damaged vehicle as "salvage," while another state may not because the damage may not reach a certain dollar or value threshold (e.g., damage estimate in relation to fair market value) required by that state's laws. In another example, a vehicle recovered from a flood or other natural disaster involving water (e.g., hurricane) may be flagged or branded as "flood" in certain states, but in other states no such designation exists. Because one state may brand or flag a vehicle as a flood vehicle does not mean that other states must also designate the vehicle as "flood." The NMVTIS is valuable because it retains and makes available to users of the system all reported brands applied to a vehicle so that relocating the vehicle from one state to another will not "wash" the brand, because the NMVTIS retains this information and makes it available to any state.

Consumers should also be aware that differences in state procedures and reporting are important to understand. For example, some states exempt vehicles of a certain age from titling, and other states may collect and report varying levels of descriptive information on vehicles (e.g., make, model, color), while several states may report on all motor vehicles, including motorcycles and heavy equipment, despite the requirement to report the NMVTIS on common automobiles only. The U.S. Department of Justice (DOJ) recommends that consumers educate themselves on these types of issues before relying on any vehicle history report information from this or any other service provider.

Understanding the National Motor Vehicle Title Information System Search Results

A National Motor Vehicle Title Information System Vehicle History Report is intentionally concise. It is intended to provide data on only five key indicators associated with preventing fraud and theft. A "clean" NMVTIS report is a GOOD thing!

While 87 percent of the United States vehicle population is in the NMVTIS, more than half of the states report data to the system and approximately 20 million salvage or total loss records are in the NMVTIS, until all entities are reporting into the NMVTIS as required, consumers should be aware of the possibility that a search may yield a false negative indication, such as "no junk or salvage history." These same gaps can exist in other, private vehicle history databases and consumers should educate themselves on these issues as well.

In addition, the NMVTIS data comes from multiple sources. These sources are independent and are not required to follow or prescribe to a uniform approach for defining vehicle conditions and titling. For example, the vehicle having been in the possession of a junk or salvage yard does not mean that a state must brand the vehicle as "junk" or "salvage." State laws vary in this regard and may not require application of such a brand, despite the fact that the vehicle was treated as salvage at some point. The bottom line is that the standards governing these matters vary from jurisdiction to jurisdiction.

Similarly, an insurance determination of "total loss" does not necessarily mean that a vehicle was destroyed or is worthless. In some cases, such as stolen vehicles that are not recovered within a 30-day period, insurance companies may label these vehicles as "total loss." If the vehicle is later recovered in perfect condition, the "total loss" determination is not removed and the insurance company or an auction company or pool may attempt to sell the vehicle in perfectly good working order.

Consumers should be aware that the information in the NMVTIS is not all of the information that a state may include in its vehicle title records. Consumers are encouraged to consider accessing the actual state title record to ensure that all relevant information is considered before making a vehicle purchase decision.

CHAPTER 52

AUTOMOBILE LOAN MODIFICATION SCAMS

About This Chapter: This chapter includes text excerpted from "Auto Loan Modification Scams," Federal Trade Commission (FTC), April 2012.

Chances are you rely on your car or truck to get you where you need to go. But, if you are late with your car payments, your vehicle could be taken away from you.

If you are having trouble paying your car loan and you are worried about having your vehicle repossessed, you may think that doing business with companies that claim they can reduce your monthly car loan or lease payment can help you avoid repossession. These companies might charge fees of several hundred dollars upfront, tout their relationships with consumer lenders, and bolster their claims to be able to significantly lower your monthly payments with glowing testimonials from "satisfied" customers. Some say that if they cannot make a deal with your lender, they will refund your money.

The promises may sound like a way to get out from under debt. But, the Federal Trade Commission (FTC), the nation's consumer protection agency (CPA), says it is smooth talk by scam artists who are out to take your money and provide nothing in return. In fact, the FTC sued companies that made claims like these, but failed to deliver the auto loan modifications they promised or honor the refund policies they "guaranteed." What is more, in many instances, the companies never even contacted any lenders.

The victims of these auto loan modification scams tell the same story: After paying a fee for the promise of a loan modification, nothing was done to secure the results that were promised. The scam artists often compounded the problem by telling their clients to stop making their car payments while the companies claimed to be in negotiations with lenders. Some victims learned that the companies had not done anything only after their lender contacted them about repossessing their vehicle. In some instances, the scam artists demanded additional fees to continue working on their client's cases.

These scams may sound familiar. Some scam artists have taken a page from the mortgage loan modification fraud playbook, moving from trying to dupe homeowners

Truth-in-Lending Disclosure

The federal Truth-in-Lending Act—or "TILA" for short—requires that borrowers receive written disclosures about important terms of credit before they are legally bound to pay the loan.

These important terms include:

- **Annual percentage rate (APR),** the cost of credit expressed as a yearly rate in a percentage
- **Finance charge,** the cost of credit expressed as a dollar amount (this is the total amount of interest and certain fees you will pay over the life of the loan if you make every payment when due)
- **Amount financed,** the dollar amount of credit provided to you (this is normally the amount you are borrowing)
- **Total of payments,** the sum of all the payments that you will have made at the end of the loan (this includes repayment of the principal amount of the loan plus all of the finance charges)

(Source: "What Is a Truth-in-Lending Disclosure? When Do I Get to See It?" Consumer Financial Protection Bureau (CFPB))

in distress to preying on drivers who cannot make their car payments. The fraud is the same: people pay in advance for a service that is either never performed, or not performed as promised.

If You Are behind on Your Car Payments

If you are having trouble making your car payments, contact your lender directly to discuss your options as early as you can. The longer you wait to call, the fewer options you will have. Typical auto loan modifications involve either deferring missed payments to the end of the loan or extending the loan term to reduce monthly payments. That choice actually increases the total amount you pay in interest, even with a lower interest rate. Creditors rarely reduce the amount of the principal or the interest rate in an auto loan modification.

If Your Vehicle Is Repossessed

If you do not—or cannot—make timely payments on your vehicle, your creditor may have the right to repossess your car without going to court or telling you in advance. Your creditor may be able to sell your contract to a third party, called an "assignee," who may have the same right to seize your car as the original creditor.

Reporting Fraud

If there is a possibility that you have been ripped off by an auto loan modification fraudster, file a complaint with the FTC and your state Attorney General.

CHAPTER 53
THINGS YOU CAN DO TO AVOID FRAUD

About This Chapter: This chapter includes text excerpted from "10 Things You Can Do to Avoid Fraud," Federal Trade Commission (FTC), August 2018.

Crooks use clever schemes to defraud millions of people every year. They often combine new technology with old tricks to get people to send money or give out personal information. Here are some practical tips to help you stay a step ahead.

Spot Imposters

Scammers often pretend to be someone you trust, such as a government official, a family member, a charity, or a company you do business with. Do not send money or give out personal information in response to an unexpected request—whether it comes as a text, a phone call, or an e-mail.

Do Online Searches

Type a company or product name into your favorite search engine with words such as "review," "complaint," or "scam." Or search for a phrase that describes your situation, such as the "Internal Revenue Service (IRS) call." You can even search for phone numbers to see if other people have reported them as scams.

Do Not Believe Your Caller ID

Technology makes it easy for scammers to fake caller ID information, so the name and number you see are not always real. If someone calls asking for money or personal information, hang up. If you think the caller might be telling the truth, call back to a number you know is genuine.

Do Not Pay Upfront for a Promise

Someone might ask you to pay in advance for things such as debt relief, credit and loan offers, mortgage assistance, or a job. They might even say you have won a prize,

Scam artists use a number of elaborate schemes to get your money, and many involve money transfers through companies like Western Union and MoneyGram. Scammers pressure people to use money transfers so they can get the money before their victims realize they have been cheated. Money transfers are virtually the same as sending cash—there are no protections for the sender. Typically, there is no way you can reverse the transaction or trace the money. Also, when you wire money, the recipient can pick it up at one of many locations. That makes it nearly impossible to identify the recipient or track the person down. In some cases, the receiving agents of the money transfer company may be cooperating with a scammer.

(Source: "Using Money Transfer Services," Federal Trade Commission (FTC))

but first, you have to pay taxes or fees. If you do, they will probably take the money and disappear.

Consider How You Pay

Credit cards have significant fraud protection built in, but some payment methods do not. Wiring money through services such as Western Union or MoneyGram is risky because it is nearly impossible to get your money back. That is also true for reloadable cards (such as MoneyPak or Reloadit) and gift cards (such as iTunes or Google Play). Government offices and honest companies will not require you to use these payment methods.

Talk to Someone

Before you give up your money or personal information, talk to someone you trust. Con artists want you to make decisions in a hurry. They might even threaten you. Slow down, check out the story, do an online search, consult an expert—or just tell a friend.

Hang Up on Robocalls

If you answer the phone and hear a recorded sales pitch, hang up and report it to the Federal Trade Commission (FTC). These calls are illegal, and often the products are bogus. Do not press one to speak to a person or to be taken off the list. That could lead to more calls.

Be Skeptical about Free Trial Offers

Some companies use free trials to sign you up for products and bill you every month until you cancel. Before you agree to a free trial, research the company and read the cancellation policy. And always review your monthly statements for charges you do not recognize.

Do Not Deposit a Check and Wire Money Back

By law, banks must make funds from deposited checks available within days, but uncovering a fake check can take weeks. If a check you deposit turns out to be a fake, you are responsible for repaying the bank.

Sign Up for Free Scam Alerts

Sign up for free scam alerts from the FTC at ftc.gov/scams. Get the latest tips and advice about scams sent right to your inbox.

If you spot a scam, report it at ftc.gov/complaint. Your reports help the FTC and other law enforcement investigate scams and bring crooks to justice.

CHAPTER 54
BANKRUPTCY: A LAST RESORT

About This Chapter: Text in this chapter begins with excerpts from "Bankruptcy," U.S. Courts, Federal Judiciary, May 15, 2010; Text beginning with the heading "Filing for Bankruptcy" is excerpted from "Filing for Bankruptcy: What to Know," Federal Trade Commission (FTC), August 2012.

Bankruptcy helps people who can no longer pay their debts get a fresh start by liquidating assets to pay their debts or by creating a repayment plan. Bankruptcy laws also protect financially troubled businesses. This chapter explains the bankruptcy process and laws.

Filing for Bankruptcy

If you plan to file for bankruptcy protection, you must get credit counseling from a government-approved organization within 180 days before you file. You also have to complete a debtor education course before your debts can be discharged.

Approved Credit Counselors and Debtor Educators

The Department of Justice's (DOJ) United States Trustee Program approves organizations to provide the credit counseling and debtor education required for anyone filing for personal bankruptcy. Only the counselors and educators that appear on the U.S. Trustee Program's lists can advertise that they are approved to provide the required counseling and debtor education. By law, the U.S. Trustee Program does not operate in Alabama and North Carolina; in these states, court officials called "Bankruptcy Administrators" approve prebankruptcy credit-counseling organizations and predischarge debtor education course providers.

Counseling and Education Requirements

Prebankruptcy credit counseling and predischarge debtor education may not be provided at the same time. Credit counseling must take place before you file for bankruptcy; debtor education must take place after you file.

You must file a certificate of credit counseling completion when you file for bankruptcy, and provide evidence of completion of debtor education after you file for bankruptcy, but before your debts are discharged. Only credit-counseling organizations and debtor education course providers that have been approved by the U.S. Trustee Program may issue these certificates. To protect against fraud, the certificates are numbered and produced through a central automated system.

Prebankruptcy Counseling

A prebankruptcy counseling session with an approved credit-counseling organization should include an evaluation of your personal financial situation, a discussion of alternatives to bankruptcy, and a personal budget plan. A typical counseling session should last about 60 to 90 minutes, and can take place in person, on the phone, or online. The counseling organization is required to provide the counseling for free for people who cannot afford to pay. If you cannot afford to pay a fee for credit counseling, ask for a fee waiver from the counseling organization before the session begins. Otherwise, you may be charged a fee for the counseling. It will generally cost about $50, depending on where you live and the types of services you receive, among other factors. The counseling organization must discuss any fees with you before you start the counseling session.

Once you complete the required counseling, you must get a certificate as proof. Check the U.S. Trustee's website to be sure that you receive the certificate from a counseling organization that is approved in the judicial district where you are filing bankruptcy. Credit-counseling organizations may not charge an extra fee for the certificate.

Postfiling Debtor Education

A debtor-education course by an approved provider should include information on developing a budget, managing money, and using credit wisely. Like prefiling counseling, debtor-education can take place in person, on the phone, or online. The education session might last longer than the prefiling counseling—about two hours—and the fee is between $50 and $100. As with prefiling counseling, if you cannot afford the session fee, ask the debtor-education provider to waive it. Check the list of approved debtor-education providers online or at the bankruptcy clerk's office in your district.

Once you have completed the required debtor-education course, you should receive a certificate as proof. This certificate is separate from the certificate you received after completing your prefiling credit counseling. Check the U.S. Trustee's website to be sure that you receive the certificate from a debtor-education provider that is approved in the judicial district where you filed for bankruptcy. Unless the debtor-education provider told you there is a fee for the certificate before the education session begins, you cannot be charged an extra fee for it.

Choosing a Credit Counselor

If you are looking for credit counseling to fulfill the bankruptcy law requirements, make sure you receive services only from approved providers for your judicial district. Check the list of approved credit-counseling providers online or at the bankruptcy clerk's office for the district where you will file. Once you have the list of approved organizations, call several to gather information before you pick one. Some key questions to ask are:

- What services do you offer?
- Will you help me develop a plan for avoiding problems in the future?
- What are your fees?
- What if I cannot afford your fees?
- What qualifications do your counselors have? Are they accredited or certified by an outside organization? What training do they receive?
- How do you keep information about me (including my address, phone number, and financial information) confidential and secure?
- How are your employees paid? Are they paid more if I sign up for certain services, if I pay a fee, or if I make a contribution to your organization?

PART 5 | IF YOU NEED MORE HELP OR INFORMATION

CHAPTER 55
LOANS—KEY TERMS

This chapter contains terms excerpted from documents produced by several sources deemed reliable.

accrue: The process in which interest accumulates on a borrower's loan.

amortization: Amortization describes the process of gradually paying off your auto loan. In an amortizing loan, for each of your monthly payments, a portion is applied toward the amount of the loan—the principal—and a portion of the payment is applied toward paying the finance charge—the interest.

annual percentage rate (APR): The annual percentage rate (APR) shows the cost of a loan expressed as a yearly interest rate, including the interest and other fees associated with the loan. Because the APR includes upfront costs paid to obtain the loan, it is usually a higher amount than the interest rate stipulated in the note.

application: The first step in the official loan process to gather and record information about the potential borrower.

assignee: An assignee is a person or a company who buys your auto loan. For example, an auto dealer who extends credit to you may sell your loan to a bank, making the bank the assignee.

automatic or direct debit: A bill-paying method you set up with the merchant or service provider. You provide the merchant or service provider (for example, your cell-phone provider or utility company) with your checking account information and they take the funds from your account each time the bill is due (for example, every month).

bank: A financial institution and business that accepts deposits, makes loans, and handles other financial transactions.

borrower: A person who has been approved to receive a loan and is then obligated to repay it and any additional fees according to the loan terms.

budget: A plan that outlines what money you expect to earn or receive (your income) and how you will save it or spend it (your expenses) for a given period of time; also called a "spending plan."

business plan: A comprehensive planning document which clearly describes the business developmental objective of an existing or proposed business applying for assistance in the Small Business Association (SBA)'s 8(a) or lending programs. The plan outlines what and how and from where the resources needed to accomplish the objective will be obtained and utilized.

buy rate: A buy rate is the interest rate that a potential lender quotes to your dealer when you apply for dealer-arranged automobile loan financing.

buying power: Also called "purchasing power," it is the amount of goods and services that can be purchased by a given unit of currency, taking into account the effect of inflation.

checking account: An account at a bank (sometimes called a "share draft account" at a credit union) that allows you to make deposits, pay bills, and make withdrawals.

cosigner: A cosigner is a person—such as a parent, close family member, or friend—who pledges to pay back a loan if you do not. This can benefit both you and your lender. A co-signer takes full responsibility for paying back the loan.

collateral: Property pledged as security for a loan to ensure repayment of a loan.

comparison shopping: The practice of comparing prices, features, benefits, risks, and other characteristics of two or more similar products or services.

compromise: The settlement of a claim resulting from a defaulted loan for less than the full amount due. Compromise settlement is a procedure available for use only in instances in which the government cannot collect the full amount due within a reasonable time by enforced collection proceedings or in which the cost of such proceedings would not justify such effort.

consumer: A person who buys or receives goods or services for personal needs or use and not for resale.

credit card: An open-ended loan that allows you to borrow money up to a certain limit and carry over an unpaid balance from month to month. There is no fixed time to repay the loan as long as you make the minimum payment due each month. You pay interest on any outstanding credit-card loan balance.

credit history: The history of an individual's debt repayment. For most types of loans, lenders use this information to gauge a potential borrower's ability to repay a loan.

credit insurance: Credit insurance is optional insurance that may pay your auto payments to your lender in certain situations, such as if you die or become disabled. If you are considering credit insurance, make sure you understand the terms of the policy being offered.

credit rating: A grade assigned to denote the net worth and credit standing of an individual or business.

credit report: A record that lists all past and present debts and the timeliness of their repayment, and documents an individual's credit history.

debit card: A plastic card used to make purchases at businesses (like grocery stores and gas stations) with money in your checking account.

debt: Amount owed to another that must be repaid.

default: The failure to repay a loan according to the terms of the loan.

deficiency balance: If your vehicle is repossessed and sold, you may be responsible for paying the difference between the amount left on your loan (plus repossession fees) and the sales price. This is known as a "deficiency balance."

delinquency: Failure of a borrower to make a timely payment on a loan.

disbursement: Payment of loan proceeds to the student or parent borrower. For a consolidation loan, this term refers to sending payoffs to the loan holders of the underlying loans you are consolidating.

down payment: A down payment is an initial, upfront payment you make toward the total cost of the vehicle. Your down payment could be cash, the value of a trade-in, or both. The more you put down, the less you need to borrow.

estate tax: A tax on the value of property you own at your death. It considers everything you own or have certain interests in at the date of death. There is a federal estate tax, and some states have their own estate taxes.

exchange rate: A number that is used to compare the value of money in two different countries. For example, you would use an exchange rate to figure out how many pesos or euros you could get for one U.S. dollar.

extended warranty: An extended warranty or vehicle service contract covers the costs of some types of repairs in addition to or after the manufacturer's warranty ends.

federal income tax: The federal government collects taxes based on the earnings of individuals and businesses, called an "income tax." The federal income tax pays for national programs such as defense, foreign affairs, law enforcement, and interest on the national debt.

federal minimum wage: The lowest national wage as established by law in the Fair Labor Standards Act (FLSA).

finance and insurance department (F&I): If you purchase a vehicle at a dealership, the salesperson may refer you to someone in the F&I or business office. This is the part of the dealership that markets loans and optional add-ons to customers after they have agreed to buy a vehicle at the dealership.

financial aid: When money is given in the form of grants, work-study, loans, and scholarships to help pay for postsecondary tuition and fees, as well as related expenses such as room and board, books, supplies, and transportation.

financial capability: The ability to manage financial resources effectively, understand and apply financial knowledge, demonstrate healthy money habits, and successfully complete financial tasks as planned.

fixed expenses: Expenses, like bills, that must be paid each month and generally cost the same amount. Some fixed expenses, like a utility bill, may also be variable because the amount changes each month depending on usage.

force-placed insurance: In order to get a loan to buy a vehicle, you must have insurance to cover the vehicle itself. If you fail to obtain insurance or you let your insurance lapse, the contract usually gives the lender the right to get insurance to cover the vehicle. This insurance is called "force-placed insurance."

foreign transaction fee: A fee your card provider charges when you use your prepaid card in a foreign country or to pay in a foreign currency. This fee is usually a percentage of your purchase, withdrawal, or other transaction, rather than a flat fee. This fee is also called a "currency conversion fee." Not all cards can be used outside the United States, so check your cardholder agreement before you travel.

grace period: A period of time after you graduate, leave school, or drop below half-time enrollment before you must begin repaying your federal student loan. If you have a Perkins Loan, your grace period is nine months; if you have a FFEL or Direct Stafford Loan, your grace period is six months. (For unsubsidized Stafford Loans, you are responsible for the interest that accrues during the grace period.)

guaranteed auto protection (GAP) insurance: GAP insurance covers the difference (or gap) between the amount you owe on your auto loan and what your insurance pays if your vehicle is stolen, damaged, or totaled. You don't have to buy this insurance, but if you decide you want it, shop around.

income tax: Federal, state, and local taxes on income, both earned (salaries, wages, tips, commissions) and unearned (interest, dividends). Includes both personal and business or corporate income taxes. Not all states and localities have income taxes.

incubator: A facility designed to encourage entrepreneurship and minimize obstacles to new business formation and growth, particularly for high-technology firms, by housing a number of fledgling enterprises that share an array of services. These shared services may include meeting areas, secretarial services, accounting services, research libraries, on-site financial and management counseling and word-processing facilities.

interest rate: The amount of interest charged on a loan, usually expressed as a percentage.

interest: A fee charged for the use of money.

intermediary organization: Organizations that play a vital or fundamental role in encouraging, promoting, and facilitating business-to-business linkages and mentor–protégé partnerships. These can include both nonprofit and for-profit organizations: Chambers of Commerce; trade associations; local, civic, and community groups; state and local governments; academic institutions; and private corporations.

lender: The entity that provides loan funds to the borrower. Depending on the type of loan, the lender may be a bank or other financial institution, or a government agency.

loan: Money borrowed from a lending institution or a government agency, usually repaid with interest.

mandatory binding arbitration: By signing a contract with a mandatory binding arbitration provision, you agree to resolve any disputes about the contract before an arbitrator who decides the dispute instead of a court. You also may agree to waive other rights, such as your ability to appeal a decision or to join a class-action lawsuit.

manufacturer incentives: Manufacturer incentives are special deals, such as zero-percent financing or cash rebates, that you may have seen advertised for new vehicles. Often, they are offered only for certain models.

manufacturer suggested retail price (MSRP): The Manufacturer Suggested Retail Price (MSRP) is the price that the automaker—the manufacturer—suggests that the dealer ask for the vehicle.

mobile banking: A service that allows you to use your smartphone or tablet to manage your bank or credit-union account without the aid of a teller. Generally, you can deposit checks into your account using this service, but not cash.

mortgage: Mortgage loans are used to buy a home or to borrow money against the value of a home you already own.

overdraft: An overdraft occurs when you don't have enough money in your bank account to cover a transaction, but the bank pays the transaction anyway.

payment: Periodic (usually monthly) installments paid to a lender to be applied toward repaying your loan. Payments are generally applied first to accrued interest and then to principal.

principal: The loan amount borrowed from a lender, not including interest or additional fees.

repayment: A loan is borrowed money that must be repaid. You have a choice of repayment plans if you received a FFEL or a Direct Loan as a student. Federal Perkins Loans don't have repayment plan choices; you generally have up to 10 years to repay, however. Your monthly payment will depend on the size of your debt and the length of your repayment period. Repaying Your Student Loans (studentaid.gov/h/manage-loans) explains available repayment options, includes examples of monthly payments for different loan amounts, and covers other topics you need to consider when managing your loans.

risk-based pricing: Risk-based pricing occurs when lenders offer different consumers different interest rates or other loan terms based on the estimated risk that the consumers will fail to pay back their loans.

salary: Compensation received by an employee for services performed. A salary is a fixed sum paid for a specific period of time worked, such as weekly or monthly.

savings account: An account at a bank (sometimes called a "share savings account" at a credit union) used to set aside money and one that pays you interest.

scholarships: Money that students receive based on academic or other achievements to help pay education expenses. Scholarships generally don't have to be repaid.

secured loans: Loans in which your property (things you own) is used as collateral; if you cannot pay back the loan, the lender will take your collateral to get their money back. The lender can also engage in debt collection, file negative information on your credit report, and may sue you.

servicer: An organization that collects loan payments on behalf of a lender.

Social Security number: The nine-digit number on a Social Security card, an important piece of identification issued by the federal government that you'll need to get a job and collect government benefits.

tax deduction: An amount (often a personal or business expense) that reduces income subject to tax.

tax refund: Money owed to taxpayers when their total tax payments are greater than the total tax. Refunds are received from the government.

total cost: This is how much you will pay to buy your vehicle, including the principal, interest, and any down payment or trade-in, over the life of the loan.

transaction fee: A transaction fee is a fee some lenders charge every time you use a debit or credit card for a certain type of transaction. Be sure to ask about fees or read the cardholder agreement associated with your card.

Truth in Lending disclosure: The federal Truth in Lending Act—or "TILA" for short—requires that borrowers receive written disclosures about important terms of credit before they are legally bound to pay the loan.

unauthorized use: Transactions to your ATM, debit, or credit card that you didn't make or approve (such as withdrawals, transfers, purchases, or charges) and for which you received no benefit.

variable-rate financing: Variable-rate financing is financing which allows the interest rate on your loan can change based on the prime rate or another rate called an "index." With a variable-rate loan, the interest rate on the loan changes as the index rate changes meaning that it could go up or down. Because your interest rate can go up, your monthly payment can also go up.

virtual currency: A kind of electronic money. It's a digital representation of value that is not issued by a government, such as a central bank or a public authority, but is accepted as a means of payment and can be transferred, stored, or traded electronically.

wage: Compensation received by employees for services performed. Usually, wages are computed by multiplying an hourly pay rate by the number of hours worked.

CHAPTER 56
ONLINE MONEY-MANAGEMENT TOOLS

Resources in this chapter were compiled from several sources deemed reliable; all websites verified and updated in February 2020.

Financial Calculators

Alliance for Investor Education (AIE)

Savings Calculator
www.investoreducation.org/cindex1.html

Bankrate LLC

Mortgage, Auto, Credit Card, Home Equity, Investment, Retirement, Personal Finance, Savings, and Tax Calculators
www.bankrate.com/calculators.aspx

Choose to Save

American Savings Education Council (ASEC) Auto, Bond, Budget, College, Credit Card, Home, Insurance, Life Expectancy, Mutual Funds, Paycheck Planning, Retiree Health, Retirement, Roth IRA, Savings, Social Security, Stock, and Tax Calculators
www.choosetosave.org/calculators/index.html

FinAid

College Costs and Savings, Integrated Saving/Borrowing, Trust Funds, Needs Analysis, Loans, Budgeting, and Insurance Calculators
www.finaid.org/calculators

Financial Calculators, Inc.

Cash Flow, College, Credit, Home and Mortgage, Tax, Insurance, Paycheck and Benefits, Qualified Plans, Retirement, Saving, Investment Calculators
www.financialcalculators.com

Investopedia
Future and Present Value, Bonds and Present Value, Currency and Forex, Retirement and Personal Finance, Stocks, Annuities
www.investopedia.com/calculator

Money Management International
Financial Wellness Test, Average Interest Rate Calculator, Available Credit Calculator, Debt-to-Income Ratio Calculator
www.moneymanagement.org/tools

Money Matters To Me
Loan, General Interest, Mortgage, and Repayments Calculators
www.moneymatterstome.com/Interactive-Tools/LoanCalculator.htm

My Money
College Planning, Group Life Insurance, Home Buying, Investing, Mortgage, Saving Bonds, Social Security, Tax Withholding, and Thrift Savings Plan Calculators
www.mymoney.gov/Fast/Pages/Results.aspx?k=Calculators&s=All

Smart about Money
National Endowment for Financial Education (NEFE) Retirement and Mutual Fund Cost Calculator
www.smartaboutmoney.org/Tools/Calculators

TimeValue Software
TCalc™
www.timevalue.com/tcalc-financial-calculators

TimeValue Software
TValue™
www.timevalue.com

TreasuryDirect®
Growth, Savings, and Tax Advantage Calculators
www.treasurydirect.gov/indiv/tools/tools_estimationcalc.htm

U.S. Securities and Exchange Commission
Mutual Fund, Tax Comparison, College Savings, Loan, Savings, Social Security Retirement, Ballpark Estimate Retirement, and 529 College Savings Plan Expense Calculator
www.sec.gov/investor/tools.shtml

Financial Quizzes

U.S. Securities and Exchange Commission (SEC)

Test Your Money Smarts Quiz
www.sec.gov/investor/tools/quiz.htm

Games

Investopedia Simulator

Stock Market Game
www.investopedia.com/simulator

LavaMind's Gazillionaire

Fantasy Business Simulation Game
www.gazillionaire.com/index.php

Market Watch

Virtual Stock Market Game
www.marketwatch.com/game

Stock Market Game

Foundation for Investor Education
www.stockmarketgame.org

CHAPTER 57

RESOURCES FOR INFORMATION ON PERSONAL AND AUTOMOBILE LOANS

Resources in this chapter were compiled from several sources deemed reliable; all contact information was verified and updated in February 2020.

Government Agencies That Provide Information about Loans

Consumer Financial Protection Bureau (CFPB)

P.O. Box 2900
Clinton, IA 52733-2900
Toll-Free: 855-411-2372
Toll-Free TTY/TTD: 855-729-2372
Website: www.consumerfinance.gov

Federal Bureau of Investigation (FBI)

935 Pennsylvania Ave., N.W.
Washington, DC 20535-0001
Phone: 202-324-3000
Website: www.fbi.gov

Federal Deposit Insurance Corporation (FDIC)

1310 Courthouse Rd.
Arlington, VA 22201
Toll-Free: 877-ASK-FDIC (877-275-3342)
Phone: 703-562-2222
Toll-Free TDD: 800-925-4618
Website: www.fdic.gov
E-mail: communications@fdic.gov

Federal Student Aid Information Center (FSAIC)

P.O. Box 84
Washington, DC 20044-0084
Toll-Free: 800-4-FED-AID (800-433-3243)
Phone: 319-337-5665
Toll-Free TTY: 800-730-8913
Website: studentaid.gov
E-mail: studentaid@ed.gov

Federal Trade Commission (FTC)

600 Pennsylvania Ave., N.W.
Washington, DC 20580
Phone: 202-326-2222
Website: www.ftc.gov

National Credit Union Administration (NCUA)

1775 Duke St.
Alexandria, VA 22314-3428
Phone: 703-518-6300
Website: www.ncua.gov

National Motor Vehicle Title Information System (NMVTIS)

U.S. Department of Justice
Washington, DC 20531
Website: www.vehiclehistory.gov
E-mail: NMVTIS@usdoj.gov

Office of the Comptroller of the Currency (OCC)

400 7th St., S.W.
Washington, DC 20219
Toll-Free: 800-613-6743
Phone: 202-649-6800
Toll-Free TTY/TTD: 855-729-2372
Fax: 713-336-4301
Website: www.occ.treas.gov

U.S. Department of Justice (DOJ)

950 Pennsylvania Ave., N.W.
Washington, DC 20530-0001
Phone: 202-353-1555
Toll-Free TTY/TDD: 800-877-8339
Website: www.justice.gov

USA.gov

Toll-Free: 844-USA-GOV1 (844-872-4681)
Website: www.usa.gov

Private Agencies That Provide Information about Loans

America Saves Campaign

The Consumer Federation of America (CFA)
1620 I St., N.W.
Ste 200
Washington, DC 20006
Phone: 202-387-6121
Fax: 202-265-7989
Website: www.americasaves.org
E-mail: save@americasaves.org

American Bankers Association (ABA)

1120 Connecticut Ave., N.W.
Washington, DC 20036
Toll-Free: 800-BANKERS (800-226-5377)
Website: www.aba.com

American Bar Association (ABA)

Chicago Headquarters
321 N., Clark St.
Chicago, IL 60654
Toll-Free: 800-285-2221
Website: www.americanbar.org
E-mail: service@americanbar.org

American College of Trust and Estate Counsel (ACTEC)

901 15th St., N.W.
Ste. 525
Washington, DC 20005
Phone: 202-684-8460
Fax: 202-684-8459
Website: www.actec.org

American Financial Services Association (AFSA) Education Foundation

919 Eighteenth St., N.W.
Ste. 300
Washington, DC, 20006-5517
Toll-Free: 888-400-7577
Fax: 202-223-0321
Website: www.afsaef.org
E-mail: info@afsaef.org

American Institute of Certified Public Accountants (AICPA)

1455 Pennsylvania Ave., N.W.
Washington, DC 20004-1081
Toll-Free: 888-777-7077
Phone: 202-737-6600
Fax: 202-638-4512
Toll-Free Fax: 800-362-5066
Website: www.aicpa.org
E-mail: service@aicpa.org

Asset Builders of America

1213 N. Sherman Ave.
Madison, WI 53704
Phone: 608-663-6332
Website: www.assetbuilders.org
E-mail: info@assetbuilders.org

Association of Credit and Collection Professionals International (ACA)

4040 W. 70th St.,
Minneapolis, MN, 55435
Toll-Free: 800-269-1607
Website: www.acainternational.org

Center for Responsible Lending (CRL)

302 West Main St.
Durham, NC 27701
Phone: 919-313-8500
Fax: 919-313-8595
Website: www.responsiblelending.org

Center for the Study of Services (CSS)

1625 K St., N.W.
Eighth Fl.
Washington, DC 20006
Phone: 202-347-9612
Website: www.cssresearch.org
E-mail: info@cssresearch.org

Choose to Save (CTS)

Employee Benefit Research Institute (EBRI)
1100 13th St., N.W.
Ste. 878
Washington, DC 20005-4204
Phone: 202-659-0670
Fax: 202-775-6312
Website: www.choosetosave.org
E-mail: info@choosetosave.org

Council for Economic Education (CEE)

122 E. 42nd St.
Ste. 1012
New York, NY 10168
Phone: 212-827-3600
Fax: 212-827-3610
Website: www.councilforeconed.org
E-mail: customerservice@councilforeconed.org

Credit Union National Association (CUNA)

5710 Mineral Pt. Rd.
Madison, WI 53705
Toll-Free: 800-356-9655
Website: www.cuna.org
Email: hello@cuna.coop

Debtors Anonymous

General Service Office (GSO)
P.O. Box 920888
Needham, MA 02492-0009
Toll-Free: 800-421-2383
Phone: 781-453-2743
Fax: 781-453-2745
Website: www.debtorsanonymous.org
E-mail: info@debtorsanonymous.org

Equifax Credit Information Services, Inc.
P.O. Box 740241
Atlanta, Georgia 30374
Toll-Free: 800-685-5000
Website: www.equifax.com
Email: cust.serv@equifax.com

Experian
475 Anton Blvd.
Costa Mesa, CA 92626
Toll-Free: 888-397-3742
Phone: 714-830-7000
Website: www.experian.com

Federal Reserve System Board of Governors
Constitution Ave., N.W.
20th St.
Washington, DC 20551
Phone: 202-452-3000
Website: www.federalreserveeducation.org

InCharge Debt Solutions
5750 Major Blvd.
Ste. 300
Orlando, FL 32819
Toll-Free: 866-904-0274
Website: www.incharge.org

Institute for Financial Literacy
P.O. Box 1842
Portland, ME 04104
Phone: 207-873-0068
Fax: 207-873-0118
Website: www.financiallit.org
E-mail: rgordon@FinancialLit.org

Insurance Information Institute (III)
110 William St.
New York, NY 10038
Website: www.iii.org
Email: info@iii.org

National Association of Insurance Commissioners (NAIC)

1100 Walnut St.
Ste. 1500
Kansas City, MO 64106-2197
Toll-Free: 866-470-NAIC (866-470-6242)
Phone: 816-842-3600
Fax: 816-783-8175
Website: www.naic.org
E-mail: help@naic.org

National Association of Personal Financial Advisors (NAPFA)

8700 W. Bryn Mawr Ave.
Ste. 700N
Chicago, IL 60631
Toll Free: 888-FEE-ONLY (888-333-6659)
Phone: 847-483-5400
Website: www.napfa.org
E-mail: info@napfa.org

National Association of Professional Insurance Agents (PIA)

419 N. Lee St.
Alexandria, VA 22314
Phone: 703-836-9340
Fax: 703-836-1279
Website: pianet.com
E-mail: web@pianet.org

National Foundation for Credit Counseling (NFCC)

2000 M St., N.W.
Ste. 505
Washington, DC 20036
Toll-Free: 800-388-2227
Phone: 202-677- 4300
Website: www.nfcc.org

National Insurance Crime Bureau (NICB)

1111 E. Touhy Ave.
Ste. 400
Des Plaines, IL 60018
Toll-Free: 800.447.6282
Phone: 847-544-7000
Website: www.nicb.org

TransUnion LLC
Law Department
555 W. Adams
Chicago, Illinois 60661
Website: www.transunion.com

INDEX

INDEX

Page numbers that appear in *Italics* refer to tables or illustrations. Page numbers that have a small 'n' after the page number refer to citation information shown as Notes. Page numbers that appear in **Bold** refer to information contained in boxes within the chapters.

A

D

E

F

J

K

L

O

P

T

U

V

W

Y

Z